The Cinematic Body

Edited by

Sandra Buckley,

Brian Massumi,

and

Michael Hardt

Theory out of Bounds

...UNCONTAINED

BY

THE

DISCIPLINES,

INSUBORDINATE...

PRACTICES OF RESISTANCE

...Inventing,

excessively,

in the between...

PROCESSES

OF

HYBRIDIZATION

The Cinematic Body

Steven
Shaviro

Theory out of Bounds *Volume 2*

University of Minnesota Press

Minneapolis • London

Published by the University of Minnesota Press
111 Third Avenue South, Suite 290, Minneapolis, MN 55401-2520
http://www.upress.umn.edu
Printed in the United States of America on acid-free paper

Third printing 2000

LIBRARY OF CONGRESS CATALOGING-IN-PUBLICATION DATA
Shaviro, Steven.
The cinematic body / Steven Shaviro.
p.   cm. — (Theory out of bounds : v. 2)
Includes bibliographical references (p.   ) and index.
1. Motion pictures — Aesthetics.   2. Film criticism — Philosophy.
I. Title.   II. Series.
PN1995.S484   1993
791.43'01 — dc20
92-41517

The University of Minnesota
is an equal-opportunity educator and employer.

Contents

Preface

The Cinematic Body is a transversal, exploratory work, one that cuts across disciplinary boundaries and seeks to engage new currents in critical thought. Although the book focuses on the dilemmas of contemporary academic film theory, and contains close readings of a number of recent films and directors' oeuvres, it is not exclusively—perhaps not even primarily—a contribution to film studies. It is also a book about postmodernism, about the politics of human bodies, about the construction of masculinity, and about the aesthetics of masochism. It intervenes in current debates on the nature and use of pornography, and it is something of a manifesto for new forms of cultural expression. This book is grounded in so-called poststructuralist theory (most notably in the work of Gilles Deleuze and Felix Guattari), but it seeks to avoid the typical academic vices of self-referential jargon, theoretical obfuscation, and scholarly detachment. It is attuned more to cheap thrills than to judicious evaluations. Its goal is not to achieve a balanced and politically responsible critical comprehension of postmodern culture, but rather to communicate a sense of the inescapable ambivalences and affective intensities of this culture, and on that basis to elaborate and affirm a thoroughly postmodern sensibility.

For all these reasons, *The Cinematic Body* is inescapably an extremely personal book. Its forms of expression and processes of writing cannot be separated from the cinematic—or more broadly cultural—forms and processes with which it is concerned and to which it refers. Precisely because postmodernism dissolves any notion of fixed personal identity or of an integral and self-contained subject, fragments and traces of subjectivity (or, better, of "personality") are strewn more or less everywhere in the postmodern landscape. I discuss this seeming paradox most explicitly in chapter VI, on Warhol, but its effects are visible throughout.

This book is "personal" first of all on account of its idiosyncratic choice of works to discuss; I'm aware of the incongruity of setting George Romero next to Robert Bresson, or Jerry Lewis beside Andy Warhol. By foregrounding my own "taste" in this manner I seek to emphasize the roles of singularity and chance, against the objectifying scholarly tendency, which seeks to reduce particulars to generals, bizarre exceptions to representative patterns, specific practices to the predictable regularities of genre. In the second place, this book is "personal" in the sense that it foregrounds visceral, affective responses to film, in sharp contrast to most critics' exclusive concern with issues of form, meaning, and ideology. Film is a vivid medium, and it is important to talk about how it arouses corporeal reactions of desire and fear, pleasure and disgust, fascination and shame. I try to evoke these prereflective responses in my own discussions of various movies. I also argue that such affective experiences directly and urgently involve a politics. Power works in the depths and on the surfaces of the body, and not just in the disembodied realm of "representation" or of "discourse." It is in the flesh first of all, far more than on some level of supposed ideological reflection, that the political is personal, and the personal political.

All these considerations lead me to criticize and reject the psychoanalytic model currently in vogue in academic discussions of film theory.

Psychoanalytic film theory has taken on all the attributes of a religious cult, complete with rites and sacred texts. Twenty years of obsessive invocations of "lack," "castration," and "the phallus" have left us with a stultifying orthodoxy that makes any fresh discussion impossible. It is time to recognize that not all problems can be resolved by repeated references to, and ever-more-subtle close readings of, the same few articles by Freud and Lacan. The psychoanalytic model for film theory is at this point utterly bankrupt; it needs not to be refined and reformed, but to be discarded altogether. Such is the main polemical thrust of this book.

Rejecting Freud and Lacan, I draw instead upon a variety of theoretical sources: Benjamin, Bataille, Blanchot, Foucault, Deleuze, and Guattari. My aim is not to promote a new orthodoxy, but to suggest that there are other alternatives besides blind faith in psychoanalysis on the one hand and alleged essentialism and apoliticism on the other. Nothing is ever definitive. The success of a work of theory should be measured by its capacity to provoke diversities of response, and not by its ability to compel unanimous acceptance. In its theoretical stance, this book once again bears explicit traces of the partial, the excessive and unbalanced, the "personal": I embrace special pleading and the enthusiasm of the fan as a way of avoiding any appearance of objectivity and universality. I trust that many of my readers will not want to follow me into certain of the more embarrassing, abject, and politically suspect byways of my argument.

Precisely to the extent that a book like this is "personal," it involves an indebtedness that can never adequately be paid or even fully enunciated. I'm aware also that any public show of gratitude is something of an aggressive gesture, since it involves the Other in what may well be an unwanted position of complicity. The ritual of acknowledgment is thus yet another instance of the excruciatingly unresolvable ambivalence that is a major theme of this book. Nonetheless, I

will state that even an incomplete list of the many people whose conscious or un-
conscious assistance was important to me in the writing of this book would have to
include the names of Kathy Acker, Charles Altieri, Safar Fathi, William Flesch,
Therese Grisham, Michael Hardt, Faye Hirsch, Katurah Hutcheson, Paul Keyes,
Filip Konstantinović, Casy McNeese, Brian Massumi, Tatjana Pavlović, Roddey
Reid, Mark Savitt, Barry Schwabsky, Steve Tackitt, Robert Thomas, Thomas
Wall, Laurie Weeks, and Philip Wohlstetter.

Film Theory and Visual Fascination

Blue Steel

KATHRYN BIGELOW'S *Blue Steel* is a relentlessly violent and beautifully photographed genre movie, with a feminist twist. The premise is familiar: a cop who's been unjustly suspended from duty for the alleged use of excessive force is the only one who can save the city from a demented serial killer. The twist is that the cop, Megan Turner (played by Jamie Lee Curtis, a veteran of John Carpenter's *Halloween* and various other slasher/psychopath movies), is female. Bigelow gleefully inverts the usual gender clichés: Turner is a woman with a big gun, and the psychotic murderer, Eugene Hunt (in Ron Silver's edgy performance) is a yuppie male who is helplessly fascinated by the phallic power of her weapon. He goes on a gory rampage, inscribing her name on the bullets with which he murders his victims. Throughout the movie, cravings for intimacy and sexual obsessions can find an outlet only in acts of gratuitous violence. The killer romances the cop, and continually places her in ambiguous, emotionally compromising positions. She momentarily falls in love with him, but finally has to kill him.

Curtis's fine performance displays a vulnerability that coexists with, but does not compromise, an underlying toughness. Megan Turner can be as cold-blooded as Clint Eastwood's Dirty Harry, but she's also open enough to acknowledge her insecurities and emotional needs—something that Eastwood's eerily repressed persona never does. Her character combines stereotypically "masculine" and "feminine" attributes, but the effect is a radical redistribution and redefinition of gender roles, rather than the projection of a drag persona. So there's more to the film than just role-reversal parody. Bigelow isn't content merely to show that girls can do it as well as boys; she entirely transforms the macho action genre by inhabiting it from within and creating it anew. *Blue Steel* is all at once— in outrageous juxtaposition—a tense thriller, a crowd-pleasing orgy of blood and destruction, an affirmative revalorization of female subjectivity and desire, a twisted and creepy but ultimately compelling love story, and a satirical send-up of psychoanalytic theories of the phallus and castration anxiety.

But I'm not doing justice to *Blue Steel* when I discuss it only in terms of script and performance, of character, plot, and genre. Bigelow pushes the action film's tired formulas to a point of delirious frenzy through specifically cinematographic means. *Blue Steel* is a perverse and powerfully stylized exercise in visual excess. The film is awash in a delicate and continually varying blue light, sometimes muted to nighttime black, at other times crossed by bars of sunlight and shadow. Bigelow's subtle tonalities and use of chiaroscuro are the updated equivalent, for color film, of the black-and-white images of 1940s film noir. But more than the film stock has changed. It is not so much a question, in Bigelow's postmodern New York, of dangers lurking in the shadows and in dark back alleys, as it is one of disturbing undercurrents in the emotional climate, of waves of anxiety and violence propagated through urban space like modulations of light. In film noir (as in German expressionism before it), light and shadow are projections of an intense subjectivity, violently at war with itself. In *Blue Steel*, this is no longer the case. There is no clear-cut opposition between night and day, or shadow and light, but rather an uncanny sense of luminous darkness. Tonal variations are diffused throughout visual space, and not projected upon it. Lighting no longer *expresses* subjectivity; it is instead almost as if subjectivity were an *effect* of atmosphere, or of variations in lighting. It is thus chillingly appropriate and entirely to the point (and not, as some critics have complained, a weakness in the film) that Silver's psychopath seems more a collocation of nervously exaggerated impersonations than a coherent, integrated, "realistic" character. The film's gender-bending strategy involves not the creation of new archetypes, but the rendering of a highly charged cinematic space in which the traditional, gender-coded expressivist archetypes— the tough male detective and his objectified *femme fatale* Other, or the grim Eastwoodian avenger and his psychotic enemy/double—are scattered and broken down like subatomic particles.

One can usefully contrast Bigelow's strategy in *Blue Steel* with that of Ridley Scott in *Blade Runner*, for many critics the quintessential postmodern film. *Blue Steel* and *Blade Runner* are superficially similar in their baroque visual styles, but these styles are employed to radically different ends. Scott's ironic recycling of film noir character types in a simulationist, postindividualist setting is entirely coherent with his use of noirish backlighting to create a series of gorgeous but essentially static tableaux. *Blade Runner's* science fiction world is oddly permeated by nostalgia. The film composes its broken-down future not out of elements from the past, but out of their absence. The desire for outmoded scenes and situations, for the easy legibility of conventions of genre and gender, is validated— rather than frustrated—by the irrelevance and unattainability of such scenes and conventions, and by the ostentatious artificiality of their postmodern reproduction. The film's sympathy for the plight of its replicants is expressed formally in Scott's self-consciously decorative pictorialism. Such a style deliberately calls attention to its own inauthenticity and transitoriness, and yet also yearns to arrest time, to make its illusions linger as long as possible. Like Rutger Hauer's replicant, we are left at the end of the film with marvelous, fading memories, visions that aren't truly our own.

Bigelow's painterly compositions, to the contrary, are disorientingly tense and unstable, always potentially explosive, and filled with suggestions of movement. Her nightmarishly lighted cityscapes are not beautiful, illusory tableaux displayed before the camera's gaze, but danger zones within which the camera itself is forced to move. Scott offers a distanced and splendidly decadent meditation on the pleasures of alienated spectatorship; Bigelow both disrupts and heightens spectatorial pleasures, by consuming distance in a frenzy of calculated excess. Her images aren't static or decorative, because she isn't concerned with the dynamics of nostalgia, memory, and loss. *Blue Steel* is not an ironic or contemplative film: it is too kinetically agitated, and puts us too perturbingly in contact with appearances. Guns are photographed, over and over again, in extreme close-up and with lovingly fetishistic attention. The camera also tends to dwell obsessively on the details of Turner's police uniform. Acts of violence erupt without narrative or psychological motivation, but they are always choreographed with exquisite precision and grace. Plot development is suspended while the camera lingers on the details of gore and destruction, as when Eugene bathes his body in the blood of a woman he has just killed. Contorted bodies aggressively fill the screen. The cool nocturnal blues of the visual field are tinged with hot blood reds. Many of the nighttime action scenes are filmed with a telephoto lens, flattening out the image and causing movement toward or away from the camera to unfold with an agonizing, hallucinatory slowness. Bigelow's style unites a continual modulation of light and an isolating, fetishistic attentiveness with concise action editing and a propensity for slaughter: the bizarre, postmodern marriage of Josef von Sternberg and Sam Peckinpah.

Blue Steel exhibits a flagrant, salutary disregard for normative standards of plausibility. It displays a logic of contamination and repetition, rather than one of linear, psychological causality. In the opening sequence, Turner—in police uniform and gun in hand—moves tensely through dingy apartment corridors and breaks in on a scene of domestic violence. She disarms a brutal husband, only to be shot unexpectedly by the battered wife she thought she was rescuing. We then learn that we have been watching not an actual event, but a police training exercise. This shock pattern recurs throughout the film. Appearances are unstable, and must continually be reinterpreted—not to discover the truth, but precisely because there is no deeper truth. There is no underlying stability against which appearances can be measured, or to which they can be referred. This is why the film is so intense. Where *Blade Runner* presents simulation as loss of the real, *Blue Steel* grasps it as a productive intensification of reality. (In the terms of current theoretical debates, Scott's view of simulation is similar to Baudrillard's, while Bigelow's has an affinity with that of Deleuze and Guattari; I am formulating this distinction along the lines suggested by Brian Massumi 1987, 1992.) Bigelow affirms and celebrates visceral immediacy as an *effect* of simulation. Her film is not grounded in nostalgia, but moves in erotically charged rhythms of apprehension and anticipation. It strains toward the explosive instability of the coming moment, rather than being turned back upon the ungraspable remnants of an ever-receding past.

  Blue Steel both generates and depicts a state of continual excitement in which desire is indistinguishable from dread. The romance between Turner and Eugene operates in this ecstatically nightmarish fashion; even when she realizes that he is the murderer (which happens relatively early in the film), she is unable to get rid of him. He continually shows up at the most gruesomely inopportune (and therefore most intimate) moments. He forces her to look on—and even virtually to pull the trigger—as he kills her closest female friend, presents himself as her fiancé to her abusive father and victimized mother, and finally attacks while she is in bed with another man. Turner has no trouble refusing Eugene's attempt to make her into a prop for *his* fantasies; she unambiguously rejects the sexual role he tries to cast her in, that of the murderous, phallic woman. (He wants to see her again as he first did, in two-handed shooting position.) But Turner has much more difficulty in repudiating Eugene insofar as his intrusions help to articulate her own desires. She clearly relishes the power and autonomy given her by her police badge—an independence in relation to men and to her parents. When other characters ask her why she has violated gender stereotypes so much as to become a cop, she replies (only half facetiously) that she likes to slam men against the wall, or to shoot guns and kill people. This sense of active empowerment is part of the feminist import of *Blue Steel*. The uniform frees Turner from conventional gender restraints; it legitimates both her need for control over her own life and her passion for violence.

But legitimation also means recuperation. The police role, in genre conventions as in actual social life, is a particular channeling of desire: violence is given free reign, precisely so that it may enforce a repressive order. A charismatic loner such as Eastwood's Dirty Harry steps outside the law, all the better to serve the normalizing goals of law and order. He gratifies our craving for spectacles of destruction, while at the same time maintaining hierarchical arrangements of power. Transgression reinforces the order being transgressed. Such service to patriarchal law cannot be an adequate outlet for Turner's desire. She isn't rejecting socially imposed stereotypes of femininity only in order to adopt those of masculinity. Although she remains conventionally heterosexual, she is impelled to move outside the binary codings of gender, and perhaps outside all fixed notions of "character" and "identity." This *outside* movement accords with Bigelow's subversive decomposition of genre formulas, her positioning of subjectivity as a simulation effect. And within the diegesis, such a movement is the reason for Turner's unstated complicity with Eugene. She "needs" him and "uses" him in order to break away from conventional subject positionings and from the socially enforced ties of job, family, and gender roles.

Eugene enters the film not as Turner's dark double, but in excited response to her own display of deadly force. He first sees her, and falls in love with her and with her gun, when she shoots and kills a thug who is holding up a convenience store. Even though Turner doesn't notice him at the time, the sequence is shot from her point of view. The camera moves with her as she tensely readies her gun and approaches the holdup man and his victims. Eugene is thus initially presented as merely a background figure within Turner's active field of vision. The center of attention is elsewhere. We are totally preoccupied by the shot/reverse shot dynamic between Turner (who is actively looking and nervously approaching) and the holdup man with his gun (who is the object and target of her gaze). It is only when Turner breaks the tension by shooting the thug that Eugene is momentarily singled out for us. The holdup man's gun floats through the air and lands right in front of Eugene, as if it had somehow magically *chosen him*. We see the gun for a moment in extreme close-up. Eugene slowly clutches it, and draws it to him. The instant passes quickly, and we return to Turner's shock in the aftermath of the shooting. Eugene's ecstatic image of Turner's "brightness" and "unflinching power" is something we never get to see. He is not the "owner" of the gaze. His voyeuristic fixation is presented only in the interstices of the main narrative, and developed largely through reverse shots. This makes for a startling inversion of the dynamics of voyeurism as articulated in Hitchcock's *Rear Window* and other classic Hollywood films. The audience doesn't "identify" with Eugene's gaze, but sees his fixation on big guns as a consequence of his own visibility, his placement in a field whose narrative/visual axis lies elsewhere. Visual fascination is a passive, irresistible compulsion, and not an assertion of the active mastery of the gaze. And it is linked with the *delegitimation* of violence, its dissociation either from the demands of social order or from the assertion of virile (stereotypically male) power and control, for Eugene "catches" violence as one catches an infection, more than he inflicts it as a willful expression of a warped self. His phallic, aggressive fantasies are decentered and unhinged in the very movement by which they are intensified. He is less an independent character than a hysterical figuration of the destabilizing excessiveness of Turner's own desire. And *Blue Steel* as a whole celebrates this excess.

Blue Steel is a blatantly fetishistic and voyeuristic film: it unabashedly revels in visual fascination. Its relation to its genre sources is something like the relation of Pasolini's *Salo* to Sade, as described by Leo Bersani (1986): "There is no Brechtian distancing from Sade; the relation of *Salo* to the literary text is one of subversive passivity.... [Pasolini] moves away from images and styles by duplicating them rather than 'criticizing' or 'opposing' them" (p. 53). In a roughly analogous way, *Blue Steel* disrupts the gender codings and power relations implicit in more conventional action films not by distancing us from but by intensifying such films' disreputable pleasures.

Blue Steel's extreme stylization and self-consciousness lead to an unbearable increase in tension that can be discharged only by random violence. The gaze is invested in a series of elaborately constructed scenarios, but it cannot be satisfied or contained by any of them. Gunfire repeatedly arises out of and ruptures the tableau; the visual becomes violently tactile. Guns thus play the same role in the diegesis that lighting does in the mise-en-scène: they are not just privileged objects of visual obsession, but, more important, the medium of its dissemination.

Blue Steel exposes visual fascination as a restless, shattering mobility—rather than as the stabilizing fixation assumed by so much film theory, or as the morose delectation of *Blade Runner*. Something has happened to the act of looking. Outbursts of violence and gradations of light arouse, agitate, and unsettle the spectator. Narcissistic gratification is interrupted, not through any recognition of loss or lack, but because I am drawn into a condition of excessive, undischargeable excitation. I am depositioned and dispossessed by the film's incessant modulations of visibility, no less than by its concise articulations of action and movement. Vision in *Blue Steel* is excruciatingly, preternaturally vivid; reality is heightened into feverish hallucination. Such a hypertrophy of the visual is Bigelow's way of undoing the security and possessiveness that have conventionally been associated with the "male gaze." She pushes fetishism and voyeuristic fascination to the point where they explode.

Film Theory and Its Discontents

I begin with Bigelow's revisionist filmmaking for a number of reasons. In its own way, *Blue Steel* touches upon most of the topics discussed in this book: the delirious excesses of postmodern vision, the excitement and passivity of spectatorship, the frenzy and fragility of images, the desires that inform social constructions of subjectivity, the pornographic allure of violence and sexuality, and the politics of the subjugated body. *Blue Steel* is at once an ostentatiously artificial construct and a passionate exploration of the dense materiality of perception and desire. It outrageously identifies what Jean Baudrillard (1988) has proclaimed to be the antagonistic and incompatible principles of the postmodern world: simulation and dissimulation, the obscenity of complete, transparent vision on the one hand, and the hidden play of seduction on the other. On a more personal level, I like this film because it is both exploitative enough to satisfy my cravings for sensationalistic shocks and "splatter" levels of blood and destruction and yet visually subtle and reflexively self-conscious enough to incite my analytic, intellectualizing impulses. In all these ways, *Blue Steel* is an exemplary postmodern work.

For the moment, however, I would like to approach *Blue Steel* as a kind of test case for the relation between film theory and "naive" film viewing. This relation is necessarily fraught with affective ambivalence and intellectual contradiction. On the one hand, theory seeks compulsively to reproduce the experiences of which it is the abstraction. In film viewing, there is pleasure and more than pleasure: a rising scale of seduction, delirium, fascination, and utter absorption in the image. The pleasures, the unpleasant constraints, the consuming obsessions of writing theory—pleasures, constraints, and obsessions that are behind every articulation of this book—cannot be separated from the bodily agitations, the movements of fascination, the reactions of attraction and repulsion, of which they are the extension and the elaboration. On the other hand, however, theory derives its particular form from its endeavor to separate itself from these founding impulses. It tries to assume as great a distance as possible from its object, whether its purpose be to praise the object or condemn it or dispassionately observe it, to trace its surfaces or analyze its hidden structures, to affirm its singularity or situate it in a larger context. Such a "scientific" attempt to distance oneself is especially problematic in the case of film theory, whose "object" is not just particular films, but the very process of film viewing itself. The subjectivity of the theorist is unavoidably engaged in this process, in ways that he or she is driven repeatedly to reflect upon, but that remain forever beyond his or her grasp. What is most important is what we are unable to acknowledge. I am too deeply implicated in the pleasures of film viewing, and too embarrassed by my complicity with or subordination to them, to be able to give a full and balanced account. Any sort of rational argumentation, theoretical generalization, or political legitimation necessarily deviates into "perverse" gratification and special pleading. Film theorists, like Sade's libertines sitting around the banquet table, find themselves constructing the most elegant, rigorous, and even lucidly self-interrogating discourses, only to ground and to justify their most singular pleasures, their most gratutious obsessions, their most untranslatable sensations.

There can be no question of escaping this twisted logic of theoretical writing; there are only different ways of coming to terms with it. What disturbs me in the founding texts of psychoanalytic and poststructuralist film theory is an almost reflex movement of suspicion, disavowal, and phobic rejection. It seems as if theorists of the past twenty years can scarcely begin their discussions without ritualistically promising to resist the insidious seductions of film. Thus Christian Metz (1982) describes his theoretical project as "an attempt to disengage the cinema-object from the imaginary and to win it for the symbolic, in the hope of extending the latter by a new province" (p. 3). This imperialistic movement of scientific rationality requires him to analyze, and ruthlessly distance himself from, his own self-confessed pathology of "loving the cinema" (pp. 14–16). Theoretical progress is the result of fascination turned against itself: "voyeuristic sadism sublimated into epistemophilia" (p. 16). Metz's acknowledgment of his own work's subjective conditions of possibility is largely a form of damage control, an endeavor to limit and neutralize the "imaginary" distortions that threaten the advance of theoretical knowledge. Metz remains attached to the great modernist belief (shared by structuralist formalism, psychoanalysis, and Brechtian aesthetics) that self-reflexive distanciation (or sublimation) is both salutary and efficacious. One of the recurrent, if implicit, arguments of the present book is that it can be neither. It is high time we rid ourselves of the notion that we can somehow free ourselves from illusion (or from ideology) by recognizing and theorizing our own entrapment within it. Such dialectical maneuvers tend, ironically, to reinforce the very objects of their critique. They achieve their explanatory power at the price of transforming local, contingent phenomena into transcendental conditions or developmental necessities. The self-reflexive theorizing that allows us to become aware of certain structural constraints also ends up echoing and amplifying those constraints, reproducing them on a larger scale. This is what Deleuze and Guattari (1983) call the "oedipalizing" effect of psychoanalysis and structural linguistics. I would find Metz more compelling if he allowed his self-analysis to contaminate and ruin his theoretical project, rather than reinforce it.

Laura Mulvey's ground-breaking and still influential essay, "Visual Pleasure and Narrative Cinema" (1988), is problematic in much the same way as Metz's work. Mulvey's analyses of fetishism and scopophilia in mainstream Hollywood cinema end up constructing an Oedipal, phallic paradigm of vision that is much more totalizing and monolithic than anything the films she discusses are themselves able to articulate. In order to theorize the *systematic* nature of patriarchal representation, Mulvey cannot avoid importing into her own theoretical model the very norms she wishes to destroy. She outlines a scenario of castration anxiety so all-encompassing that no form of narrative or visual enjoyment or engagement is exempt. A forbiddingly formalistic avant-garde cinema is posited as the *only* alternative to co-optation by the dominant patriarchal system. The unintended effect of Mulvey's argument is to foreclose whatever potentials for resistance and subversion, or Deleuzian "lines of flight," *are* latent within mainstream, narrative film. (I have been arguing that *Blue Steel* is an exemplary instance of just such a subversion from within.) Mulvey, like Metz, can distance herself from what she regards as the fundamental sadism of the voyeuristic position only by turning that sadism back upon film viewing itself. Thus she calls for the "destruction" of cinematic pleasure (p. 58) and insists that this destruction be carried out "not in favor of a reconstructed new pleasure" (p. 59), but only in the direction of an

aesthetics of distance, "dialectics, passionate detachment" (p. 68). The psychoanalytic theorist's need for control, his or her fear of giving way to the insidious blan-
dishments of visual fascination, and his or her consequent construction of a theoretical edifice as a defense against a threatening pleasure—all this tends uncannily
to resemble the very drama of trauma and disavowal that psychoanalytic film
theory attributes to the normative male spectator.

Recent work in semiotic and psychoanalytic film theory has of
course become a lot less totalizing, and a lot more nuanced and various, than was
the case in these texts of the mid-1970s. For instance, an increasing number of
theorists—Mary Anne Doane (1987), Tania Modleski (1988), Kaja Silverman
(1988), Constance Penley (1989), Linda Williams (1983, 1989), and Carol Clover
(1992), among others—have sought to identify alternative possibilities of female
pleasure in mainstream cinema, and thus to palliate the grim "either/or" of Mulvey's account. But most of these revisionary readings, interesting and insightful as
they often are, still operate within the semiotic/psychoanalytic model proposed
initially by Metz and given a powerful feminist dimension by Mulvey. D. N.
Rodowick is right to observe that Mulvey's article is a founding, paradigmatic,
"transdiscursive" text in film study, one of those works that (like the works of
Freud himself) "open problematics and set theoretical agendas that inaugurate
whole fields of investigation" (in Bergstrom & Doane 1989, 274).

Whatever revisions have been proposed, the grounding con-
tours and assumptions of psychoanalytic film theory, which the writings of Metz
and Mulvey articulate in so powerful and polemical a manner, are still largely accepted. It is less a question of particular arguments and positions than of the continued maintenance of an all-encompassing, hegemonic *paradigm* for the critical
and theoretical discussion of film. With a few singular exceptions (such as Dudley
Andrew's [1985] defense of phenomenology, or Noel Carroll's [1988] cognitive

theory), psychoanalysis remains the sole and ubiquitous horizon of "serious" (read: academic) discourse on film. The languages of Freud and Marx, or more precisely of Lacan and Althusser, as they have been reductively superimposed upon a certain formalization of the cinematic apparatus, have long been the reigning master discourses for any interrogation of desire and politics, gender and sexuality, culture and ideology in the movies.

How much longer can such a situation go on? "As Italian film theorist Francesco Cosetti has suggested, the field of film theory is undergoing a paradigm shift, its future uncertain" (Hammett 1992, 86). But even as film theorists have come to be increasingly aware that their paradigm is shaky, they have for the most part continued to uphold it, adding refinements and subtleties to the basic Metz/Mulvey model, like the Ptolemaic astronomers with their epicycles. My intention in this book is different: to accentuate the crisis in film theory, to help blow the paradigm apart. Not to survey, critique, and work forward from recent developments (as Rodowick, for instance, has admirably done in *The Difficulty of Difference*, 1991), but to suggest the possibility of thinking *otherwise* about film and culture.

Fear of Images

I have suggested above that film theory is written out of the tension between a desire to reproduce and a desire to keep at a distance the voyeuristic excitations that are its object. The problem with paradigmatic contemporary film theory is that the latter, reactive side has all too completely gained control. This theory still tends to equate passion, fascination, and enjoyment with mystification; it opposes to these a knowledge that is disengaged from affect, and irreducible to images. Beneath its claims to methodological rigor and political correctness, it manifests a barely contained panic at the prospect (or is it the memory?) of being affected and moved by visual forms. It is as if there were something degrading and dangerous about giving way to images, and so easily falling under their power. Theory thus seeks to ward off the cinema's dangerous allure, to refuse the suspect pleasures that it offers, to dissipate its effects by articulating its hidden but intelligible structure. Behind all these supposedly materialist attacks on the ideological illusions built into the cinematic apparatus, should we not rather see the opposite, an idealist's fear of the ontological instability of the image, and of the materiality of affect and sensation?

Indeed, the fear and distrust of images is traditional in Western thought. Ever since Plato, philosophers have warned us against being seduced by reflections and shadows. Metaphysics prefers the verbal to the visual, the intelligible to the sensible, the text to the picture, and the rigorous articulations of signification to the ambiguities of untutored perception. It posits a radical distinction between the perceptible realm of mere appearances and the invisible realm of truth. And Lacanian psychoanalysis remains within this Platonic tradition, at least to the extent that it denounces the delusions of the optical system or metaphor and privileges the Symbolic order of language in opposition to an Imaginary defined primarily in visual terms. An appeal to Lacan in recent film theory is usually the occasion for a Platonic attack upon the illusionism of cinema and the image's powers of falsity and deception.

In another classic text, Jean-Louis Baudry (1986a) reads Plato's allegory of the cave as a prototype of the cinematic apparatus: Plato describes a machine for projecting a simulated, hallucinatory "impression of reality" (p. 302). Baudry self-consciously reproduces Plato's idealist logic in the very act of criticizing it; his analysis of the regressive, fantasmatic desire underlying film spectatorship takes its cues from Plato's own account of the illusions of the prisoners in the cave. Film images are equated with the shadows in the cave: vacuous, degraded, and insubstantial projections that, by a kind of ideological-optical illusion, are mistakenly but unavoidably taken for reality. The Lacanian film critic, like the Platonic philosopher, warns us not to be deceived by the apparent immediacy of what we see in the mirror, for no visual presentation can capture the complex textual play of absences and mediations; none can be adequate to the severe demands of dialectical comprehension. The word is the death of the thing, and the falsity of the image is a necessary consequence of the truth of discourse. Percept and affect must be subordinated to textuality and the Law of the signifier. Film theory endeavors to subdue and regulate the visual, to destroy the power of images, or at least to restrain them within the bounds of linguistic discursivity and patriarchal Law.

I am trying to suggest that semiotic and psychoanalytic film theory is largely a phobic construct. Images are kept at a distance, isolated like dangerous germs; sometimes, they are even made the object of the theorist's sadistic fantasies of revenge. What is usually attacked is the emptiness and impotence of the image, its inability to support the articulations of discourse or to embody truth. Images are condemned because they are bodies without souls, or forms without bodies. They are flat and insubstantial, devoid of interiority and substance, unable to express anything beyond themselves. They are—frustratingly—static and evanescent at once, too massively present in their very impalpability. The fundamental characteristic of the cinematic image is therefore said to be one of *lack*. As Kaja Silverman (1988) summarizes this line of argument, "Film theory has been haunted since its inception by the specter of a loss or absence at the center of cinematic production, a loss which both threatens and secures the viewing subject." This lack is primarily one of "the absent real and the foreclosed site of production," though it is secondarily projected onto female bodies (p. 2). Images are false, since they have been separated from the real situations of which they claim to be the representations, as well as from the material conditions in which they have been produced. They are suspect, unreliable, and "ideological," because they presume to subsist in this state of alienation, and even perpetuate it by giving rise to delusive "reality effects," rituals of disavowal, and compensatory fantasies of plenitude and possession.

But is it really *lack* that makes images so dangerous and disturbing? What these theorists fear is not the emptiness of the image, but its weird fullness; not its impotence so much as its power. Images have an excessive capacity to seduce and mislead, to affect the spectator unwarrantedly. What is the source of this mysterious power? Much has been written about the "lost object" as a mainstay of cinematic desire (e.g., Silverman 1988, ch. 1). To the contrary: the problem for the cinema spectator is not that the object is lost or missing, but that it is never quite lost, that it is never distant or absent enough. Maurice Blanchot (1981) suggests that the image is not a representational substitute for the object so much as it is—like a cadaver—the material trace or residue of the object's failure to vanish completely: "The apparent spirituality, the pure formal virginity of the image is fundamentally linked to the elemental strangeness of the being that is present in absence" (p. 83). The image is not a symptom of lack, but an uncanny, excessive residue of being that subsists when all *should* be lacking. It is not the index of something that is missing, but the insistence of something that refuses to disappear. Images are banally self-evident and self-contained, but their superficiality and obviousness is also a strange blankness, a resistance to the closure of definition, or to any imposition of meaning. Images are neither true nor false, neither real nor artificial, neither present nor absent; they are radically devoid of essence. Empty simulacra, copies for which there is no original, they tend to proliferate endlessly, repetitiously, without hope of regulation or control. The fleeting insistence of weightless images, of reflections and projections, of light and shadow, threatens to corrupt all standards, to exceed all limits, and to transgress every law.

- critique of lacanian lack .

The vapid "givenness" of the image is at the same time its secret openness to passion and desire. This is the affirmative lesson of Andy Warhol's early films. Voyeuristic fascination is always already at work in these films, even in the absence of editing or other "suturing" techniques (though many of them do, in fact, employ such techniques); even, we might say, in the absence of a viewing subject. On the side of production, this subject is elided by Warhol's notorious habit of simply letting the camera run unattended. And on the side of consumption it is equally elided, in the sense that a film such as *Empire* is not vitiated by the failure of anyone actually to see it. These films almost seem like a parodic *reductio ad absurdum* of Andre Bazin's (1967) claims for the fundamental realism of photographic images:

> *For the first time, between the originating object and its reproduction there intervenes only the instrumentality of a nonliving agent. For the first time, an image of the world is formed automatically, without the creative intervention of man. . . . Photography affects us like a phenomenon in nature, like a flower or a snowflake whose vegetable or earthly origins are an inseparable part of their beauty. (v. 1, p. 13)*

Bazin offers the utopian vision of an originary, phenomenological plenitude of perception, preserved and extended by the cinematic apparatus. Warhol's films ruin this idealized vision, precisely through their excessive fidelity to the Bazinian project. They eagerly embrace the nonhuman, nonliving passivity of mechanical reproduction. They are content merely to record; at the limit they are indeed nothing more than unmediated *traces* of a visual and spatial "real." But such traces are Blanchotian, cadaverous residues—far from manifesting any Bazinian "transference of reality from the thing to its reproduction" (p. 14). Reality is not preserved and sustained so much as it is *altered* by the very fact of passive, literal reproduction—or what could better be called hypermimetic simulation.

Simulation, as Deleuze and Guattari (1983) suggest, disqualifies both the original and the copy: "It carries the real beyond its principle to the point where it is effectively produced" (p. 87).

The decadent beauty of Warhol's films comes from their failure to refer, as copies, back to some authentic original, and therefore their irreducibility to Bazin's genetic model of the growth of flowers and snowflakes. When the eye and hand of the artist are removed, nature also disappears. The human figures portrayed in such films as *Sleep* and *Blow Job* are all the more thoroughly "de-originated" and objectified in that they are not submitted to the mastery of any gaze. Subjective agency is indeed not necessary; the mere presence of the camera as recording device corrupts and corrodes the pure self-evidence of vision. Warhol's images have an obsessive force *because* they seem not to require an active subject of perception, and *because* they are banal, flat, unresonant, and devoid of motion. They insidiously solicit an impersonal, interminable attentiveness. They risk provoking boredom only because they so disconcertingly threaten to draw us into their involuntary, presubjective realm of visual fascination.

Warhol's films are not as random, unformed, or minimal as conceptual descriptions have sometimes made them seem. (I discuss them in greater detail in chapter VI.) Still, they mark a certain "degree zero" of cinematic experience, all the more so in that their reductive literalism is patently arbitrary and constructed, and not a "natural" origin. At this zero point, an impersonal structure of visual fascination is already in place, even though there is no subject present to assume it. Warhol's images, like those Blanchot evokes, flicker in an anonymous space of cadaverous resemblances. Their radical ambiguity—what Blanchot (1981) calls preoriginary "dissimulation" (p. 89)—precedes and ruins any split between being and representation, any opposition between phenomenal presence and linguistic signification. These images cannot be described in terms of

Why images do not respond to any
— Structural logic of
subjectivity. No presence / lack.

— Why language does not...

"lack," precisely because they do not take the place of any prior reality, and thus do not elicit the lost "presence" upon which all notions of lack or absence dialectically depend. They have always already subtracted themselves from the psychoanalytic narrative of traumatic separation, disavowal, phobic projection, and compensatory, fetishistic reconstruction. Visual fascination is thus a precondition for the cinematic construction of subjectivity, and not a consequence of it. It is not the gaze that demands images, but images that solicit and sustain—while remaining indifferent to—the gaze. Warhol's cinematic apparatus does not respond to any structural logic of subjectivity; rather, it is a machine for inducing and implanting voyeuristic effects. In Foucault's (1979) terms, Warhol's cinema is "the diagram of a mechanism of power . . . a figure of political technology" (p. 205)—a presubjective articulation of power and pleasure.

Lines of Flights

The example of Warhol's films, no less than that of *Blue Steel*, is meant to point to functions of the cinematic apparatus, and forms of visual fascination, that cannot be theorized adequately by psychoanalysis. The psychoanalytic narrative is at best a countereffect, a normalization or "oedipalization," of historically specific mechanisms of mechanical reproduction, and of a corresponding visual obsession. Indeed, psychoanalysis has been most useful in film theory precisely in the study of modes of normalization. Feminist critics from Mulvey to Silverman have profoundly anatomized the anxious efforts of the normative male spectator to reassert power and control in the face of cinematic dispossession. It is highly problematic, however, to deploy the notions of lack, castration, and the phallus structurally rather than just symptomatically, to transform them into master terms for the interpretation of cinematic narrative per se. As Linda Williams (1989) rightly argues:

right on.

Psychoanalysis itself should not be regarded as the key to understanding the cinematic apparatus; instead, like the cinema itself, it should be seen simply as another late-nineteenth-century discourse of sexuality, another apparatus for aligning socially produced sexual desires with oedipal and familial norms. Considered in this light, cinema and psychoanalysis are both historically determined—and determining—mechanisms of power and pleasure. (p. 46)

The insistent psychoanalytic focus upon the *representation* of sexual difference may lead us to elide or forget more fundamental questions about *how* power relations—especially including the hierarchized binary oppositions of gender—are in fact socially *produced*.

Gender and sexuality cannot and should not be regarded primarily as functions of ideology, symbolization, and representation, because gender and sexuality are embedded in, and produced by, a whole range of complex power relations and effects operating in multiple registers throughout the socius. Foucault (1980) proposes that "power must be understood in the first instance as the multiplicity of force relations immanent in the sphere in which they operate and which constitute their own organization" (p. 92). Such immanent relations of force serve (among many other things) to regulate the processes of production and distribution, to colonize bodies, to channel the modes of sensory perception, and to articulate divisions of space and time. These forces themselves are continually being captured, appropriated, deviated, and redirected by other forces. Foucault (1983a) defines the exercise of power as "a set of actions upon other actions"; power "incites, it induces, it seduces, it makes easier or more difficult" (p. 220). Larger orders of domination and oppression are not the structural preconditions for, but precisely the empirical effects of, such multiple and ever-changing force relations. For instance, the cinematic mechanisms that objectify and fetishize women's bodies are not *consequences* of phallocentrism; rather, it is phallo-centrism—understood not as a transcendental structure, but as a historically spe-cific way of distributing gender roles and normalizing and regulating desire—that is a consequence of particular technologies of power, among which the mecha-nisms of cinema must be included. Thus Williams (1989) links the emergence of the cinema in the late nineteenth century to the contemporaneous "implantation of perversions" and elaboration of a *scientia sexualis* as described by Foucault (pp. 34–37).

The oppression of women by men obviously predates the nine-teenth-century regime of sexual normalization, just as class divisions (and class struggle) precede the emergence of capitalism, but it would be a mistake in either case to posit a uniform and transhistorical form of domination. Psychoanalysis ex-plains the fetishization of sexual difference as a result of the reigning phallic or Symbolic order, while a Foucaultian approach regards the phallic order as itself something that needs to be derived, historicized, and explained as an effect. Fou-cault's historical nominalism leads him radically to question any notion of "deep structure." The forms of ideology and the canons of representation must indeed be included *among* immanent power relations, but they are not the basic, ultimate forms of power's efficacy and intelligibility. The import of Foucault's analyses of modern society's disciplinary and sexualizing mechanisms is that desire cannot be conceived in terms of lack, and power relations cannot be subsumed by a single master narrative of "castration," or the subject's "entry into" patriarchal law and the Symbolic order.

Foucault's "analytics of power" is complemented by Deleuze and Guattari's endeavor to articulate a post-Freudian theory of sexuality. (I discuss this theory in greater detail in the appendix to this chapter.) Deleuze and Guattari argue, along with Foucault, that power in postmodern society works as a process of production, rather than as a drama of representation—an affirmative play of affects and effects, and not a series of splits and absences unfolding according to a logic of negativity. They seek to overthrow what they call "the anthropomorphic representation of sex" (1983, 294). Such a formulation is almost a redundancy, for sex is anthropomorphized—which means that it is subjected not just to "human" norms (whatever that might mean), but specifically to male heterosexual ones— precisely when it is compelled to pass through the defiles of representation or the signifier. Deleuze and Guattari are not utopians; they do not believe in any sponta- neous and natural being of sex, prior to societal regimentation and repression. They do argue, however, that it is insufficient merely to contest the abusive nature of particular structures of sexual representation. Too much has already been con- ceded to the forces of patriarchal order when representation is accepted as the bat- tlefield. It is necessary to go further, to discover the conflicting forces, the "molec- ular" movements, that subtend and invest—and often contradict—the global, "molar" order of phallic representation. There is always already a socius and a pol- itics prior to that mythical moment when the Symbolic order or system of norms is instituted in society, or implanted in the individual. Deleuze and Guattari in- sist that social formations be defined not by their hegemonic institutions and ideologies but by their potentials for change, not by their norms but by their "lines of flight." Foucault argues much the same thing when he says that unstable, mut- able relations of force precede any fixed structures of domination and repre- sentation. No form of domination is ever final: every structure nourishes within itself the forces that potentially lead to its destruction. For Deleuze and Guat- tari, as for Foucault, the point of theory is to oppose the finality of deep struc- tures, and to elicit and amplify the forces of potential change. Theory is neither a re-presentation of reality nor a critique of representations, but a new, affirmative construction of the real.

In what follows, I take my cues from Foucault and from Deleuze and Guattari, in order to articulate a subversive micropolitics of post-modern cinema. I address many of the concerns raised so urgently by both femi-nist and psychoanalytic theorists, but without recourse to Freud's and Lacan's metapsychological structures. My path leads from the paradoxical nature of cine-matic perception, through the mechanisms by which cinema generates affect, and on to the position of the cinematic spectator (the form of subjectivity that not only experiences but is in large measure produced by cinematic affect). I consider the ontology of the single image, the ways in which images are connected through editing, and the overall problem of temporality in film. And I offer a theory of cin-ematic fascination that is a radical alternative to the psychoanalytic paradigm. Such an approach is affirmative and transformative, rather than critical or evaluative: it evokes the capacity of the cinematic apparatus to produce and multiply "lines of flight" instead of dwelling on its role in confirming and enforcing oppressive stan-dards and ideologies. It is radically antinormative, both in the political sense that it questions and opposes socially sanctioned norms and in the more aesthetic (Dadaist or 'pataphysical) sense that its "theory" of cinematic experience is con-structed out of exceptions rather than typical instances, extremes rather than aver-ages, singular aberrations rather than (against) repeated patterns. My goal is not to establish the (phenomenological or psychoanalytic) "truth" of cinematic experi-ence and the cinematic apparatus, but to follow these images in their seductive drift away from any such truth.

My guiding principle is that cinematic images are not repre-sentations, but *events*. Foucault (1982) writes (following Deleuze):

An event is neither substance, nor accident, nor quality, nor process; events are not corporeal. And yet, an event is certainly not immaterial; it takes effect, becomes effect, always on the level of materiality. . . . Let us say that the philosophy of event should advance in the direction, at first sight paradoxical, of an incorporeal materialism. (p. 231)

An event is something like the blow job that we do not get to see in Warhol's film of that name, or the bursts of gunfire that at once articulate and shatter vision in *Blue Steel*. My own fascination with such images or events is the source of my "perverse" investment in the project of this book. If, as I have suggested, theory writing is always divided between mimetic participation and phobic rejection, then I am driven by the hope of abolishing the latter—although my attempt to do so will inevitably be as futile as are those of most theorists to extinguish the former. Psychoanalytic film theory projects its phobia toward images back upon the images themselves. My own masochistic theoretical inclination is to revel in my bondage to images, to celebrate the spectatorial condition of metaphysical alienation and ideological delusion, rather than strive to rectify it. But I can't escape the fatality that heightens self-consciousness whenever one seeks to abolish it, and that turns every gesture of ecstatic, "sacrificial mutilation" (Bataille 1985, 61–72) into yet another instance of self-assertion and self-validation.

Literal Perceptions

Cinematic perception is different from "natural" perception. This troubles film theorists a great deal: How can cinema have so powerful a "reality effect" when it is so manifestly unreal? The antinomy of cinematic perception is the following: film viewing offers an immediacy and violence of sensation that powerfully engages the eye and body of the spectator; at the same time, however, it is predicated on a radical dematerialization of appearances. The cinematic image is at once intense and impalpable. On one hand, film (even more than other visual forms, and in sharp contrast to the articulations of language) is inescapably literal. Images confront the viewer directly, without mediation. What we see is what we see; the figures that unroll before us cannot be regarded merely as arbitrary representations or conventional signs. We respond viscerally to visual forms, before having the leisure to read or interpret them as symbols. On the other hand, this literalness is empty and entirely ungrounded; it does not correspond to any sort of presence. Nothing is there except the image. The film viewed does not present objects, but merely projects them. We see images and hear sounds, but there is no substance beneath these accidents. The film is composed only of flickering lights, evanescent noises, and insubstantial figures.

But what can it mean to say that cinematic perception is unmediated or literal? Hegel, in his discussion of "Sense-Certainty," argues that singular, immediate experience is radically impossible: I cannot designate a "this," cannot identify a "here" and a "now," without already having assumed the universal forms of subjectivity, time, and space. No experience is possible without a concept. Hegel's intellectualist argument has become axiomatic in recent theory, which claims that there can be no perception or other experience without textualization and linguistic articulation. Nevertheless, such logic remains circular or tautological: it can subsume sensation within universal (linguistic or conceptual) forms only because it has already deployed those forms in order to describe sensation in the first place. The starting and ending points of Hegel's argument are interdependent and interchangeable, because the acts of designating and identifying a sensation are *already* those of placing it within symbolic or textual categories. But this is to make the idealist assumption that human experience is originally and fundamentally cognitive. It is to reduce the question of perception to a question of knowledge, and to equate sensation with the reflective consciousness of sensation. The Hegelian and structuralist equation suppresses the body. It ignores or abstracts away from the primordial forms of raw sensation: affect, excitation, stimulation and repression, pleasure and pain, shock and habit. It posits instead a disincarnate eye and ear whose data are immediately objectified in the form of self-conscious awareness or positive knowledge.

These Hegelian, cognitive strictures legislate the "truth" of sensation; they subordinate experience to, and contextualize it within, an order of references and significations. Perception presupposes a context of dialectical relations, or at the very least a grounding in certain transcendental conditions of possibility. It must be articulated, on one hand in relation to a system of representations in the structure of language or the mind of the spectator, and on the other in relation to the supposed stability of the objective world. Indeed, my own stability as a subject is dependent upon my ability to recognize and order my impressions, to comprehend them in communicable meanings, and to refer them to actual objects. I am able to reflect and act only insofar as I can both read my perceptions as non-immediate signs and identify them with things that are really there. "Natural" perception is thus never raw or immediate: it is always already subordinated to a *double articulation*. Deleuze and Guattari (1987, pp. 39–74) argue that this double articulation is a principle not just of linguistic systems, but of all forms of what they call *stratification*: the hierarchical ordering, coding, and territorializing of previously multiple and heterogeneous forces. It is not the case that everything is linguistic or textual, but rather that language is one particular instance (although an important one) of the processes of stratification. The alternative between presence and mediation, or phenomenological immediacy and linguistic deferral, is therefore a false one: experience is *at once* textualized (or opened to the play of negations and differences) and anchored in a living present. Signification and presence are two coexistent dimensions of perceptual "truth."

If cinematic perception differs from "natural" perception, this is because it undermines both sides of the double articulation. Film viewing resists the canons of perceptual "truth." The insubstantial flicker of "moving pictures" cannot easily be contained within systems of stratification. Images on the screen are violently torn away from any external horizon or context, as from any actual presence. One may recall Godard's notorious (and not entirely facetious) comment that what is presented in *Weekend* is not blood, but merely the color red. The immediacy of the image short-circuits the processes of signification, while its simulacral incorporeality precludes any objective reference. The antinomy of cinematic perception is resolved by the way in which film undoes both dimensions of perceptual "truth," both sides of the double articulation, at once. The Hegelian argument against raw sensation is valid only to the extent that sensation is equated with cognition and attributed to a fixed subject. But now, perception can no longer be subsumed under reflective consciousness, or under cognition and judgment; instead, it marks a limit beyond which these can never extend. Sensation is disengaged from the transcendental conditions that are supposed to ground and organize it, as from the referential coordinates that allow us to locate and preserve it. Sheer appearance precedes any possible act of recognition; film shows before it says.

Contrary to the assertions of much recent theory, then, we need not assume that the visual order is dependent upon the order of the signifier. Blanchot (1981) defines the nontruth of the image in its radical disjunction from language:

- The aesthetic destabilizes
  recognition and perception.
                                        28,9
- The poetic: strip rejects language
                  as a referential object.

The image has nothing to do with signification, meaning, as implied by the existence of the world, the effort of truth, the law and the brightness of the day. Not only is the image of an object not the meaning of that object and of no help in comprehending it, but it tends to withdraw from its meaning by maintaining it in the immobility of a resemblance that has nothing to resemble. (p. 85)

The way in which we apprehend the image of a pebble is vastly different from the way in which we comprehend the signifier "pebble"; the former cannot be reduced to the latter, even if it is only the latter that allows us to recognize what we see *as* a pebble, to classify it under a general concept, to refer to it as an object, and to specify it as something that we can negate, manipulate, and transform.

   Consider Godard's images, in extreme close-up, of a pebble held in a hand in *Weekend*, and of coffee swirling in a cup in *Two or Three Things I Know about Her*. These images are invested with a surprising, alien beauty; they are "aestheticized" precisely to the extent that they insist before, and persist beyond, the act of recognition that stabilizes and rationalizes perception. Both shots are introduced, almost didactically, in response to the question, What is this? or What is an object? The pebble is displayed on a hand like a pediment, against a dark background, its indentations—almost like the features of a ravaged face—harshly contoured in the sharp light. The coffee is a dark and unsettled liquid mass, in continual flux, punctuated by unstable flecks of white foam. The aberrant scale and unfamiliar lighting of these images defamiliarizes their objects—or, better, forces us to stop regarding them *as* referential objects. They appear in fixed shots, held for a long time: duration has become an independent dimension of the image, and is no longer a function of the time needed for cognition and action. The pebble and the coffee are neither useful nor significant; they work neither as things nor as signs. They are nothing but images, mutely and fascinatingly soliciting our

> - the nonsignifying image [word]
>
> - a liberation of the (textle, poetic) from the objectifying's linguistic categories.

attention. The pebble rests, the coffee swirls, filling the screen. Our gaze is suspended; we are compelled merely to regard these images, in their strangeness, apart from our knowledge of what they represent. Meanwhile, a voice off-screen comments on the irreducibility of the pebble to human meanings and instrumentalities, and on the failure of a linguistically bound self-consciousness to subsume or coincide with the images that surround and engulf it. The only response to questions regarding the use and nature of objects is a liberation of the visual from objectifying linguistic categories. The disjunction between speech and image reflects the incapacity of language (metaphor and metonymy) to abolish and replace appearance (the literal). Apart from all speech, or at its limit, the image subsists, a trace or residue, alien to the process of signification.

Filmmakers have frequently called attention to the radical potentialities of the nonsignifying image, as have theorists who have gotten beyond the simplistic binary opposition between Bazinian realism and Metzian semiotics. Deleuze (1986) begins his account of cinema with a Bergsonian equation between "the infinite set of all images" and the incessant "movements of matter," in a "world of universal variation, of universal undulation, universal rippling" (p. 58); human perception and consciousness are only secondary differentiations within this field of images in play. Blanchot's insistence on the radical disjunction between sight and language is picked up by Foucault and—in the specific context of film—by Deleuze (see 1988a, 60–69; 1989, 241–61). For his part, Walter Benjamin (1969) claims in his crucial essay, "The Work of Art in the Age of Mechanical Reproduction," that "evidently a different nature opens itself to the camera than opens to the naked eye—if only because an unconsciously penetrated space is substituted for a space consciously explored by man" (pp. 236–37). Benjamin seems to echo Dziga Vertov (1984), according to whom "the kino-eye lives and moves in time and space; it gathers and records impressions in a manner wholly

— freeing perception from the norms of human agency + human cognition.

different from that of the human eye. . . . Within the chaos of movements, running past, away, running into and colliding—the eye, all by itself, enters life" (pp. 15, 18). And in yet another register, Robert Bresson (1986) notes that "what no human eye is capable of catching, no pencil, brush, or pen of pinning down, your camera catches without knowing what it is, and pins it down with a machine's scrupulous indifference" (p. 26).

Benjamin, Vertov, Bresson, and Deleuze are as fascinated as is Bazin with cinema's capacity for freeing perception from the norms of human agency and human cognition. Such a viewpoint is directly opposed to the one that sees the cinematic apparatus as primarily a device of ideological reproduction. But the radical theorists I am citing here obviously reject Bazin's belief in the "natural" status of mechanically reproduced images. They insist, rather, that film dislodges sensation from its supposed "natural" conditions, which is to say from the anthropocentric structures of phenomenological reflection that realists such as Bazin take for granted. Deleuze (1986) proposes a Bergsonian theory of cinema because, whereas "what phenomenology sets up as a norm is 'natural perception' and its conditions," for Bergson, to the contrary, "the model cannot be natural perception, which does not possess any privilege" (p. 57).

Cinematic perception is primordial to the very extent that it is monstrously prosthetic. It is composed, one might say, of the unconscious epiphenomena of sensory experience. It affirms those very empirical contingencies that are sublated and denied by the Hegelian dialectic, and bracketed by the Husserlian *epoche*. The dematerialized images of film are the raw contents of sensation, without the forms, horizons, and contexts that usually orient them. And this is how film crosses the threshold of a new kind of perception, one that is below or above the human. This new perception is multiple and anarchic, nonintentional and asubjective; it is no longer subordinated to the requirements of representation and idealization, recognition and designation. It is affirmed before the intervention of concepts, and without the limitations of the fixed human eye: "the sensory exploration of the world through film . . . the exploration of the chaos of visual phenomena that fills space" (Vertov 1984, 14–15).

The camera does not invent, and does not even represent; it only passively records. But this passivity allows it to penetrate, or to be enveloped by, the flux of the material world. The automatism and nonselectivity of mechanical reproduction make it possible for cinema to break with traditional hierarchies of representation and enter directly into a realm of matter, life, and movement. The movie camera dehumanizes and deidealizes perceptual experience: it is at opposite poles from the Platonic dream of escaping the transitory and transcending mere material sensation. The cinematic apparatus responds, rather, to Georges Bataille's (1985) demand for the affirmation of transience, for the "apotheosis of that which is perishable" (p. 237). It opens the door to a "base materialism" (p. 45), defined as "the direct interpretation, *excluding all idealism*, of raw phenomena, and not a system founded on the fragmentary elements of an ideological analysis" (p. 16).

The experience of watching a film remains stubbornly concrete, immanent, and prereflective: it is devoid of depth and interiority. Sitting in the dark, watching the play of images across a screen, any detachment from "raw phenomena," from the immediacy of sensation or from the speeds and delays of temporal duration, is radically impossible. Cinema invites me, or forces me, to stay within the orbit of the senses. I am confronted and assaulted by a flux of sensations that I can neither attach to physical presences nor translate into systematized abstractions. I am violently, viscerally affected by *this* image and *this* sound, without being able to have recourse to any frame of reference, any form of transcendental reflection, or any Symbolic order. No longer does a signifying structure anticipate every possible perception; instead, the continual metamorphoses of sensation pre-empt, slip and slide beneath, and threaten to dislodge all the comforts and stabilities of meaning. As Benjamin (1969) says, "No sooner has [the spectator's] eye grasped a scene than it is already changed. It cannot be arrested" (p. 238).

      The materiality of sensation remains irreducible to, and irrecuperable by, the ideality of signification. It is the shock and surprise of this movement, and not the complacency of being able to recognize the real in its reproduction, that amazed the first film spectators at the end of the nineteenth century. Godard evokes this amazement very well, in a sequence in *Les Carabaniers* in which his young protagonist goes to the movies for the first time. Upon viewing the Lumière shot of a train directly approaching the camera (and therefore the audience), the boy's immediate reaction is not—as we might suppose—to try to run away, but to cover his eyes. He is not responding as if a train were really there; he is responding, rather, to the actual image of a train. He is affected not by any supposed representational verisimilitude of the image, but by its visceral insistence and its movement. A train is indeed heading directly at him, not of course for his seat in the theater, but for his line of sight. It is not a question here of cinema's "reality effect"; the boy's reaction cannot be characterized as a hallucinatory belief in the reality of an illusion. His heightened involvement with the image is more on the order of a direct stimulation of the optic nerves, bypassing the cognitive and reflective faculties altogether. The agitation of the senses and compulsive fascination that overtake the viewer cannot be reduced to effects of lack, disavowal, and ideological or Imaginary misrecognition. What Benjamin (1969) calls the "physical shock effect" (p. 238) of film viewing disrupts the traditional, historically sedimented habits and expectations of vision; it undoes the transcendental and phenomenological structures that claimed to regulate perception and to ground and unify the ego. Film produces, instead, a new *automatism* of perception.

Materialist Constructions

I have been writing primarily about film as a visual experience. But in cinema, sounds as well as visual images tend toward the condition of nonsignifying traces that escape, resist, and prove refractory to the dominant order of discursive comprehension. Kaja Silverman (1988, 42) notes that even theorists (like Metz and Baudry) who insist on the secondariness and constructedness of the cinematic image nonetheless posit film sound as a realm of originary plenitude. These theorists argue that, whereas there is a radical discontinuity between an image and the object of which it is an image, no such distinction can be made in the case of sound. A sound that is recorded and played back is still the "same" sound, rather than the "image" or simulacrum of a sound. Silverman counters these arguments by citing Lacan to the effect that "speech produces absence, not presence," and "the discoursing voice is the agent of symbolic castration" (p. 43). I would suggest that—just as in the case of images—both sides of the debate are wrong. Silverman makes her case by explicitly reducing sound to speech, and by implicitly reducing particular speech acts (*parole*) to overall linguistic structure (*langue*). But the work of reproduction in the cinematic apparatus in fact moves in precisely the opposite direction from the one Silverman evokes. The passivity of mechanical recording devices tends to isolate sounds, as well as images, from their discursively regulated contexts. Speech acts in film, like nonlinguistic noises, have their own "physical shock effect"; they are events whose immediacy is also their evanescence. Far from reducing sound to the condition of language, cinema tends to "deterritorialize" and disarticulate linguistic utterance, to pull it in the direction of nonsignifying sound. In Godard's films—to take the example of a filmmaker usually thought to mark the *ne plus ultra* of cinematic discursivity—bits of language, whether spoken in voice-overs or visually presented in titles, always have a gratuitous, material, and literal insistence, exceeding their discursive signification. Godard's method of insistent citation has the effect not of turning his films into "texts," but of affirming the "incorporeal materiality" of sounds as well as images. This insertion or inscription of language within film makes all the more impossible the reduction of cinematic structures to linguistic ones.

Deleuze and Guattari (1987, 75–110) argue that the classic structuralist opposition of *langue* and *parole* is untenable: no clear conceptual distinction can be maintained between individual speech acts and the underlying structures of language in which speakers supposedly participate (see also Grisham 1991). A "continuous, immanent process of variation" (Deleuze and Guattari 1987, 103) moves transversally through the sociolinguistic field, undercutting the hierarchized distinctions of competence and performance, norm and deviation, structural law and empirical instance. Under different social and political conditions, language of course has a greater or lesser degree of fluidity, but structural linguistic theory tends to deny this fluidity altogether. Such theory is thus particularly inappropriate for film, which by its very forms pushes fluidity and immanent variation to the maximum. Even language, we might say, isn't really "structured like a language" in the famous Saussaurian and Lacanian sense; all the less is cinema so structured. No matter how much film relies on syntactic conventions, rhetorical punctuations, and symbolic abbreviations, these do not and cannot have the autonomy and the self-referentiality that are attributed to linguistic structures. The sheer duration of a film, and the continually varying visual and aural impressions that compose that duration, are important in a way that the material content of language (according to structural linguistics) is not. Language as a synchronic structure is said to be independent of its material base, as of the time needed for actual expression, but cinema cannot survive the elimination or sublimation of sensation and temporality. If we try to abstract from the immanent phenomena of a film in order to reach a hidden but intelligible deep structure—as linguists do with the phenomena of language—there is literally nothing left.

The cinematic apparatus radically deoriginates sounds and linguistic utterances, as well as visual images. This process of deracination, the freeing of sounds and images from their referents, is of course what the psychoanalytic theorists have in mind when they compare film to language and describe it in terms of lack, absence, and castration. I am arguing, to the contrary, that the deterritorializing and deoriginating force of the apparatus leads directly to the visceral immediacy of cinematic experience. What I have claimed with regard to images is all the more apparent in the case of sounds: that their *reproduction* cannot be equated with or reduced to their *representation*. The indiscernibility of initial and reproduced sounds points to the simulacral logic that we have already seen at work in Warhol's silent films: it becomes impossible to identify definitively either the original or the copies. "By making many reproductions [the technology of mechanical reproduction] substitutes a plurality of copies for a unique existence. And in permitting the reproduction to meet the beholder or listener in his own particular situation, it reactivates the object reproduced" (Benjamin 1969, 221). Sounds and images are "reactivated," multiplied and intensified, precisely by being cut off from their source or origin. Mechanical reproduction marks the withering of the aura, the radical subversion of the hierarchy of original and copy upon which the theories of mediation and representation, or lack and substitution, depend.

Film theorists usually posit a radical opposition between the direct presentation of sounds and images through recording and the manipulation of them through editing. This is as much the case for realists such as Bazin and

contemporary phenomenological theorists such as Dudley Andrew as it is for formalists from Eisenstein and Balázs on to semiotic and psychoanalytic critics writing in the wake of Metz. For Bazin, montage compromises the perceptual realism
of cinema; for the latter group, without the imposition of cinematic grammar and
syntax through aggressive editing, there would scarcely be such a thing as a film at
all. I want to argue, against both positions, that there isn't really any discontinuity between these two dimensions. In Godard's *La Chinoise*, Jean-Pierre Leaud
rejects traditional descriptions of Lumière as a naturalist and Méliès as a fantasist.
He claims that Lumière's art is equivalent to that of the impressionist painters,
since it endeavors to disengage fleeting perceptions from scenes of everyday life,
while Méliès is best seen as a proto-Brecht, a critical social realist, documenting,
analyzing, and anticipating the actual technological transformations of modern
society.

One might argue, in a similar spirit, that the lines joining and
separating the realism of cinema from its illusionism cannot be drawn as simply as
is usually thought. We can assert, against Bazin, that a style based on long takes
and depth of field is no less artificial and constructed than one based on montage;
but we can also argue, against formalists and semioticians, that this constructedness in no way compromises the perceptual intensity/immediacy of images and
movements in time and space. Rather, constructedness and immanent materiality
go hand in hand. Bazin fails to realize that it is the very devices of abstraction and
construction he attacks that can alone produce the very "realism" he values. But
the complementary mistake of formalist and semiotic theory is to assume that,
since the cinematic image is constructed (since it cannot be a direct presentation of
reality in the manner Bazin too naively claims), it must be deciphered as a mode of
ideological representation. This is to ignore the way in which the sensorial imme-

diacy of cinema is the direct consequence of its overt denial of theatrical presence. Cinematic images and sounds are neither immediately present objects nor their mediated representations, precisely because they are traces and reproductions of the real. In this netherworld of simulacra and traces, the combined immediacy and impalpability of the cinematic image is the common condition for the long-take, deep-focus realism of Renoir and for the montage style of Eisenstein, for the anti-illusionism of Bresson and Godard and for the delirious hyperillusionism of Raul Ruiz, for the deadpan minimalism of early Warhol and the elegant maximalism of *Blue Steel*.

Thus, editing neither vitiates the integrity of mechanically reproduced images nor compensates for their inadequacy. Everything I have been saying about the immediacy and irrecuperability of singular images and sounds is only accentuated by the necessities of framing, cutting, and montage. The radical discontinuity that editing makes possible serves yet further to dislodge the spectator. It undermines any notion of a fixed center of perception, in relation to which there could be a single standard of size and movement, and at which experience would obey the laws of spatial contiguity and linear causal succession. As Deleuze (1986) puts it, "The frame ensures a deterritorialization of the image," because it "gives a common standard of measurement to things which do not have one—long shots of countryside and close-ups of the face, an astronomical system and a single drop of water" (pp. 14–15). More generally, William Flesch (1987) argues that, due to editing, "the virtual space of film ... is alien to the laws of causality," so that "film provides a perfect analogy to Hume's epistemology of flux" (p. 278). Flesch goes on to show that the Humean or Heraclitean logic of film—its anarchic play of images at once literal and disembodied, and connected to one another only by convention or habit—remains irreducible to the space and structures of theatrical representation, however much Hollywood continuity rules strive to mimic and reimpose this latter.

In film, there can be no firm guarantees of identity and presence. Even the most naturalistic mise-en-scène is fragmented and framed in ways that are incompatible with monocular representational space, or with that of a proscenium theater. And even the most seamless and "invisible" editing style involves incessant violations of continuity and coherence, numerous ruptures of point of view. Neither mise-en-scène (the initial choice of what the camera will record) nor editing (the ulterior arrangement of what the camera has recorded) provides a release from contingency and instability. The "lines of flight" opened up by the material practice of film editing are never entirely effaced, even when they are recuperated in the stratifications of continuity rules. Every attempt to manipulate and to order the flow of images only strengthens the tendential forces that uproot this flow from any stability of meaning and reference. Cinematic vision pushes toward a condition of freeplay: the incessant metamorphoses of immanent, inconstant appearances.

In the realm of mechanical reproduction, the alternative between realism and illusionism is thus a false one. Benjamin, Vertov, and Bresson, whom I have already cited for their claims that cinematography is a materialist practice that produces a new form of direct contact with the real, are *also* among those who most stringently insist upon the constructed nature of the cinematic image. For Benjamin (1969), film penetrates into material and social reality not in spite of, but directly as a result of, its constructedness:

The equipment-free aspect of reality here has become the height of artifice; the sight of immediate reality has become an orchid in the land of technology.... [Film] offers, precisely because of the thoroughgoing permeation of reality with mechanical equipment, an aspect of reality which is free of all equipment. (pp. 233–34)

More cryptically, Bresson (1986) makes the same point in his maxim "ON FRAG-MENTATION: This is indispensable if one does not want to fall into REPRE-SENTATION. See beings and things in their separate parts. Render them independent in order to give them a new dependence" (p. 84). When the real is fragmented as a result of being permeated with machines, the opposition between subjectivity and objectivity, or between the observer and the observed, vanishes. The machines used by the filmmaker can no longer be regarded as tools to manipulate reality from a distance, for there no longer is any distance. In a world of mechanical reproduction, fragmentation and construction are not modes of representation, but processes of the real itself.

It is in this sense that Vertov (whose filmmaking practices anticipate Benjamin's theoretical formulations) embraces the real through editing and the manipulation of images. Deleuze (1986) rightly criticizes Jean Mitry for

condemning in Vertov a contradiction for which he would not dare to reproach a painter: a pseudo-contradiction between creativity (montage) and integrity (the real). What montage does, according to Vertov, is to carry perception into things, to put perception into matter.... In this respect all procedures are legitimate, they are no longer trick shots. (p. 81)

Consider some famous sequences in *Man with a Movie Camera*: the montage of the opening and closing of an eye, a camera lens, and window shutters; or the overlaying of a documentary sequence involving rapid motion, the editor cutting that very sequence, and the audience watching the same sequence unroll on the screen. It is inadequate merely to say (as Baudry 1986b, 296, for instance, does) that such sequences reveal the constructedness of the film image and unveil the mediating presence of the cinematic apparatus. Vertov is reveling in the cinema's powers of recording and montage; he relies upon them absolutely, rather than alienating the audience from them.

Cinema is at once a form of perception and a material perceived, a new way of encountering reality and a part of the reality thereby discovered for the first time. The kino-eye does not transform reality, so much as it is itself caught up in the dynamic transformations that constitute the material and social real. In presenting the cinematic apparatus within the film, the sequences I have cited do not suspend or put into doubt the reality of the spectacle; they affirm and expand precisely that reality, by setting up a series of equivalencies and relays. Vertov's exploration of the real *through* montage (fragmentation and reconstruction) is a way of subverting or short-circuiting representation. He brings the audience directly into the process of the film, just as he brings his own activity as filmmaker directly into the larger processes of social production and reproduction. Far from questioning the cinematic image with critical and hermeneutical suspicion, he celebrates its multiple registers of efficacy. It is in such terms that Vertov earns his claim to be a Marxist, materialist filmmaker: like Benjamin, he understands social relations (including the cinema) as material forces in their own right, rather than just as effects of ideological representation.

It is odd that semiotic and psychoanalytic film theory—in striking contrast to Benjamin and Vertov—remains so preoccupied with the themes of ideology and representation, that it associates visual pleasure almost exclusively with the illusion of a stable and centered subject confronting a spatially and temporally homogeneous world, and that it regards editing primarily as a technique for producing such an illusion, by "suturing" the spectator and perspec-

tivizing the gaze. A wide variety of cinematic pleasures are predicated explicitly
X upon the decentered freeplay, the freedom from the constraints of subjectivity,
that editing and special effects make possible. This is not the case only with a film
such as *Man with a Movie Camera*, whose delirious explorations of nonsubjective
perception are directly linked to a revolutionary political practice. One can cite,
just as readily, the weird alienation effects that proliferate throughout Jerry
Lewis's comedies (discussed in chapter III) or the implausible arrangements of
bodies, impossible points of view, nonnaturalistic transformations of decor, and
other forms of visual and narrative discontinuity that characterize the classic
American musical. Films such as Vincente Minnelli's *The Band Wagon* and Stanley Donen's *Singin' in the Rain* are as self-conscious, and as radically disruptive
in terms of form, as any of the works of Alexander Kluge or Yvonne Rainer. They
liberate space from the constraints of Renaissance perspective, and time from
the constraints of causal narrative logic—and delight spectators all the more in
doing so.

My point is obviously not to deny the radical differences—in
political stance and in the kind of pleasure offered the spectator—between a film
by Donen and one by Kluge. I am suggesting, rather, that these differences cannot
be grounded in formal procedures, and especially that ideological positions cannot
be correlated with a simplistic opposition between "invisible editing" that works to
conceal itself and editing that calls attention to its own artifice. From Busby
Berkeley's delirious choreography to Minnelli's mannerist stylizations, American
musicals have produced pleasure for mass audiences by highlighting, and reveling
in, those very processes that—according to the suppositions of psychoanalytic film
theory—the commercial cinema needs to dissimulate and repress in order to function successfully. These musicals dissipate the illusion of subjective plenitude; they

foreground their own constructedness, and they even unveil and bring into play the presence of the camera. The cheerfully aggressive dislocations practiced in these films push well beyond the formal symmetries (Berkeley's patterns of dancing girls, Astaire's elegantly controlled movements) that they are needed to support. The surplus enjoyment provided in American musicals—produced by the very techniques that in other contexts have been regarded as ones of "alienation"—continually exceeds those functions of fantasy and of ideological resolution that are highlighted in the most important recent discussions of the genre (see Altman 1987; Feuer 1982).

Passivity and Fascination

The crucial point is that, contrary to the claims of psychoanalytic film theory, cinematic pleasure does not put the spectator in a position of active mastery of the gaze, and does not necessarily depend upon specular identification. Pleasure can just as well be linked to the destruction of identification and objectification, to the undermining of subjective stability, and to an affirmation of the multiple techniques that denaturalize (or de-Cartesianize) cinematic perception. Contemporary film theorists seek to disrupt the supposed illusion of "naturalness" in cinema, just as Brecht disrupted the naturalistic conventions of bourgeois theater. But these theorists fail to notice that Brechtian techniques have an entirely different impact when they are transferred from the stage to the screen. The fact is that distancing and alienation-effects serve not to dispel but only to intensify the captivating power of cinematic spectacle. Precisely because film is already predicated on what Benjamin (1969) calls the destruction of the aura, because it is already an "alienated" art, its capacity to affect the spectator is not perturbed by any additional measure of alienation. Devices whose purpose is to distance actors from their roles make little sense in a medium that has already abolished the physical presence of the actors' bodies in space. As Benjamin puts it:

For film, what matters primarily is that the actor represents himself to the public before the camera, rather than representing someone else.... The stage actor identifies himself with the character of his role. The film actor very often is denied this opportunity. (pp. 229–30)

Flesch (1987), following Benjamin, therefore speaks of "the *proximity without presence* of the virtual space of film" in opposition to the power of the aura as implied by "charismatic, theatrical presence" (p. 287). In film's virtual space, visual pleasure and fascination are emphatically *not* dependent upon any illusion of naturalness or presence. And consequently, this pleasure and fascination cannot be reduced by traditional modes of critical reflection. Alienation-effects are already in secret accord with the basic antitheatricality of cinematic presentation.

　　　　Psychoanalytic film theory's claims for the centrality of the active gaze, of Renaissance perspective, and of narcissistic identification are at best archaic—they refer to a much older technology, which the photographic and cinematic apparatuses and the social developments of nineteenth- and twentieth-century capitalism have rendered obsolete. Film theory usually traces cinematic representation back to the model of the *camera obscura*: the device for projecting an inverted image, composed of light admitted through a pinhole, onto a wall in a dark chamber. The camera obscura was used by Renaissance painters in order to establish the rules of perspective; in the seventeenth and eighteenth centuries it became a favored philosophical model or metaphor of vision. But Jonathan Crary (1988a) argues that the camera obscura "collapse[d] as a model for an observer and for the functioning of human vision" precisely at the time that photography was being invented, in the early nineteenth century (p. 31). The camera obscura's disembodied, interiorizing, monocular paradigm of vision was replaced by a paradigm that "dramatized the productive role played by the body in vision" (p. 34). In this new epistemological regime, "the privileging of the body as a visual producer began to collapse the distinction between inner and outer upon which the camera obscura depended"; at the same time, "subjective vision [was] found to be distinctly temporal, an unfolding of processes within the body" (p. 35). Physiology replaces Cartesian mental privacy as the model for subjective action and response; vision is now unthinkable without reference to the "opacity or carnal density of the observer" (p. 43).

This nineteenth-century embodiment of vision is just one aspect of a larger epistemological shift. In response to an emergent capitalism's need to mobilize and control labor power on a massive scale, the human body's actions and reactions were analyzed, dissected, and quantified as never before. But Crary also mentions the "strange intensity and exhilaration" of early nineteenth-century research on vision, in the course of which experimenters blinded themselves by repeatedly staring at the sun (p. 34). Cinema is one important product of this new episteme and technology of vision. Even at its most manipulative, it is premised less on the ideological mystification of the spectator than on his or her calculated physiological responses. But beyond and as a result of these very calculations, film also tends toward the blinding ecstasy of Bataillean expenditure. In the cinematic apparatus, vision is uprooted from the idealized paradigms of representation and perspective, and dislodged from interiority. It is grounded instead in the rhythms and delays of an ungraspable temporality, and in the materiality of the agitated flesh.

Art in the age of mechanical reproduction thus cannot be equated with illusionistic representation. In film, Benjamin (1969) says, "art has left the realm of the 'beautiful semblance' which, so far, had been taken to be the only sphere where art could thrive" (p. 230). Mass-produced images "demand a specific kind of approach; free-floating contemplation is not appropriate to them. They stir the viewer; he feels challenged by them in a new way" (p. 226). On one hand, the rush of film images is simply too quick, too immediate, to allow the spectator the breathing room necessary for traditional, detached aesthetic contemplation. On the other hand, this immediacy or speed is not authenticated by any illusion of concrete or actual presence. The immediacy of cinema is always excessive: it is too strong, too insistent, to be contained by any "metaphysics of presence." Film's virtual images do not correspond to anything actually present, but *as* images, or *as* sensations, they affect me in a manner that does not leave room for any suspension of my response. I have already been touched and altered by these sensations, even before I have had the chance to become conscious of them. The world I see through the movie camera is one that violently impinges upon me, one that I can no longer regard, unaffected, from a safe distance. But this *also* means that cinema involves the violation of presence and the irreversible alienation of the viewer. The cinematic image, in its violent more-than-presence, is at the same time immediately an absence: a distance too great to allow for dialectical interchange or for any sort of possession. In its disruptive play of immediacy and distance, film is not just an art without an aura; it is an art that enacts, again and again, what Bataille calls the sacrifice of the sacred (auratic) object, or what Benjamin calls the disintegration of the aura in the experience of shock.

Blanchot (1981) makes a radical distinction between the realm of subjective action and perception and the passive regime of the image. In "natural" perception, seeing is an initiative and a power of the subject. "Seeing implies distance, the decision that causes separation, the power not to be in contact and to avoid the confusion of contact" (p. 75). By placing things (and other people) at the proper distance from myself, I am able to constitute them *as* objects, and have them always ready and at my disposal. This is also what allows me to constitute myself as an active subject. This form of seeing corresponds to what Derrida calls the metaphysics of presence. It is the realm of traditional subject/object dualism, but also of phenomenological intentionality, and of the countermovement of objectification in the play of gazes as described, for instance, by Sartre. The important thing to note is that, in this realm, domination (through objectification) and reciprocity (through a dialectic of mutual recognition, a dialogic relationship, or an interplay of gazes) cannot be opposed. They are alternate terms of one and the same movement. Bakhtinian dialogism and Lacanian Symbolic intersubjectivity are still played out against the background of this phallocratic regime of power and possession.

On the other hand, the power of the ego is ruptured at the point of what Blanchot (1981) calls *fascination*:

But what happens when what you see, even though from a distance, seems to touch you with a grasping contact, when the matter of seeing is a sort of touch, when seeing is a contact at a distance? What happens when what is seen imposes itself on your gaze, as though the gaze had been seized, touched, put in contact with appearance? (p. 75)

It is the moment when "the thing we are staring at has sunk into its image, [and] the image has returned to that depth of impotence into which everything falls back" (p. 80). The release of the image takes place when we are no longer able to separate ourselves, no longer able to put things at the proper distance and turn them into objects. The distance between subject and object is at once abolished and rendered infinite. On one hand, I am no longer able to evade the touch or contact of what I see, but on the other, since the image is impalpable, I cannot take hold of it in return, but always find it shimmering just beyond my grasp. The thing has dissolved into its image, and no longer offers me the prospect of reciprocity, or the hope of mastery by means of possession. Instead, the image becomes an obsession, it *haunts* me: "What haunts is the inaccessible which one cannot rid oneself of, what one does not find and what, because of that, does not allow one to avoid it. The ungraspable is what one does not escape" (Blanchot 1981, 84). My gaze has lost its power of initiative and sunk into a strange passivity:

the gaze of what is incessant and interminable, in which blindness is still vision, vision that is no longer the possibility of seeing, but the impossibility of not seeing, impossibility that turns into seeing, that perseveres—always and always—in a vision that does not end: a dead gaze, a gaze that has become the ghost of an eternal vision. (p. 75)

Blanchot is not writing specifically about cinema, but his description powerfully evokes what actually happens when I am sitting in a dark room, confronted by a parade of images moving across a screen. Blanchot's discussion contradicts the usual psychoanalytic notion that scopophilia and voyeurism are "active" affects or perversions, for the overwhelming experience of visual fascination in the cinema, of what Blanchot calls "passion for the image" (p. 75), is one of radical passivity. I do not have power over what I see, I do not even have, strictly speaking, the power to see; it is more that I am powerless not to see. The darkness of the movie theater isolates me from the rest of the audience, and cuts off any possibility of "normal" perception. I cannot willfully focus my attention on this or on that. Instead, my gaze is arrested by the sole area of light, a flux of moving images. I am attentive to what happens on the screen only to the extent that I am continually distracted, and passively absorbed, by it. I no longer have the freedom to follow my own train of thought. As Benjamin (1969) puts it, "The spectator's process of association in view of these images is indeed interrupted by their constant, sudden change. This constitutes the shock effect of the film" (p. 238). The unstable screen image holds my distracted attention captive; I do not have the ability to look away. There is no way to watch a film without allowing this to happen; I can resist it only by giving up on the film altogether, by shutting my eyes or walking out. But as I watch, I have no presence of mind: sight and hearing, anticipation and memory, are no longer my own. My responses are not internally motivated and are not spontaneous; they are forced upon me from beyond. Scopophilia is then the opposite of mastery: it is rather a forced, ecstatic abjection before the image, much like the psychopath's fixation on the female cop's gun in *Blue Steel*. Voyeuristic behavior is not willed or controlled by its subject: it is a form of captivation, in which passivity is pushed to the point of automatism. Film viewing is neither self-concerned nor in the traditional aesthetic sense disinterested; when I watch a film, an alien interest is forced upon me, one from which I cannot escape, but that I also cannot make my own.

The compulsion that determines cinematic fascination is brilliantly rendered in a scene from Stanley Kubrick's *A Clockwork Orange*: Alex's eyes are propped open forcibly, so that he is compelled to watch a series of atrocities unfold on the screen before him. Ostensibly this is a totalitarian-behaviorist "cure" for Alex's unremitting social deviance, but actually it exposes the continuity and resonance between Alex's anarchic, "freely willed" violence and the standardizing violence of the state. A similar mechanism is presented even more cogently and cruelly in Dario Argento's *Terror at the Opera*. The heroine, an opera singer, is compelled to witness a psychopath committing his gruesome murders: before each one, he immobilizes her and attaches rows of sharp little stakes above and below her eyes. She is literally forced to stare at the action unfolding directly before her, but in which she cannot actively participate, for if she so much as blinks, the tiny knives will lacerate her eyeballs. The resulting nauseating intimacy and complicity between the female viewer (who is not directly the victim) and the male murderer is closely akin to the ambiguous dynamic between Eugene and Turner that I've already discussed in *Blue Steel*. Looking is an obsessive passivity, a violent forcing, that yet cannot entirely be reduced to a situation of being manipulated, enslaved, subjugated, or controlled. The cop in *Blue Steel* and the opera singer in *Terror at the Opera* are overtly appalled by the violence they are compelled to see, yet there's a latent—secretly desirable—erotic thrill in the way these gory spectacles are being produced for *them*. They do not "identify" with the murderers, but they are transformed, and even energized, by their involuntary participation. It is precisely to the extent that these scenarios are so blatantly prurient and pornographic that they resist being classified according to the conventional binary opposition of sadistic male violence and helpless female passivity. I am proposing them as a singular counterparadigm for film spectatorship on account of both their extremity and their subversive, complicitous, and irreducibly ambiguous blurring of traditional polarities between male and female, active and passive, aggressor and victim, and subject and object. They point not to Lacanian specular dynamics, but to a radically different economy/regime/articulation of vision.

The Tactile Image

Benjamin (1969) argues that the experience of film, like that of Dadaist art works, is ultimately *tactile*: "It hit[s] the spectator like a bullet, it happen[s] to him, thus acquiring a tactile quality" (p. 238). The equation of vision and gunfire in *Blue Steel* is more than just a metaphor. Images literally assault the spectator, leaving him or her no space for reflection. Violence is at work even on the most basic physiological level, in the much-disputed phenomenon of "persistence of vision." Film movement appears continuous only because of the eye's retention of virtual images. When I watch a film, images excite my retina, 24 times a second, at a speed that is slow enough to allow for the impact and recording of stimuli, but too fast for me to keep up with them consciously. Perception has become unconscious. It is neither spontaneously active nor freely receptive, but radically passive, the suffering of a violence perpetrated against the eye. Images themselves are immaterial, but their *effect* is all the more physical and corporeal. They are continually being *imprinted* upon the retina, and as Derrida has shown, the imprint, or trace, that thus constitutes perception can never be taken up into the self-consciousness of a living present.

The retention of virtual images is concomitant with an irreducible gap between stimulus and response, or more precisely between the imprinting of a sensation and its reception. This gap or interval is, for Deleuze (1986), constitutive of but irreducible to subjectivity: it is the ungraspable nonperception that alone makes subjective perception possible (see pp. 61–66). The gap is a wound at the heart of vision: the phenomenon of shock that fascinates Benjamin, or the exorbitation of the eye, the blindness at the heart of sight, that so obsesses Bataille. In Blanchot's (1981) words, "The split [between eye and object], which had been the possibility of seeing, solidifies, right inside the gaze, into impossibility. In this way, in the very thing that makes it possible, the gaze finds the power that neutralizes it" (p. 75). The disengagement of a primordial or preoriginary level of perception violently excites, and thereby fascinates and obsesses, the film viewer. Perception is turned back upon the body of the perceiver, so that it affects and alters that body, instead of merely constituting a series of representations for the spectator to recognize.

We neglect the basic tactility and viscerality of cinematic experience when we describe material processes and effects, such as the persistence of vision, merely as mental illusions. Cinema produces real effects *in* the viewer, rather than merely presenting phantasmic reflections *to* the viewer. The cinematic image is not an object for some (actual or ideal) spectator; instead, the spectator is drawn *into* the fragmented materiality and the "depth without depth" (Blanchot 1981, 75) of the image. In film, the old structure of aesthetic contemplation collapses. I am solicited and invested by what I see: perception becomes a kind of physical affliction, an intensification and disarticulation of bodily sensation, rather than a process either of naive (ideological and Imaginary) belief or of detached, attentive consideration. Contemplation is replaced by "tactile appropriation," which "is accomplished not so much by attention as by habit" (Benjamin 1969, 240).

When I am caught up in watching a film I do not really "identify" in a psychoanalytic sense with the activity of the (male) protagonist, or with that protagonist's gaze, or even with what theorists have called the "omnivoyeuristic" look of the camera. It is more the case that I am brought into intimate contact with the images on the screen by a process of *mimesis* or *contagion*. Benjamin specifically opposes "the mimetic faculty" (even within language) to the movement of signification. Mimesis in this sense involves a participatory and tactile contact between what post-Cartesian thought calls the object and the subject, as in the rituals of sympathetic magic and the assaults of capitalist advertising. As Michael Taussig (1992) summarizes this aspect of Benjamin, "The connection with tactility is paramount, the optical dissolving, as it were, into touch and a certain thickness and density.... mimesis implies *both* copy and substantial connection, *both* visual replication and material transfer" (pp. 144–45). Mimesis culminates in the production of what Benjamin (1985a) calls "nonsensuous similarities," which cannot be assimilated by or reduced to the canons of meaning and representation (pp. 160–63).

According to orthodox psychoanalysis, the subject is stabilized and rigidified by means of its identifications; but following Benjamin and Taussig, we must radically redefine the very notion of *identification*, and say rather that the subject is captivated and "distracted," made more fluid and indeterminate, in the process of sympathetic participation. Mimesis and contagion tend to efface fixed identities and to blur the boundaries between inside and outside. The viewer is transfixed and transmogrified in consequence of the infectious, visceral contact of images. Transformations of this sort are the explicit subject of many recent horror films, most notably of George Romero's "living dead" trilogy. The viewer of these films does not identify with their active protagonists so much as he or she is touched by—drawn into complicitous communication with—the passive, horrific, and yet strangely attractive zombies. (I discuss these films in more detail in chapter II.)

Much work remains to be done on the psychophysiology of cinematic experience: the ways in which film renders vision tactile, short-circuits reflection and directly stimulates the nervous system, produces and invests social power relations that are not just matters of ideology, and reinstates a materialistic—rather than a signifying—semiotics. This latter is one of the themes of Deleuze's (1986, 1989) two volumes on cinema, in which he deploys Peirce's theory of signs explicitly against Metz's notion that cinema is structured like a language, and against the psychoanalytic tenet of "lack," of a radical gap or opposition between material processes and signifying ones. It is thus necessary to take issue with Silverman's (1988) seemingly commonsensical claim that "within cinema there are, of course, no tactile convergences, and the gap between viewer and spectacle remains irreducible" (p. 6). On the contrary, the allure and the danger of cinema are the direct consequences of such "tactile convergences."

If cinema is similar to dream, this is not because it would disavow lack and "castration" by offering a compensatory illusion of subjective omnipotence and narrative continuity. Rather, film moves and affects the spectator precisely to the extent that it lures him or her into an excessive intimacy, one so extreme that it is also, immediately, a distance precluding identification. It dissolves the contours of the ego and transgresses the requirements of coherence and closure that govern "normal" experience. In this new realm, the gaze is at once fascinated and distracted, but in any case passive and not possessive. The world of static, stabilizing self-representations slips out from under me. I am drawn instead into a realm of Heraclitean flux, a time and space from which all fixed points of reference and self-reference, all lines of perspective, and all possibilities of stabilizing identification and objectification are banished. Contrary to the usual assertions of orthodox film theory, then, nothing could be further removed from egocentric fantasy, or from the fetishistic disavowal of lack and the delusive self-confirmations of narcissism, than is the experience of film viewing.

The question is ultimately one of what affects and passions are constructed or expressed by the mechanisms of cinema. I am taking issue with the conservative, conformist assumption—shared by most film theorists—that our desires are primarily ones for possession, plenitude, stability, and reassurance. I am thereby also rejecting this assumption's complementary underside: the notion of the Oedipal structuration of a "split subject," which must assume the burdens of "lack" (alienation from the real), and of the exclusive, binary disjunction of gender, as the price for entering into society. I am suggesting, rather, that what film offers its viewers is something far more compelling and disturbing: a Bataillean ecstasy of expenditure, of automutilation and self-abandonment—neither Imaginary plenitude nor Symbolic articulation, but the blinding intoxication of contact with the Real.

In affirming raw sensation, in communicating the violent contents of visual excitation apart from its pacifying forms, and in provoking visceral excitation, film hyperbolically aggravates vision, pushing it to an extreme point of implosion and self-annihilation. As Buñuel says of *Un chien andalou*, a film's "object is to provoke instinctive reactions of revulsion and attraction in the spectator" (quoted in Aranda 1976, 64). And Buñuel adds that "nothing in the film symbolizes anything." All cinema tends away from the coagulation of meaning and toward the shattering dispossession of the spectator, the moment of the razor slicing the eyeball in *Un chien andalou*. Film extinguishes the *power* of sight, but this extinction is not a definitive conclusion. Horror fans know that the dead always walk again, even as consumers of pornography know that no orgasm is ever the last. Film is a mode of what Rosalind Krauss (1986) (commenting on Bataille) calls *antivision*. The disempowering of the gaze opens a space of horror and obscenity, in which "we see that which exceeds the possibility of seeing, that which it is intolerable to see" (Bataille 1986, 268; translation modified). And it occurs in a time of repetition, without a living present, a time that linear narrative cannot fill, like the interminable time of Chantal Akerman's *Jeanne Dielman*, or what Blanchot (1981) describes in another context as "the time in which nothing begins, in which initiative is not possible, where before the affirmation there is already the recurrence of the affirmation" (p. 72).

The extinction of sight is the positive condition for a new space and time, the strange realm of fascination and the image. And this is why pornography and horror are so crucial to any account of cinematic experience. In the realm of visual fascination, sex and violence have much more intense and disturbing an impact than they do in literature or any other medium; they affect the viewer in a shockingly direct way. Violent and pornographic films literally anchor desire and perception in the agitated and fragmented body. These "tactile convergences" are at once the formal means of expression and the thematic content of a film like *Blue Steel*.

Masochism

All this suggests the need for a new approach to the dynamics of film viewing: one that is masochistic, mimetic, tactile, and corporeal, in contrast to the reigning psychoanalytic paradigm's emphasis on sadism and separation. Leo Bersani (1986)—whose approach has strong affinities to Bataille—provocatively suggests that "sexuality is ontologically grounded in masochism," and even that sexuality is "a tautology for masochism" (p. 39). Bersani argues, through a deconstructive reading of several of Freud's crucial texts, that the escalating process of sexual excitation undoes conventional oppositions between pleasure and pain. Bersani presents his argument as a contribution to psychoanalytic discourse, but he continually approaches the point where the entire psychoanalytic paradigm—and particularly the Oedipal/structural version of it that informs film theory—threatens to break down. The same can be said for Deleuze's (1971) early work, *Masochism*. In contesting Freud's thesis on the reversibility between masochism and sadism, and in arguing that these libidinal formations correspond to radically different logics and "aesthetics," Deleuze begins his dismantling of the psychoanalytic paradigm, something that is explicitly accomplished in *Anti-Oedipus* (Deleuze and Guattari 1983). Following both Bersani and Deleuze, we may say that the violent stimulation of the body and the loss of ego boundaries that are foregrounded in masochism, but that characterize sexual play in general, are at once desirable and threatening. The self is repetitively shattered by an ecstatic excess of affect, and not primordially "split" by the imposition of "lack." And I do not try merely to defend myself against slipping into this delicious passivity, this uncontainable agitation; I compulsively, passionately seek it out. Anxiety over the disruption of identity is concomitant with, and perhaps necessary to, the very intensity of sensual gratification. Fearfulness is itself a thrill and a powerful turn-on, as any devotee of horror films knows. It is impossible to reduce sexual passion, and within it the "passion for perceiving" that animates the cinematic spectator, to a desire for self-identity, wholeness, security, and recognition. The masochist seeks not to reach a final consummation, but to hold it off, to prolong the frenzy, for as long as possible. Cinema seduces its viewers by mimetically exacerbating erotic tension, in an orgy of unproductive expenditure. Visual fascination is a direct consequence of this masochistic heightening, rather than of any secondary movements of suturing and satiation.

In their intensified form, the states of excitation, *which are comparable to toxic states, can be defined as the illogical and irresistible impulse to reject material and moral goods that it would have been possible to utilize rationally (in conformity with the balancing of accounts). (Bataille 1985, 128)*

What inspires the cinematic spectator is a passion for that very loss of control, that abjection, fragmentation, and subversion of self-identity that psychoanalytic theory so dubiously classifies under the rubrics of lack and castration.

       Psychoanalytic film theory has belatedly started to pay more attention to questions of masochism, passivity, and the body. In her recent book *Male Subjectivity at the Margins*, Kaja Silverman (1992) is usefully attentive to the ways in which male masochism, at least, potentially subverts patriarchal order, and thereby constitutes for Freud "a veritable hermeneutic scandal" (p. 210). Nonetheless, much of Silverman's discussion reads as a kind of policing action, seeking to contain the theorization of masochism within the boundaries of Oedipal structuration. She stigmatizes approaches that derive masochism—or any formation of subjectivity—from sources other than "the categorical imperatives of the Oedipus complex and symbolic law" (p. 417) as being either wishfully and delusively "utopian" (referring to Deleuze and to Gayle Rubin; pp. 211, 417) or "determinedly apolitical" (referring to Gaylyn Studlar; p. 417). As a result, Silverman hedges all her claims for the subversive potentialities of masochism; she seems nervous about the possibility that these "perverse" sexualities might work as "lines of flight," or open up trajectories other than the familiar phallocentric one. She is right to recall that "masochism in all its guises is as much a product of the existing symbolic order as a reaction against it" (p. 213), but it's strange and disappointing that she presents this ambiguity as a limitation on the political consequentiality of masochism. Change can take place only at the strange and ambiguous boundary between inside and outside, between complicity and resistance; the very ambivalence that a masochistic aesthetic so beautifully heightens and intensifies is a necessary condition for any political intervention. Silverman makes what Nietzsche (1968) denounced long ago as *the error of mistaking cause for consequence*" (p. 47); she regards our society's "symbolic order" as the transcendental cause of gender and sexual oppressions, rather than as a concrete (and therefore contingent and changeable) effect and instrument of practices of oppression. She seeks to master the disturbing, preoriginary ambiguity of film images by writing it off to the account of the castration complex and the law of the father.

Gaylyn Studlar (1985) is closer to the mark than Silverman, in that she aligns cinema directly with masochistic pleasure—as opposed to the sadistic drive to control and extinguish the objects of one's gaze—and thus "opens the entirety of film to the existence of spectatorial pleasures divorced from issues of castration, sexual difference, and female lack" (p. 610). (Studlar works through this thesis in much greater detail in *In the Realm of Pleasure*, 1988.) Studlar uses object-relations theory, rather than Lacan, as her main frame of reference in psychoanalysis. Further, she takes up Deleuze's point that masochism and sadism are radically distinct formations, rather than "vicissitudes" of the same underlying drive. She thereby rejects the Lacanian view that (as in Silverman) sees masochism as a defense against castration anxiety and the other rigors of the Symbolic order. Studlar presents masochism instead as a defense against the more primal fears (associated

— The ambivalent pleasures of the
Masochistic body...

with the mother, not the father) of separation, abandonment, and oral frustration. To pose the question of masochism in these terms is not merely to substitute one structural cause, or one parental figure, for another. Studlar's theory has the great and radical virtue of grounding spectatorial response in prereflective affect (the primordial experience of pain) rather than in the cognitive terms of Oedipal law. The sensations and reactions of the body precede, and never cease to subtend, the categorical demands of the Symbolic order, of conscience and the superego. The ambivalent pleasures of the masochistic body provide a rich field for contesting, evading, or eroding phallic power and the global binarization of gender.

Silverman (1992) is wrong to assert that a view like Studlar's is apolitical and essentialist, and that it "comes close to grounding [masochism] in biology" (p. 417), for it is Silverman, not Studlar, who is implicitly making the metaphysical assumption that the body is somehow prior to history, outside politics. Studlar's work helps to remind us, to the contrary, that the opposition between the biological and the cultural is a false one, for the pre-Oedipal, pre-Symbolic, infantile body is already steeped in and invested by culture. It is a question of learning to analyze the politics of the regulation of bodies, and of the distribution of pleasures and pains: a politics more fundamental than the one located in the structural constraints and rationalizing processes of law and ideology. (I discuss this question of the politics of bodies at greater length in chapter IV, in relation to the films of David Cronenberg.) Studlar remains within the somewhat limiting confines of orthodox psychoanalytic notions of fantasy; nonetheless, she takes an important step toward theorizing the *embodiment* of cinematic vision.

For all their differences, Studlar and Silverman both posit masochism as what psychoanalysis calls a mechanism of defense. But to do so is to see masochism only as a secondary, reactive phenomenon, connected to compensatory fantasy, the disavowal of difference, and the struggle to preserve an

— they are affirmative passions, rather than defensive or recuperative ones.

imaginary state of plenitude. I am arguing instead for an *active* and *affirmative* reading of the masochism of cinematic experience. Commenting on Nietzsche, Deleuze (1983) suggests that a body can be defined as a force (or conjunction of forces) endowed with a certain "capacity for being affected"; such a capacity is "an *affectivity*, a sensibility, a sensation" (p. 62). A force or body is active and affirmative to the extent that it does not merely seek to preserve and capitalize itself, but expends and actualizes its capacity to the maximum, "goes to the limit of what it can do" (p. 61). Bersani's ontologically primordial masochism and Bataille's notion of expenditure are active expressions of force in this Nietzschean sense. They are affirmative passions rather than defensive or recuperative ones. The drives and enjoyments of the body cannot be equated with the safety and stability of the ego. They reject the tendency toward equilibrium that Freud so curiously associated with both the "pleasure principle" and the death drive lying "beyond" it. The masochism of the cinematic body is rather a passion of disequilibrium and disappropriation. It is dangerous to, and cannot remain the property of, a fixed self. The agitated body multiplies its affects and excitations to the point of sensory overload, pushing itself to its limits: it desires its own extremity, its own transmutation.

Possession and appropriation—the defense mechanisms of the ego or the capitalizations/constrictions of power and domination—are only countereffects, secondary and partial recuperations, of this passionate, masochistic excess. Bataille (1985) insists that utility serves and supports expenditure, rather than the reverse: "Men assure their own subsistence or avoid suffering, not because these functions themselves lead to a sufficient result, but in order to accede to the insubordinate function of free expenditure" (p. 129). Deleuze and Guattari similarly argue that power relations are parasitic upon virtualities, becomings, and movements of variation and deterritorialization that they remain unable to capture or to normalize. It is by a just such a logic that in horror films, our primary excitement and involvement is with the victims, not with the monsters or the murderers. Our "identification" or investment is with the very bodies being dismembered, rather than with the agents of their destruction. This is why it is so wrong to regard the films of someone such as Dario Argento as being misogynistic or vengefully patriarchal fantasies. Even when the heroine's survival is at issue—as in *Suspiria* or *Terror at the Opera*—the protagonist's dread, shared by the viewer in a state of fearful anticipation, blends into a kind of ecstatic complicity at the convulsive point of danger and violence. Argento's hyperbolic aestheticization of murder and bodily torment exceeds any hope of comprehension or utility, even as it ultimately destabilizes any fixed relations of power. The spectatorial affect of terror is an irrecuperable excess, produced when violated bodies are pushed to their limits. Terror subsists as a surplus affect, an "incorporeally material" image/effect, a kind of ghostly emanation that survives the extinction of the victim's body and escapes being appropriated to the account of the killer's insatiable *ressentiment*.

Another way to put this is to say that, in horror films, we are complicitous with the monster precisely to the extent—and *only* to the extent— that the latter does not operate from a position of power, but is in its own right victimized and driven by a passive compulsion. Such a dynamic of vulnerability drives Boris Karloff's monster in James Whale's *Frankenstein*, not to mention George Romero's pathetic zombies. This pattern of complicitous counterinvestment is the explicit subject of Michael Powell's overt meditation on sexism and scopophilia in *Peeping Tom*. Mark Lewis (Carl Boehm), the young male protagonist, literally murders women as he films them: one of the legs of his camera's tripod is equipped with a knife. He also attaches an enormous reflector to the camera, so that the victims are forced to watch their own expressions of terror as he slices their throats. They are thus seeing, in real time, the film of their own deaths—and this involuntary spectacle marks the deepest level of voyeuristic fascination. At home, Mark furtively watches the films he has made of his murders, motivated not by sadistic gratification but by a desperate need to experience, in himself, his victims' terminal fear. His murders are ultimately imperfect rehearsals for his own spectacular suicide, which (with the aid of the reflector) he simultaneously films and views. *Peeping Tom* thus amply indicates cinema's capacity to reproduce, or to serve as a relay for, traditional gender-coded patterns of murderous domination. But it also shows how this capacity is subverted by the very mechanisms that make it possible. The aggressive act of filming is only a detour en route to the passivity and self-abandonment of spectatorship. And violence against the Other is finally just an inadequate substitute for the dispossession of oneself. The reflections of masochistic spectacle create a space of superfluity, of violently heightened ambivalence, in which every exercise of power gets lost.

In order to register affects and effects like these, in order to affirm the full measure of the movies' masochistic ambivalence, in order to push cinema to the limit of what it can do, we need to shatter, scatter, and violently displace the psychoanalytic paradigm that has dominated academic film theory for the past twenty years or so. Linda Williams's (1989) careful and circumspect historicization of psychoanalytic theory is a useful first step in this direction. Carol J. Clover (1992) makes a more radical and decisive challenge to the psychoanalytic paradigm—even as she still locates herself within it—in her incisive (pun intended) discussion of certain "low" genres of horror: slasher, demonic possession, and rape/revenge films. Clover suggests, for instance, that the usually despised genre of the slasher—which is related to the Argento films I have touched upon above, but without Argento's possibly recuperative aestheticism—is in fact far less misogynistic, and far more open to subversive gender ambiguity, than has usually been imagined. Clover is wonderfully attentive—as so few film theorists are—to the pleasures of "exploitation" genres and sleaze, and to the importance of visceral excitation in film viewing. Her focus on the body leads her to dismantle the psychoanalytic theory that ostensibly serves as the framework of her discussion.

Clover's essay concentrates on the figure that she calls the "Final Girl," the character in the slasher genre who escapes from the psychopathic murderer and finally succeeds in killing him. Clover's crucial move is to oppose a "literal" reading of the Final Girl to the traditionally psychoanalytic "figurative" reading of her. A figurative reading "begins with the processes of point of view and identification" (p. 44) and goes on to assert that the Final Girl is "nothing more than a figurative male" (p. 55), and that therefore the slasher film "has very little to do with femaleness and very much to do with phallocentrism" (p. 53). But from a body-centered, literalistic viewpoint, these films "re-represent the hero as an anatomical female," so that "at least one of the traditional marks of heroism, triumphant self-rescue, is no longer strictly gendered masculine" (p. 60). An ambiguously fluctuating androgyny or gender ambiguity is thus the product not of Symbolic coding, but of the irreducible excess of actual bodies in opposition to that coding.

It becomes ironically apparent that the traditional psychoanalytic reading regulates and normalizes these films, disarms or disavows their subversive potential for gender fluidity, precisely to the extent that it imprisons the literal insistence of bodies within the categorical grid of Symbolic figuration. The psychoanalytic paradigm finally reinforces the very order of oppression that it claims, or wishes, to comprehend and critique. In her most theoretical chapter, Clover not only proposes a masochistic model of spectatorship, but explicitly takes orthodox film theory to task for its "repeated denial or avoidance" of the dimension of masochistic pleasure in film spectatorship "in contrast to the wealth of attention lavished on male sadism" (p. 225). She rightly takes this pattern of disavowal as a sign that even explicitly politicized psychoanalytic critics have too much of a "stake in the dominant fiction" of masculine sadism (p. 230). Clover focuses mostly upon the way in which the (male) spectator's masochistic identification with the (female) victim authorizes him vicariously to enjoy her subsequent revenge and triumph; to that extent her account remains centered upon self-possession and power, rather than giving an adequate account of the more difficult (and ultimately more subversive and troubling) dynamics of expenditure and abject enjoyment. The secret links between masochistic humiliation and submission and the pressure of excessive desire are more complex than is indicated by Clover's model of victimization and revenge. Nonetheless, Clover's work goes a long way toward reclaiming, and toward affirmatively valorizing and celebrating, the aesthetics of masochism, the visceral embodiment of film viewing, the pleasures and agitations of the flesh, and the literal insistence of the cinematic body.

As Clover helps to suggest, practical filmmaking is far more radical, in its subversive explorations of gender ambiguity, than is the theory that claims to recognize its accomplishments and to criticize its defects. In what follows, I seek to push film theory to the limits of what it can do, to develop a mode of criticism that dares to be "as radical as reality itself." It is in terms of passivity and expenditure that we should begin to construct both a materialist aesthetics and a radical politics of the cinema. And in particular, it is by affirming the primacy of involuntary fascination, of free-floating anxiety, over the reactive movements by which the ego seeks to master and regulate that anxiety that we can best approach the politics of gender in film. Even those all-too-common movies that—on the level of character and narrative—purvey the most reactionary stereotypes of gender and sexuality have their own potentialities for change and reversal, their "lines of flight." The cinematic apparatus has at least this virtue: that it tends to subvert the metaphysics that would privilege an intelligible, phallocratic order at the expense of the contingency and multiplicity of sensation, and to rupture the acquisitive mastery of the gaze. This is obviously not to claim that all films are somehow automatically progressive or liberating in their political effects. I *am* asserting, however, that we need to abandon the notions of representation, identification, lack, and so on, if we are to be able to map out the political lines of force, the plays of power and resistance, that inhabit and animate the cinematic image. I am urging that we surrender to and revel in cinematic fascination, rather than distance ourselves from it with the tools of psychoanalytic reserve and hermeneutic suspicion. And I am quite definitely suggesting that film's radical potential to subvert social hierarchies and decompose relations of power lies in its extreme capacity for seduction and violence (even though—or rather, precisely because—this capacity is also the source of its effectiveness as a tool of manipulation and propaganda). Film should be neither exalted as a medium of collective fantasy nor condemned as a mechanism of ideological mystification. It should rather be praised as a technology for intensifying and renewing experiences of passivity and abjection.

Appendix: Deleuze and Guattari's Theory of Sexuality

Avoid Freud

TODAY, THE most crucial task for any theory of sexuality remains how to get away from Freud. We are tired of endless discussions of the phallus, the castration complex, and the problematics of sexual representation. Psychoanalytic discourse, even at its ostensibly most critical, does nothing but reinscribe a universal history of lack and oppression. We cannot really oppose the dominant male-heterosexual order when our only language is the code that defines and ratifies precisely that order. We cannot move toward new articulations of bodies and pleasures so long as we think the body only through the defiles of language, signification, and representation. Hence the importance of Deleuze and Guattari's intervention in current debates on sexual theory. One of the many virtues of *Anti-Oedipus* (1983) and *A Thousand Plateaus* (1987) is that they permit us to rethink sexuality in radically a-Freudian terms, without, on the other hand, retreating to the outmoded, "precritical" discourses of behaviorism, sexology, and clinical psychiatry.

Deleuze and Guattari are far from denying the importance of Freud; rather, they assign him a crucial role analogous to that played by Kant in ethics and by Adam Smith and David Ricardo in political economy. Deleuze (1984) discusses Kant's radical break with all previous theories of the Good when he posits the moral law as "the pure form of universality," a subjective essence "with no content other than itself" (p. x). In a similar way, as Marx and Foucault both show, Smith and Ricardo are the first—in accordance with the development of capitalism—to deterritorialize wealth, to disengage it from extrinsic determinations, and to define its abstract essence as productive labor (Deleuze and Guattari 1983, 299–300). And finally, Freud's "greatness lies in having determined the essence or nature of desire, no longer in relation to objects, aims, or even sources (territories), but as an abstract subjective essence—libido or sexuality" (1983, 270). Freud is the last great thinker of the nineteenth century. In his formulations, desire is no longer (as it was for classical thought) the clearly delineated attribute of a preexisting subject, but rather the ungraspable movement that produces and positions the subject in its finitude. Psychoanalysis discovers desire as exchange value, and delineates the Symbolic or exchange economy of desire. Libido is like money, and the laws of its transformation are of the utmost importance.

Why, then, does psychoanalysis seem so unsatisfactory today? Just as the actual process of exploitation is necessary to the functioning of capital, and yet remains an unthought, unrecognized presupposition of Ricardo's model of political economy, so concrete practices of sexual subjectivation and domination are intrinsic to, and yet not taken into account by, Freud's representations of desiring economy. The processes of exploitation, domination, and subjectivation mark the reterritorialization of production and desire. Just as capitalism subjugates abstract labor by representing it in the form of private property, so psychoanalysis subjugates desire, recaptures and restratifies it, by recourse to the infinite representations of a structural unconscious. "Thus subjective abstract Labor as represented in private property has, as its correlate, subjective abstract Desire as represented in the privatized Family" (Deleuze and Guattari 1983, 303–4). In a very real sense, Freud's theories are the best model we have for the deployment of sexuality under advanced capitalism. But the difficulty lies precisely in this exem-

plary status of psychoanalysis, that it is so imposing as a *model*, for a model is never ✕
just a neutral tool for understanding. It internalizes, perpetuates, and reproduces
the norms and hierarchies whose genesis and structure it puts on display. To build
a model is to proclaim a necessity. It is very well for the Freudians to claim that
sexual difference is socially constructed and not naturally given; nothing is really
changed, since for them this social construction is as inevitable as any natural
necessity might have been. To comprehend the world in this way is to accept too
many assumptions, to take too much for granted—to *interpret* the world in such a
way that it becomes all the more difficult to *change* it. Psychoanalysis is never part
of the solution, but always part of the problem. To change the nature of sexual ✕
relations in our society it is necessary to *think* them differently.

Deleuze and Guattari seek not to interpret sexuality, but to
change it; not to construct a model of its essence, but to elucidate the concrete
ways in which it functions, and to open up possibilities of its becoming otherwise.
They do not provide a critique: the mode of critique is insufficiently radical, since
it always remains in silent complicity with the model it criticizes. They do not provide a hermeneutics: they seek liberation from social significations that are all too
firmly in place, rather than the recovery of meanings that have supposedly been
distorted or lost. Their project of schizoanalysis is an *affirmative* form of opposi-
tional, revolutionary thought. Implicitly anarchistic, it is closer to Foucault's analytics of power, and to the antihierarchical currents of May 1968, than it is to any
version of psychoanalysis. It inscribes the question of power at the heart of sexuality, in contrast to Freud and Lacan, who see power—if they see it at all—only as a
function of representation. And the history it recounts is one of contingency, not
one of law or necessity. Like Foucault (1979), Deleuze and Guattari seek to
rewrite "the history of the present" (p. 31) rather than—in psychoanalytic fashion—to reconstruct or retrospectively bring to light a hidden history of the past.

The task of schizoanalysis is not merely to demonstrate (as critical thought does) the all-too-evident presence of laws, oppressive institutions, and alienated conditions of existence, but to call forth the forces of resistance, the desires, and the lines of flight that already inhabit, and that can be turned against, such fixed configurations of power.

A radical rethinking of sexuality must be concerned not with Imaginary and Symbolic representations, but with a rewriting of the Real itself. "The objective being of desire is the Real in and of itself. . . . Desire always remains in close touch with the conditions of objective existence; it embraces them and follows them, shifts when they shift, and does not outlive them" (Deleuze and Guattari 1983, 26–27). And the texts that most closely embrace the Real, and that are most useful for Deleuze and Guattari's own discourse on sexuality, are invariably "fictional" rather than "theoretical" ones, those not of Freud and Lacan, but of Proust, Artaud, D. H. Lawrence, and Virginia Woolf—above all, Proust. The great twentieth-century work on the theory of sexuality is not Freud's *Three Essays*, but *Sodome et Gomorrhe*. When Proust's narrator observes the sexual encounter between the Baron de Charlus and Jupien, that seemingly predestined yet infinitely improbable event, he at the same time discovers something of far greater import: the existence of an entire field of multiple, molecular sexualities, of radical differences that are irreducible to the binary code of sexual opposition, and that explode, by their sheer excess as by their vegetal innocence, the hypocritical requirements of social morality and the constraints of what Deleuze and Guattari (1983) call the "anthropomorphic representation of sex" (p. 294).

Compulsory Heterosexuality

Deleuze and Guattari discern three levels, or three degrees of intensity, in Proust's articulation of sexuality. "We are statistically or molarly heterosexual, but personally homosexual, without knowing it or being fully aware of it, and finally we are transsexual in an elemental, molecular sense" (1983, 70). All these levels coexist in bourgeois society, but this does not mean that they are of equal status. In fact, they constitute a sequence that must be traversed in both directions. The initiation of Proust's narrator (and reader) proceeds from the gross evidence of molar hetero- sexuality to the discovery of a microscopic world of hidden and innocent pleasures. But the relations of power in our society operate in the reverse direction. They select and organize the singularities of an anarchic, molecular sexuality, subject them to the laws of morality and of the signifier, arrange them hierarchically, dis- tribute them around a statistical norm, and finally construct heterosexuality as a majoritarian standard or as a transcendent model.

Heterosexuality is a dominant formation in our society. It is important to define precisely the nature of its dominance. As a molar entity, het- erosexuality is the privileged representation of desire. But, as Deleuze and Guat- tari continually remind us, the mere existence of a given representation tells us nothing about its use. Nor is it possible to argue from the existence of a represen- tation (even assuming it to correspond to a moment of primary repression and consequent libidinal fixation) to any conclusions regarding the nature of what is represented or repressed. A transcendental condition never resembles what it con- ditions; the link between the two is purely arbitrary and external. Contrary to Lacanian theory, "Law" (even the law of sexual difference) cannot be said to con- stitute desire, or to circumscribe the effects of power. Deleuze and Guattari con- cur with Foucault in rejecting the dialectical or "juridico-discursive" representa- tion of power/desire in terms of law and negativity. Just as desire must be seen as immanent and productive, rather than grounded in lack, so power must be seen as positive and incitative, rather than negative and prohibitive. A representation of sexual difference (like the Lacanian Symbolic) can be viewed as a *model* of unequal (hierarchical) power relations. But it remains on the level of mere representation; invoking it doesn't get at the question of how power actually functions, how it *uses* the various regimes of signs or social representations.

All this leaves open the question of just how the norm of heterosexuality (implying male domination on the one hand and the binary articulation of sexual difference on the other) *does* function in our society. Heterosexuality is structural, superpersonal, and Symbolic—not an intrinsic determination, but an external form of domination. It is "compulsory" (as Adrienne Rich puts it), imposed on everybody; but this means also that it is *only* imposed. It is ubiquitous, enforced by the severest penalties, required by law and by convention, but at the same time it is strangely superficial, nominal, and not essential. The very fact that so much energy is invested in presenting it as the norm or *telos* of human sexual behavior and development points to its purely ideal function. In Kantian terms, heterosexuality is regulative and not constitutive. Just as it is impossible for any individual, *qua* empirical individual in the phenomenal world, to act in accordance with the disinterested rationality of the Kantian moral law, so there can be no pure, immanent experience of heterosexuality *as such*. Even those particular desires commonly classified as "heterosexual" are only inadequate approaches to the ideal. This is why, in Freud's normalizing view, everybody is more or less neurotic, more or less maladjusted, more or less guilty in the eyes of the superego.

The error of psychoanalysis is to assign an intrinsic and internal status to this imposition of the ideal and of the norm. Or rather, this is not its error but its positive function, for it is precisely by enforcing internalization, by imposing a deformed representation of desire, that psychoanalysis works as an apparatus of power. Even the ostensibly most politicized psychoanalytic thinkers are wont to proclaim that the castration complex, the binary organization of gender, and hence implicitly the imposition of heterosexuality as a norm, are "the price of being human," "the difficulty at the heart of being human," or "the *sine qua non* of the construction of the human subject" (I quote Juliet Mitchell, in her introduction to Lacan 1983, 17, 25). Maybe so, but shouldn't this then lead us to question our definitions of what it means to be "human"? And to suggest, as Deleuze and Guattari (1983), following Marx, suggest, that "the true difference is not the difference between the two sexes, but the difference between the human sex and the 'nonhuman' sex" (p. 294)? Lacan ironically appears as the last human- ist, since his entire theory hinges on an "anthropomorphic representation of sex," a metaphysical distinction of essence between human beings (who speak) and ani- mals (who allegedly don't).

To put it as plainly as possible: psychoanalysis, despite its protestations to the contrary, cannot stop being a humanist and theological con- struct. It both proposes a false interpretation of desire and functions effectively to manage and normalize desire insofar as it induces us to regard desire as essentially a matter of (true or false) interpretation and representation. It teaches us not a Nietzschean *amor fati* or love of otherness and change, but rather the grim wor- ship of necessity, of an all-too-human destiny: "resignation to Oedipus, to castra- tion ... in short, 'assumption of one's sex'" (Deleuze and Guattari 1983, 59). In "positioning" the subject, it completes a task initiated by nineteenth-century psy- chiatry, what Foucault has analyzed as the positive investment of sexualities by power.

Psychoanalysis is merely the last word in the "incorporation of perversions" and "specification of individuals" (Foucault 1980, 42–43), in the "hys- terization of women's bodies" and the "psychiatrization of perverse pleasure" (pp. 104–5). It creates an eternal image of (hetero-)sexual difference, instead of recog- nizing it as a specific and highly contingent political arrangement (*agencement*). The crucial point is that Freud and Lacan internalize the norm as a fundamental principle of human psychic functioning, as unattainable as it is ineluctable, whereas Proust, Foucault, and Deleuze and Guattari recognize it for what it is: purely formal, purely extrinsic, and hence purely oppressive.

All Desire Is Homosexual

Let us return to Proust's three regimes. Heterosexuality is a molar aggregate; it operates on a level of generality greater than the simply personal. It is a standard to which no single identity can ever fully correspond. Which is to say, the individual will always be located on a different plane than that of compulsory, molar heterosexuality. In order to function concretely, the Symbolic or heterosexual model requires a whole series of techniques of an entirely different order: practices of subjectivation, the construction of interiority under the twin rubrics of signification and guilt. It is only on this secondary level that individuals are defined as being uniquely of one sex or the other. Under the tyranny of an exclusive either/or, a reductive binarization of difference, "desire at the same time receives a fixed subject, an ego specified according to a given sex, and complete objects defined as global persons" (Deleuze and Guattari 1983, 70). Where psychoanalysis sees a "law" of difference as threatening the Imaginary notion of self-identity, Deleuze and Guattari show how the imposition of a "global and specific" regime of difference in fact imprisons us within fixed identities. So-called Symbolic articulation is what specifies the subject, not what subverts it. Possibilities of connection are closed off, bodies are constrained by their representation as psyches, subjectivities, or "selves." As Foucault (1979) puts it, "The soul is the effect and instrument of a political anatomy; the soul is the prison of the body" (p. 30). For Proust also, multiple sexual potentialities are trapped within the envelope of a molar specification of gender. This is a world of universal imprisonment, the famous "assumption" of masculinity or femininity leading only to Proust's somber prophecy that the sexes will each die alone ("Les deux sexes mourront chacun de son côté"). The public sphere of heterosexual "normality" can enforce its standards, and perpetuate itself, only insofar as it is doubled by an inner world of fear, isolation, secrecy, and guilt.

Hence the crucial role of homosexuality in Proust's novel. Since the social norm of heterosexuality induces us to adopt a sexual identity, but cannot inwardly prescribe that identity, we are perpetually split between an outward appearance and an inner "reality." Our societally sanctioned, public existence is heterosexual. But there can be no such thing as an innate heterosexual identity. As males, or as females, our secret, inner existence—even if we are consciously aware of this—is homosexual. Like Proust's narrator, we begin by assuming that everybody (including ourselves) is heterosexual, only to end by discovering that in fact nobody is. This is the reason for Proust's notorious theme of *la race maudite*, the accursed and exiled progeny of Sodom and Gomorrah. From the point of view of heterosexual normality, homosexual desire can only be stigmatized as a guilty secret. But this biblical or patriarchal curse is merely the counterpart of a deeper truth: that this secret is everybody's, that "homosexuality is the truth of love" (Deleuze 1972, 78), that *all desire is homosexual*. And this is why, Deleuze says, the guilt that Proust associates with homosexuality "is more apparent than real.... guilt is experienced socially rather than morally or internally" (pp. 118–19). It is the "black humor" (Deleuze and Guattari 1983, 318) of Proust that disengages, beneath socially imputed guilt, the radical innocence of a "vegetal" or molecular desire. "More than vice, says Proust, it is madness and its innocence that disturb us" (p. 69).

All the ambiguities of Proustian desire are played out on the middle level, the level on which we are constituted as persons: the level of the divergent homosexual series of Sodom and Gomorrah. Our sexual identities are traversed by lines of force moving in opposite directions. In one direction, we are imprisoned by our individuality, territorialized, fixed in place, in accordance with the superpersonal model of an ideal heterosexuality. We are held accountable for who we are, expected to conform to the image of ourselves, hounded into secrecy and tormented by an ascription of guilt because of our inevitable failure so to conform. Hence the sufferings of Charlus and the jealous suspicions the narrator brings to bear upon Albertine. But in the other direction, the two homosexual series mark a refusal of guilt, an escape, a point of resistance, a "line of flight" from the heterosexual norm. "The entire theme of the accursed or guilty race is intertwined, moreover, with a theme of innocence, the theme of the sexuality of plants" (Deleuze 1972, 118–19). Homosexuality is no longer "Oedipal, exclusive, and depressive," induced, specified, managed, contained, and stigmatized by the dominant social order; instead it is "anoedipal, schizoid, included, and inclusive," an active, revolutionary multiplication of the potentialities of the body. Affirming a radical "innocence of becoming," homosexuality marks a threshold of transformation; the approach to Proust's third or molecular level, "an ultimate level, constituted by the behavior of organs and of elementary particles" (Deleuze 1972, 119).

Molecular Sexuality

This ultimate level is infrapersonal, composed of multiplicities, becomings, and asubjective singularities. Proust proposes a strange vegetal sexuality, an initial hermaphroditism that may be contrasted with the more familiar Freudian hypothesis of bisexuality. The hermaphrodite is an aggregate of contiguous but noncommunicating singularities: as in certain plants, male and female partial organs are both present, but separated from one another, in the same individual. Freudian bisexuality implies a "Logos-as-Organism," a phantasmic originary undifferentiation; to the contrary, hermaphroditism is perfectly actual and perfectly differentiated: "not the property of a now-lost animal totality, but the actual partitioning of the two sexes in one and the same plant" (Deleuze 1972, 120). Hermaphroditism, then, does *not* imply or refer back to a lost unity. But neither are its separations and nonidentities the result of lack or prohibition. It avoids the Freudian/Lacanian alternative between an Imaginary illusion of wholeness and a Symbolic law of difference via castration, for the hermaphrodite lacks nothing, even though it cannot be characterized as a totality. It contains the different sexes within itself, but also the enormous distances that separate and isolate those sexes. Its constituents are partial objects, parts of machines, micro-organs that remain open to the outside, that cannot function by themselves, but that also cannot be referred back to any closure, to any organic unity of which they would be the parts. They are "fragments whose sole relationship is sheer difference," and that cannot be referred to "a primordial totality that once existed" or to "a final totality that awaits us at some future date" (Deleuze and Guattari 1983, 42). Together they constitute not a unity (for unities are themselves only statistical abstractions), but a preoriginary multiplicity in which parts continually refer to other parts outside of themselves, without any possibility of closure, without beginning or end.

Proust's narrator thus discovers a molecular world of transsexuality, of partial and nonspecific homosexualities, of "nonhuman" sex. This is the level on which desiring production escapes from the codings and classifications of power: an explosion into "relations of production of desire that overturn the statistical order of the sexes," and that move "beyond the anthropomorphic representation that society imposes on the subject, and with which [the subject] represents its own sexuality" (Deleuze and Guattari 1983, 296). On this molecular level, desire implies a continual process of *transversal communication*: separations that do not imply lack are bridged along paths that do not create unity. Connections are always being established, but these connections do not imply the abolition of distance and difference. Quite the contrary, for transversal connections always require the fortuitous intervention of outside terms, additional pieces of the machine that perform the connection without themselves being integrated within it. "It will be with them as with plants: the hermaphrodite requires a third party (the insect) so that the female part may be fertilized, or so that the male part may fertilize. An aberrant communication occurs in a transversal dimension between partitioned sexes" (Deleuze 1972, 121). The sexes remain separate, even after they have communicated at a distance. And the insect will puruse its aberrant course elsewhere, since it has no intrinsic, organic relation to the terms that only its accidental passage could have put into contact.

If these connections form a "whole," it is one that remains at the same time bizarrely "peripheral": "It is a whole of these particular parts but does not totalize them; it is a unity of all of these particular parts but does not unify them; rather, it is added to them as a new part fabricated separately" (Deleuze and Guattari 1983, 42). And the molecular components of this machine, the particular partial organs, each may be biologically "male" or "female," but they no longer function, or do not yet function, in terms of the molar, binary code of gender. "An individual of a given sex (but no sex is given except in the aggregate or statistically) bears within itself the other sex with which it cannot communicate directly" (Deleuze 1972, 120). Just as subjectivity, for Proust, is statistically compounded out of innumerable *petits moi*, none of which, individually, has the monadic or self-enclosed form of the ego, so men and women are composed of innumerable little sexes, none of which conforms (whatever their biological particularity) to the gregarious social constructions of gender. Rather, they are multiple potentialities of the body, so many *puissances* or affects that have not yet been subordinated to the constraints of the organism and its organic, hierarchical organization. "The Body without Organs is opposed not to the organs but to that organization of the organs called the organism ... to the organic organization of the organs" (Deleuze and Guattari 1987, 158). There is no longer a sexual norm, and no longer a range of deviations from that norm, since we have reached a realm "where homosexuality and heterosexuality cannot be distinguished any longer" (Deleuze and Guattari 1983, 319). And finally, in this space of nomadic multiplicities, the outside or additionial term that is always necessary to effect a transversal communication is itself random, partial, and nomadic. It is not a transcendental regulator, like the phallus, that separates and prohibits, that distributes exclusive differences. The insect, although extrinsic to the parts of the plant it puts into contact, remains in the same dimension, on the same plane of immanence with them. Its flight follows and records their divergences, affirms their disjunctions, tracing out the inclusive "either ... or ... or ... [soit ... soit ...] of the combinations and permutations where the differences amount to the same without ceasing to be differences" (Deleuze and Guattari 1983, 70).

For Deleuze and Guattari, as for Proust, and as also for Foucault, "a molecular sexuality bubbles away beneath the surface of the integrated sexes" (Deleuze 1988a, 76). It is always present, if only virtually, in every sociosexual arrangement. The problem with which we are faced is not an abstract, theoretical one, but always something concrete, pragmatic, and political: how, in a given situation, to mobilize this molecular sexuality, how to turn it against the molar imposition of heterosexuality, against the assignment of identities based on degrees of deviation, against the stratification and hierarchization of gender. It is not enough to appeal to some inscrutable Law, or merely to critique or chronicle our society's long history of oppressive hegemonic representations. More important, it is necessary to discover, to invent, new forms of resistance, new collective articulations of desire, new lines of flight, and even, perhaps, new ecstasies of abjection.

Contagious Allegories
George Romero

Postmodern Zombies

GEORGE ROMERO'S "living dead" trilogy—*Night of the Living Dead, Dawn of the Dead*, and *Day of the Dead*—offers all sorts of pleasures to the willing viewer. These films move effortlessly among sharp visceral shocks, wry satirical humor, and a Grand Guignolesque reveling in showy excesses of gore. They are crass exploitation movies, pop left-wing action cartoons, exercises in cynical nihilism, and sophisticated political allegories of late capitalist America. Their vision of a humanity overrun by flesh-eating zombies is violently apocalyptic; at the same time, they remain disconcertingly close to the habitual surfaces and mundane realities of everyday life. Business as usual bizarrely coexists with extremes of tension and hysteria, in a world on the verge of vertiginous destruction. Everything in these movies is at once grotesque and familiar, banal and exaggerated, ordinary and on the edge. Romero's zombies seem almost natural in a society in which the material comforts of the middle class coexist with repressive conformism, mind-numbing media manipulation, and the more blatant violence of poverty, sexism, racism, and militarism. Romero is at once the pornographer, the anthropologist, the allegorist, and the radical critic of contemporary American culture. He gleefully uncovers the hidden structures of our society in the course of charting the progress of its disintegration.

What can it mean for the dead to walk again? The question is discussed endlessly in the three films, but no firm conclusion is ever reached. Some characters search for scientific explanations, others respond with mystical resignation. Maybe it is an infection brought back from an outer space probe, or maybe there is no more room in hell. Of course, the whole point is that the sheer exorbitance of the zombies defies causal explanation, or even simple categorization. The living dead don't have an origin or a referent; they have become unmoored from meaning. They figure a social process that no longer serves rationalized ends, but has taken on a strange and sinister life of its own.

Deleuze and Guattari (1983) aptly remark that "the only modern myth is the myth of zombies—mortified schizos, good for work, brought back to reason" (p. 335). The life-in-death of the zombie is a nearly perfect allegory for the inner logic of capitalism, whether this be taken in the sense of the exploitation of living labor by dead labor, the deathlike regimentation of factories and other social spaces, or the artificial, externally driven stimulation of consumers. Capitalist expropriation involves a putting to death, and a subsequent extraction of movement and value—or simulated life—from the bowels of that death. Whereas precapitalist societies tend to magnify and heroicize death, to derive grandeur from it, capitalism seeks rather to rationalize and normalize it, to turn it to economic account. Romero's zombies have none of the old precapitalist sublimity, but they also cannot be controlled and put to work. They mark the rebellion of death against its capitalist appropriation. Their emergence—and this is one of the thrills of watching these films—reminds us of the derisory gratuitousness of death, and of Bataille's equation of death with expenditure and waste. Our society endeavors to transform death into value, but the zombies enact a radical refusal and destruction of value. They come after, and in response to, the capitalist logic of production and transformation; they live off the detritus of industrial society, and are perhaps an expression of its ecological waste.

Indeed, Romero has called to life the first postmodern zombies. (There have been many imitations since, in scores of other films: superficial imitation, or proliferating repetition, is the definitive feature of such undefinable not-quite-beings.) These walking corpses are neither majestic and uncanny nor exactly sad and pitiable. They arise out of a new relation to death, and they provoke a new range of affect. They are blank, terrifying, and ludicrous in equal measure, without any of these aspects mitigating the others. Romero's zombies could almost be said to be quintessential media images, since they are vacuous, mimetic replications of the human beings they once were. They are dead people who are not content to remain dead, but who have brought their deaths with them back into the realm of the living. They move slowly and affectlessly, as if in a trance, but the danger they represent is real: they kill and consume. They are slower, weaker, and stupider than living humans; their menace lies in numbers, and in the fact that they never give up. Their slow-motion voracity and continual hungry wailing sometimes appears clownish, but at other times emerges as an obsessive leitmotif of suspended and ungratified desire.

The zombies' residual, yet all-too-substantial, half-lives reproduce the conditions both of film actors separated from their charismatic presence (which the camera has appropriated) and of film audiences compulsively, vicariously participating in events that they are unable to control or possess. The zombies embody a phenomenological loss that—precisely because it is so viscerally embodied—cannot be figured in terms of "lack." They continue to participate in human, social rituals and processes—but only just enough to drain them of their power and meaning. For instance, they preserve the marks of social function and self-projection in the clothes they wear, which identify them as businessman, housewife, nun, Hare Krishna disciple, and so on. But this becomes one of the films' running jokes: despite such signs of difference, they all act in exactly the same way. The zombies are devoid of personality, yet they continue to *allude* to personal identity. They are driven by a sort of vestigial memory, but one that has become impersonal and indefinite, a vague solicitation to aimless movement.

The zombies are impelled by a kind of desire, but they are largely devoid of energy and will. Their restless agitation is merely reactive. They totter clumsily about, in a strange state of stupefied and empty fascination, passively drawn to still-living humans and to locations they once occupied and cherished. Only now they arrive to ravage, almost casually, the sites to which their vague memories and attractions lead them. They drift slowly away from identity and meaning, emptying these out in the very process of replicating them. The zombies are in a sense all body: they have brains but not minds. That is to say, they are nonholistic, deorganicized bodies: lumps of flesh that still experience the cravings of the flesh, but without the organic articulation and teleological focus that we are prone to attribute to ourselves and to all living things. They are empty shells of life that scandalously continue to function in the absence of any rationale and of any interiority. All this is particularly evident when active characters, with whom the audience has identified, are killed and monstrously reborn. In their artificial second life, these characters are both the same and not the same. They are still recognizable beneath their gruesome features, but their corpses shamble along or jerk convulsively, graceless and uncoordinated, drained of the tension of purposive activity.

These strange beings, at once alive and dead, grotesquely literal and blatantly artificial, cannot be encompassed by any ordinary logic of representation. In their compulsive, wavering, deorganicized movements, the zombies are *allegorical* and *mimetic* figures. They are allegorical in the sense that allegory always implies the loss or death of its object. An allegory is not a representation, but an overt materialization of the unbridgeable distance that representation seeks to cover over and efface. (I am defining allegory here in terms that derive ultimately from Walter Benjamin's *The Origin of German Tragic Drama*, 1985b; for a discussion of the importance of allegory, so conceived, to postmodernism, see especially Owens 1984; Olalquiaga 1992). The "living dead" emerge out of the deathly distance of allegory; their fictive presence allows Romero to anatomize and criticize American society, not by portraying it naturalistically, but by evacuating and eviscerating it. Allegory is then not just a mode of depiction, but an active means of subversive transformation.

The zombies do not (in the familiar manner of 1950s horror film monsters) stand for a threat to social order from without. Rather, they resonate with, and refigure, the very processes that produce and enforce social order. That is to say, they do not mirror or represent social forces; they are directly animated and possessed, even in their allegorical distance from beyond the grave, by such forces. Thus they are also mimetic figures, in Benjamin's (1985a, 160–63) sense of magical participation, perception become tactile, and nonsensuous (nonrepresentational) similarities (I am indebted to Michael Taussig for calling this essay to my attention). The movement from allegory to mimesis is a passage from passive reanimation to active, raging contagion. This progression is the source of the zombies' strange appeal. Forever unequal to themselves, they are figures of affective blockage and intellectual undecidability. They can be regarded both as monstrous symptoms of a violent, manipulative, exploitative society and as potential remedies for its ills—all this by virtue of their apocalyptically destructive, yet oddly innocuous, counterviolence. They frighten us with their categorical rapacity, yet allure us by offering the base, insidious pleasures of ambiguity, complicity, and magical revenge. Romero's films knowingly exploit the ambiguity of their position: they locate themselves both inside and outside the institutions and ideologies—of commercial film production and of American society generally—from which they have evidently arisen.

Survival or Sacrifice?

But what of horror's traditional themes of struggle and survival, of rescuing the possibilities of life and community from an encounter with monstrosity and death? The "living dead" trilogy plays with these themes in a manner that defies conventional expectations. (Indeed, it is this aspect of the films that has been most thoroughly discussed by sympathetic commentators. See especially Wood 1986, 114–21; Newman 1988, 1–5, 199–201, 208–10.) All three films have women or blacks as their chief protagonists, the only characters with whom the audience positively identifies as they struggle to remain alive and to resist and escape the zombies. The black man in *Night* is the sole character in the film who is both sympathetic and capable of reasoned action. The woman protagonist in *Dawn* rejects the subordinate role in which the three men, wrapped up in their male bonding fantasies, initially place her; she becomes more and more active and involved as the film progresses. The woman scientist in *Day* is established right from the start as the strongest, most dedicated, and most perspicacious of the besieged humans. In both *Dawn* and *Day*, the women end up establishing tactical alliances with black men who are not blindly self-centered in the manner of their white counterparts. All these characters are thoughtful, resourceful, and tenacious; they are not always right, but they continually debate possible courses of action, and learn from their mistakes. They seem to be groping toward a shared, democratic kind of decision making.

In contrast, white American males come off badly in all three films. The father in *Night* considers it his inherent right to be in control, although he clearly lacks any sense of how to proceed; his behavior is an irritating combination of hysteria and spite. The two white men among the group in *Dawn* both die as a result of their adolescent need to indulge in macho games or to play the hero. The military commanding officer in *Day* is the most obnoxious of all: he is so sexist, authoritarian, cold-blooded, vicious, and contemptuous of others that the audience celebrates when the zombies finally disembowel and devour him. These white males' fear of the zombies seems indistinguishable from the dread and hatred they display toward women. The self-congratulatory attitudes that they continually project are shown to be ineffective at best, and radically counterproductive at worst, in dealing with the actual perils that the zombies represent. The macho, paternalistic traits of typical Hollywood action heroes are repeatedly exposed as stupid and dysfunctional.

Romero dismantles dominant behavior patterns; he gives a subversive, left-wing twist to the usually reactionary ideology and genre of survivalism. To the extent that the films maintain traditional forms of narrative identification, they divert these forms by providing them with a new, politically more progressive content. Carol J. Clover (1992) argues that slasher and rape-revenge films of the 1970s and 1980s enact a shift in the gender identification of traditional attributes of heroism and struggle, whereby women take on these attributes instead of men; *Dawn* and *Day* present us with a more self-conscious, radical, and thoroughgoing version of the same shift in cultural sensibilities. But, as I mentioned in chapter I, the scope of Clover's argument is limited by the fact that it too easily valorizes heroic triumph. In Romero's trilogy, to the contrary, the success of the sympathetic characters' survival strategy is limited; it does not, and cannot be expected to, resolve all the tensions raised in the course of the three films. Unlike in the slasher and revenge films described by Clover, here the protagonists' survival is not the same as their triumph. The zombies are never defeated; the best that the sympathetic living characters of *Dawn* and *Day* can hope for is the reprieve of a precarious, provisional escape.

And this tenuousness leads us back to the zombies. The "living dead" trilogy does not simply or unequivocally valorize survival; perhaps for that reason, it ultimately does not rely for its effectiveness on mechanisms of spectatorial identification. The zombies exercise too strong a pull, too strange a fascination. The three films progress in the direction of ever-greater contiguities and similarities between the living and the nonliving, between seduction and horror, and between desire and dread. In consequence, identities and identifications are increasingly dissolved, even within the framework of conventional, ostensibly sutured narrative.

The first film in the series, *Night of the Living Dead*, is the one most susceptible to conventional psychoanalytic interpretation, for it is focused on the nuclear family. It begins with a neurotic brother and sister quarreling as they pay a visit to their father's grave, and moves on to the triangle of blustering father, cringing mother, and (implicitly) abused child hiding from the zombies in a farmhouse basement. Familial relations are shown throughout to be suffused with an anxious negativity, a menacing aura of tension and repressed violence. In this context, the zombies seem a logical outgrowth of, or response to, patriarchal norms. They are the disavowed residues of the ego-producing mechanisms of internalization and identification. They figure the infinite emptiness of desire, insofar as it is shaped by, and made conterminous with, Oedipal repression. The film's high point of shock comes, appropriately, when the little girl, turned into a zombie, cannibalistically consumes her parents. But at the same time, the film's casual ironies undercut this allegory of the return of the repressed. The protagonists not only experience the zombie menace firsthand, they also watch it on TV. Disaster is consumed as a cheesy spectacle, complete with incompetent reporting, useless information bulletins, and inane attempts at commentary. The grotesque, carnival-esque slapstick of these sequences mocks survivalist oppositions. Even as dread pulses to a climax, as plans of action and escape fail, and as characters we expect to survive are eliminated, we are denied the opportunity of imposing redemptive or compensatory meanings. There is no mythology of doomed, heroic resistance, no exalted sense of pure, apocalyptic negativity. The zombies' lack of charisma seems to drain all the surrounding circumstances of their nobility. And for its part, the family is subsumed within a larger network of social control, one as noteworthy for its stupidity as for its exploitativeness.

Romero turns the constraints of his low budget—crudeness of presentation, minimal acting, and tacky special effects—into a powerful means of expression: he foregrounds and hyperbolizes these aspects of his production in order to depsychologize the drama and emphasize the artificiality and gruesome arbitrariness of spectacle. Such a strategy doesn't "alienate" us from the film so much as it insidiously displaces our attention. Our anxieties are focused upon events rather than characters, upon the violent fragmentation of cinematic process (with a deliberate clumsiness that mimes the shuffling movement of the zombies themselves) rather than the supposed integrity of any single protagonist's subjec-tivity. The zombies come to exemplify not a hidden structure of individual anxiety and guilt, but an unabashedly overt social process in which the disintegration of all communal bonds goes hand-in-hand with the callous manipulation of individual response. It is entirely to the point that *Night* ends on a note of utter cynicism: the zombies are apparently defeated, but the one human survivor with whom we have identified throughout the film—a black man—is mistaken for a zombie and shot by an (implicitly racist) sheriff's posse.

The other films in the cycle are made with higher budgets and have a much slicker look to them, but they are even more powerfully disruptive. The second film, *Dawn of the Dead*, deals with consumerism rather than familial tensions. The zombies are irresistibly attracted to a suburban shopping mall, because they dimly remember that "this was an important place in their lives." Indeed, they seem most fully human when they are wandering the aisles and escalators of the mall like dazed but ecstatic shoppers. But the same can be said for the film's living characters. The four protagonists hole up in the mall and try to re-create a sense of "home" there. Much of the film is taken up by what is in effect their delirious shopping spree: after turning on the background music and letting the fountains run, they race through the corridors, ransacking goods that remain sitting in perfect order on store shelves. Once they have eliminated the zombies from the mall, they play games of makeup, acting out the roles of elegance and wealth (and the attendant stereotypes of gender, class, and race) that they dreamed of, but weren't able actually to afford, in their previous middle-class lives. This consumers' utopia comes to an end only when the mall is invaded by a vicious motorcycle gang: a bunch of toughs motivated by a kind of class resentment, a desire to "share the wealth" by grabbing as much of it as possible for themselves. They enter by force and then pillage and destroy, enacting yet another mode of commodity consumption run wild. One befuddled gang member can't quite decide whether to run off with an expensive TV set or smash it to bits in frustration over the fact that no programs are being broadcast anymore.

The still alive and the already dead are alike animated by a mimetic urge that causes them to resemble *Dawn*'s third category of humanoid figures: department store mannequins. The zombies are overtly presented as simulacral doubles (equivalents rather than opposites) of living humans; their destructive consumption of flesh—gleefully displayed to the audience by means of lurid special effects—immediately parallels the consumption of useless commodities by the American middle class. Commodity fetishism is a mode of desire that is not grounded in repression; rather, it is directly incited, multiplied, and affirmed by artificial means. As Meaghan Morris remarks, "A Deleuzian account of productive desire ... is more apt for analyzing the forms of modern greed ... than the lack-based model assumed by psychoanalytic theories" (in Bergstrom & Doane 1989, 244). Want is a function of excess and extravagance, and not of deficiency: the more I consume, the more I demand to consume. "I shop, therefore I am" (Barbara Kruger).

The appearance of the living dead in the shopping mall thus can no longer be interpreted as a return of the repressed. The zombies are not an exception to, but a positive expression of, consumerist desire. They emerge not from the dark, disavowed underside of suburban life, but from its tacky, glittering surfaces. They embody and mimetically reproduce those very aspects of contemporary American life that are openly celebrated by the media. The one crucial difference is that the living dead—in contrast to the actually alive—are ultimately not susceptible to advertising suggestions. Their random wandering might seem to belie, but actually serves, a frightening singleness of purpose: their unquenchable craving to consume living flesh. They cannot be controlled, for they are already animated far too directly and unconditionally by the very forces that modern advertising seeks to appropriate, channel, and exploit for its own ends. The infinite, insatiable hunger of the living dead is the complement of their openness to sympathetic participation, their compulsive, unregulated mimetic drive, and their limitless capacity for reiterated shock. The zombies mark the dead end or zero degree of capitalism's logic of endless consumption and ever-expanding accumulation, precisely because they embody this logic so literally and to such excess.

In the third and most complex film of the series, *Day of the Dead*, Romero goes still further. A shot near the beginning shows dollar bills being blown about randomly in the wind: a sign that even commodity fetishism has collapsed as an animating structure of desire. The locale shifts to an isolated underground bunker, where research scientists endeavor to study the zombies under the protection of a platoon of soldiers. All human activity is now as vacant and meaningless as is the zombies' endless shuffling about; the soldiers' abusive, macho posturings and empty assertions of authority clash with the scientists' futile, misguided efforts to discover the cause of the zombie plague, and to devise remedies for it. All that remains of postmodern society is the military-scientific complex, its chief mechanism for producing power and knowledge. But the technological infrastructure is now reduced to its most basic expression, locked into a subterranean compound of sterile cubicles, winding corridors, and featureless caverns. Everything in this hellish, underground realm of the living is embattled, restricted, claustrophobically closed off. This microcosm of our culture's dominant rationality tears itself apart as we watch: it teeters on the brink of implosion, destroying itself from within even as it is literally under siege from without. The bunker is like an emotional pressure cooker: fear, fatigue, and anxiety all mount relentlessly, for they cannot find any means of relief or discharge. As the film progresses, tensions grow between the soldiers and the scientists, between the men and the one woman, and ultimately among the irreconcilable imperatives of power, comprehension, survival, and escape. The entire film is a maze of false turns, blocked exits, and dead ends, with the zombies themselves providing the only prospect of an outlet.

Day of the Dead is primarily concerned with the politics of insides and outsides: the social production of boundaries, limits, and compartmentalizations, and their subsequent affirmative disruption. The zombies, on the outside, paradoxically manifest a "vitality" that is lacking within the bunker. Their inarticulate moans and cries, heard in the background throughout the film, give voice to a force of desire that is at once nourished and denied, solicited and repulsed, by the military-scientific machine. Inside the bunker, in a sequence that works as a hilarious send-up of both behaviorist disciplinary procedures and 1950s "mad scientist" movies, a researcher tries to "tame" one of the zombies. The dead, he explains, can be "tricked" into obedience, just as we were tricked as children. He eventually turns his pet zombie, Bub, into a pretty good parody of a soldier, miming actions such as reading, shaving, and answering the telephone, and actually capable of saluting and of firing a gun. This success suggests that discipline and training, whether in child rearing or in the military, is itself only a restrictive appropriation of the zombies' mimetic energy. Meanwhile, the zombies mill about outside in increasing numbers, waiting with menacing passivity for an opportunity to break in. From both inside and outside, mimetic resemblances proliferate and threaten to overturn the hierarchy of living and dead. The more rigidly boundaries are drawn between reason and desire, order and anarchy, purpose and randomness, the more irrelevant these distinctions seem, and the more they are prone to violent explosion.

The climax occurs when one of the soldiers—badly wounded (literally dismembered, metaphorically castrated), and motivated by an ambiguous combination of heroic desperation and vicious masculine resentment—opens the gates and lets the zombies into the bunker, offering his own body as a first sacrifice to their voracity. The controlling boundary is ruptured, and the outside ecstatically consumes the inside. Allegory entirely gives way before a wave of contagious expenditure and destruction. The zombies take their revenge, but, as Kim Newman (1988) notes, "American society is cast in the role usually given to an individually hatable character" (p. 209). If the zombies are a repressed by-product of dominant American culture in *Night*, and that culture's simulacral double in *Dawn*, then in *Day* they finally emerge—ironically enough—as its animating source, its revolutionary avenger, and its sole hope of renewal. They are the long-accumulated stock of energy and desire upon which our militarized and technocratic culture vampiristically feeds, which it compulsively manipulates and exploits, but cannot forever hope to control.

The Seductiveness of Horror

Everything comes back to the zombies' weird attractiveness: they exercise a perverse, insidious fascination that undermines our nominal involvement with the films' active protagonists. The rising of the dead is frequently described as a plague: it takes the form of a mass contagion, without any discernible point of origin. The zombies proliferate by contiguity, attraction, and imitation, and agglomerate into large groups. The uncanny power of Romero's films comes from the fact that these intradiegetic processes of mimetic participation are the same ones that, on another level, serve to bind viewers to the events unfolding on the screen. The "living dead" trilogy achieves an overwhelming affective ambivalence by displacing, exceeding, and intensifying the conventional mechanisms of spectatorial identification, inflecting them in the direction of a dangerous, tactile, mimetic participation. Perception itself becomes infected, and is transformed into a kind of magical, contagious contact. The films mobilize forms of visual involvement that tend to interrupt the forward movement of narrative, and that cannot be reduced to the ruses of specular dialectics. We cannot in a conventional sense "identify" with the zombies, but we are increasingly seduced by them, drawn into proximity with them. The participatory contact that they promise and exemplify is in a deep sense what we most strongly desire; or, better, we gradually discover that it is *already* the hidden principle of our desire. Romero's trilogy amply justifies Bataille's (1985) suggestion that "extreme seductiveness is probably at the boundary of horror" (p. 17).

The first of these modes of seductive implication is a kind of suspension or hesitation. We watch alongside a protagonist who does not see anything—but who is waiting, anxiously, for the zombies to appear, or for dead bodies to rise. Nothing happens, the instant is empty. Of course, such scenes are a classic means of building suspense. But Romero gives the blank time of anticipation a value in its own right, rather than just using it to accentuate, by contrast, the jolt that follows. Sometimes he even sacrifices immediate shock effect, the better to insist upon the clumsy, hallucinatory slowness of the zombies' approach, for even after the zombies have finally appeared, we are still held in suspense—waiting for them to come near enough to devour us, to embrace us with their mortifying, intimate touch. Such a pattern of compulsive, fascinated waiting is especially important in *Dawn*. In one excruciatingly drawn-out scene, one of the barricaded humans waits for the moment when his comrade, having just died in bed from zombie-inflicted wounds, will come back to life as one of *them*. There is nothing he can do; he simply sits, gun in hand, taking swigs from a bottle of whiskey. Ever so slowly, the sheets covering the corpse begin to move.... Again, at the very end of the film, the same character is tempted to remain behind and shoot himself in the head, instead of joining the woman survivor in a last-minute departure by helicopter. No true escape is possible; running away now only means accepting the horror of having to fight the zombies again someplace else. One can put an end to this eternal recurrence only by not delaying, by shooting oneself immediately in the head, directly destroying the physical texture of the brain. The man hesitates for a long, unbearable moment, his gun at his temple, as the zombies approach— ravening after his flesh, but still shuffling along at their usual slow pace. Only at the last possible instant is he finally able to tear himself away.

The dread that the zombies occasion is based more on a fear of infection than on one of annihilation. The living characters are concerned less about the prospect of being killed than they are about being swept away by mimesis—of returning to existence, after death, transformed into zombies themselves. The screams of the dying man in *Dawn* sound very much like (and are equated by montage with) the cries of the zombies. The man is most horrified not by his pain or his impending death, but by the prospect of walking again; he promises with his last breath that he will try not to return. Of course, he fails: revivification is not something that can be resisted by mere force of will. To die is precisely to give up one's will, and thus to find oneself drawn, irresistibly, into a passive, zombified state. In these scenes, the protagonist's momentary hesitation is already, implicitly, a partial surrender to temptation. A chain of mimetic transference moves from the zombies, to the man who dies and returns as a zombie, to the other man who watches him die and return, and to the audience fascinated by the whole spectacle. As the moments are drawn out, a character with whom we identify seems on the verge of slipping into a secretly desired incapacity to act, a passionate wavering and paralysis. Living action is subverted by the passivity of waiting for death; indecision debilitates the self-conscious assertion of the will. In *Dawn*, the protagonists end up resisting this temptation and returning to a stance of action and resolve. But it's only a small step from them to the wounded soldier in *Day*, who gives himself over entirely to the zombies.

At such moments in the three films, it is as if perception were slowed down and hollowed out. As I wait for the zombies to arrive, I am uncannily solicited and invested by the vision of something that I endlessly anticipate, but that I cannot yet see. Deleuze (1986, 155–59) argues that the sensorimotor link, the reflex arc from stimulus to response, or from affection to action, is essential to the structure of action narrative. But at such moments of waiting for the zombies' awakening or approach, the link between apprehension and action is hollowed out or suspended, in what Deleuze (1986, 197–215) calls a "crisis" in the act of seeing. The stimulating sensation fails to arrive, and the motor reaction is arrested. The slow meanders of zombie time emerge out of the paralysis of the conventional time of progressive narrative. This strangely empty temporality also corresponds to a new way of looking, a vertiginously passive fascination. The usual relation of audience to protagonist is inverted. Instead of the spectator projecting him- or herself into the actions unfolding on the screen, an on-screen character lapses into a quasi-spectatorial position. This is the point at which dread slips into obsession, the moment when unfulfilled threats turn into seductive promises. Fear becomes indistinguishable from an incomprehensible, intense, but objectless craving. This is the zombie state *par excellence*: an abject vacancy, a passive emptying of the self. But such vacuity is not nothingness, for it is powerfully, physically felt. The allure of zombiehood cannot be represented directly—it is a kind of mimetic transference that exceeds and destroys all structures of representation—but it lurks in all these excruciating, empty moments when seemingly nothing happens. Passively watching and waiting, I am given over to the slow vertigo of aimless, infinite expectation and need. I discover that implication is more basic than opposition; a contagious complicity is more disturbing than any measure of lack, more so even than lack pushed to the point of total extinction. The hardest thing to acknowledge is that the living dead are not radically Other so much as they serve to awaken a passion for otherness and for vertiginous disidentification that is already latent within our own selves.

A second mode of voyeuristic participation in the "living dead" trilogy comes into play when the zombies finally do arrive. Romero gleefully exploits his viewers' desires to experience and enjoy, vicariously, the rending apart and communal consumption of living flesh. These films literalize obscenity. In their insistence on cannibalism and on the dismemberment of the human body, their lurid display of extruded viscera, they deliberately and directly present to the eye something that should not be seen, that *cannot* be seen in actuality. Audiences attend these films largely in the hope of being titillated by a violence that is at once safely distant and garishly immediate—extravagantly hyperreal. I'm taken on a wild ride, through a series of thrills and shocks, pulled repeatedly to the brink of an unbearable and impossible consummation. The zombies' almost ritualistic violation of the flesh allows me to regard, for an ephemeral instant, what is normally invisible: the hidden insides of bodies, their mysterious and impenetrable interiority. At the price of such monstrous destructiveness, I am able to participate in a strange exhibition and presentation of physical, bodily affect. These films enact the making evident, the public display, of my most private and inaccessible experiences: those of wrenching pain and of the agonizing extremity of dying. I am fixated upon the terrifying instant of transmogrification: the moment of the tearing apart of limb from limb, the twitching of the extremities, and the bloody, slippery oozing of the internal organs. Fascination resides in the evanescent and yet endlessly drawn-out moment when the victim lives out his own death, an instant before the body is finally reduced to the status of dead meat.

Cheap Thrills

And this is the real reason people flock to see—indeed, why we passionately enjoy—horror films such as Romero's. What is the nature of this fascination, this dread, this enjoyment? In what position does such sensationalistic excess place the spectator, and how does it address him or her? Horror shares with pornography the frankly avowed goal of physically *arousing* the audience. If these "base" genres violate social taboos, this is not so much on account of *what* they represent or depict on the screen as of *how* they go about doing it. Horror and porn are radically desublimating; they make a joke of the pretensions of establishing aesthetic distance and of offering "redeeming social value." They exceed the boundaries usually assigned to mass entertainment, by ludicrously hyperbolizing and literalizing what are supposed to be merely the secondary, deferred, compensatory satisfactions of fantasy. More precisely, they short-circuit the mechanism of fantasy altogether: they are not content to leave me with vague, disembodied imaginings, but excitedly seek to incise those imaginings in my very flesh. They focus obsessively upon the physical reactions of bodies on screen, the better to assault and agitate the bodies of the audience. This is precisely why porn and horror films epitomize "bad taste." They do not bring me gratified fulfillment or satiation, but insidiously exacerbate and exasperate my least socially acceptable desires.

Romero's trilogy, and the many horror films produced in its wake, do not try to suture the spectator into a seamless world of false plenitude and ideological mystification. Rather, they blithely dispense with the canons of realistic conviction. They indulge themselves in the production of "special effects," in the double sense of grotesque visual effects and of affective and physiological effects upon the viewer. What counts is not the believability of the events depicted, but only the immediate response they elicit from the spectator. Whereas the scenes of anticipation previously discussed hollow out the space between stimulus and response, the present scenes of carnage and gore overload this space to the point of explosion. A behaviorist model of discontinuous shock effects replaces the traditional, representational or naturalistic model of apparent depths and plausible causal connections. Indeed, these films go out of their way to call attention to their own irreality, the hilarious and ostentatious artificiality of their spectacular, outrageous special effects.

Romero's movies are filled with marvelously tasteless sight gags, reminiscent of 1950s comic books, such as the scene in *Dawn* in which one character is so absorbed in using a machine to test his blood pressure that he virtually fails to notice the zombies tearing him apart (final blood pressure reading: zero), or the shot in *Day* of eyes still fluttering frantically in a head that has been sliced in two. These films do not try to disguise, but openly revel in, their recourse to mechanistic, technological means of manipulation. This cynicism on the plane of expression goes hand-in-hand with a self-conscious celebration of simulation and monstrosity on the plane of content. Just as the zombies cannot be categorized within the diegesis (they cannot be placed in terms of our usual binary oppositions of life and death, or nature and culture), so on the formal level of presentation they transgress, or simply ignore, the boundaries between humor and horror, between intense conviction and ludicrous exaggeration.

These films are wildly discontinuous, flamboyantly antinaturalistic, and nonsensically grotesque. Yet the more ridiculously excessive and self-consciously artificial they are, the more literal is their visceral impact. They can't be kept at a distance, for they can't be referred to anything beyond themselves. Their simulations are radically immediate: they no longer pretend to stand in for, or to represent, a previously existing real. Horror thus destroys customary meanings and appearances, ruptures the surfaces of the flesh, and violates the organic integrity of the body. It puts the spectator in direct contact with intensive, unrepresentable fluxes of corporeal sensation. I respond with a heightened tingling of the flesh, with an odd mixture of laughter, anxiety, and disgust. As Romero's films increasingly subvert the pragmatics of survival and slide into a realm of ambivalent, gory fascination, they come to exemplify a base counteraesthetics grounded in shock, hilarity, relentless violence, delirious behaviorism, contagion, tactile participation, and aimless, hysterical frenzy.

I watch these films, finally, with an alarming, ambivalent, and highly charged exhilaration. At the end of *Day*, especially, I am seduced and transfixed by the joy and the terror—the disgusting, unspeakable pleasure—of the human body's exposure and destruction. As the flesh of the last few soldiers is deservedly torn to shreds, more and more zombie hands thrust themselves into the frame, grasping, tearing, avidly yet impersonally claiming their gobbets of skin and entrails. The zombie potlatch marks a democratic, communal leveling of all invidious distinctions; it is an ephemeral instant of universal participation and communication. As I witness this cannibal ferment, I enjoy the reactive gratifications of *ressentiment* and revenge, the unavowable delights of exterminating the powerful Others who have abused me. But such intense pleasures are deeply equivocal, ironically compromised from the outset, participatory in a way that implicates my own interiority. For one thing, I can scarcely distinguish the agonies of the victims from the never-satisfied cravings of the avengers, the continuing disquiet of the already dead. What is more, the nervous, exacerbated thrills of destruction, the jolts and spasms that run through my body at the sight of all this gore, threaten to tear me apart as well. I enjoy this sordid spectacle only at the price of being mimetically engulfed by it, uncontrollably, excitedly swept away. I find myself giving in to an insidious, hidden, deeply shameful passion for abject self-disintegration.

On a formal no less than on a thematic level, the "living dead" trilogy destabilizes structures of power and domination. It accomplishes this by being absurdly reactive, by pushing to an outrageous extreme the consequences of manipulation, victimization, and Nietzschean "slave morality." It does not negate, but appropriates and redirects, the simulationist technologies of postmodern control. It does not provide a cathartic release for, but self-consciously channels and intensifies, our aggressive and destructive drives. It abolishes reflective distance, and desublimates affective response. It does not propose any redemptive or utopian vision, but overtly imbricates control with the loss of control. These painful ambiguities continue to pursue those few protagonists who do manage to escape. The survivors who reach a tropical island at the end of *Day* have nothing to look forward to but an empty, eventless, nightmare-ridden time—or, worse, the eventuality that the zombies will reach them by learning how to swim. There is no possibility of evasion, just as there is none of mastery, and none of firm and stable identification, for the zombies always come in between: they insinuate themselves within the uncanny, interstitial space that separates (but thereby also connects) inside and outside, the private and the public, life and death. In this liminal position, they are the obscene objects of voyeuristic fascination.

In a deeper sense, however, the zombies are the bearers or the subjects of this fascination as well: their endless desire, their deindividuated subjectivity, infects and usurps my own. They literalize and embody an extremity of agitation, an ecstatic emptying out of the self, a mimetic contagion, in which I can participate, alas, only vicariously. Yet in the long run, this inauthentic, vicarious participation is more than enough. The most intense and disturbing passion is the most factitious. Voyeurism implies a strange complicity, less with the agent of destruction than with the victim. I have survived the vision of hell and apocalypse, I am only sitting in a movie theater after all. My intense enjoyment of this spectacle, my thrilling, pornographic realization that humankind "can experience its own destruction as an aesthetic pleasure of the first order" (Benjamin 1969, 242), is not something to moralize against, but something to be savored. In the postmodern age of manipulative microtechnologies and infectious mass communication, such a pleasure marks the demoralization and collapse of the fascist exaltation Benjamin was warning against, and the birth instead of a politics of mimetic debasement, a subtle and never-completed opening to abjection.

...

Comedies of Abjection
Jerry Lewis

Embarrassment and Abjection

IT IS hard to find anybody who likes the comedy of Jerry Lewis, at least on this side of the Atlantic. Even in France, I am told, the smug intellectualism of Woody Allen is currently more popular than Lewis's infantile shenanigans. But in North America, Lewis is almost universally vilified, when he is not simply ignored. There has been no revival of interest in his movies, despite several recent signs: *hommages* in Fassbinder's *In a Year of 13 Moons* and in Godard's *Prénom Carmen* and *Soigne ta droite*, his noncomic performances in Scorsese's *The King of Comedy* and in episodes of the television series *Wise Guy*, his recent appearance in Emir Kusturica's *American Dreamers*, and his palpable influence on current film comedians as diverse as Steve Martin and Pee-wee Herman. Lewis survives as a media figure today only as the host of his yearly telethon for muscular dystrophy. Otherwise, he has no pull at the box office; his stance as a comedian seems too narrowly entrenched in the sensibilities of the 1950s to have much interest for the culture criticism of the 1990s. Even Lewis's best films—his eleven comedies as a "total filmmaker," directing himself, and often producing and screenwriting as well—remain beyond the pale of respectable discussion. The now-discredited exaggerations of *auteur* criticism, and the past excesses of Lewis's French and Francophile admirers, have perhaps only made the situation worse: today there is something rather embarrassing in even admitting that I have enjoyed a Jerry Lewis film, let alone in taking an active interest in his work.

It is with my own sense of embarrassment that I want to begin this discussion of Jerry Lewis, for my argument is precisely that the affects of embarrassment and humiliation are central to Lewis's work, and define his uniqueness as a comedian and as a filmmaker. Most commonly, comedy liberates through aggression: the comedian achieves a kind of self-redemption by turning the tables on his or her tormentors, or simply by violating and overturning social taboos. Lewis's comedy, however, moves in the direction not of liberation and redemption, but of utter abjection. What is more, this abjection undermines the integrity of the individual personality, and marks the point of an inscription of the social. The painful, negative emotions that surprisingly proliferate in Lewis's movies are never those of an isolated self; they always imply the gaze and judgment of others. Within the narrative situations of Lewis's films, embarrassment and abjection are the direct consequences of subordination: of being assigned a low position in the social hierarchy and being compelled to take orders. But these affects are not experienced only by Lewis's various screen personas; they are also shared, beyond the frame, in a kind of process of contagion, by the audience. My embarrassment at having to defend an enthusiasm for Lewis's movies is not unrelated to the embarrassment I feel while actually watching those movies—a sense of being somehow implicated in the Idiot's bumbling, spastic misadventures. Embarrassment, in Lewis's comedy, results in a strange complicity between actor and spectators, one that inverts the traditional mechanisms of cinematic identification. In this sense, Lewis's films are not only an acute form of social commentary, they also reflect directly upon the issues in film theory that I am discussing throughout this book.

Talking about embarrassment and abjection may be one of the few things that is even more difficult than talking about humor, about why something is funny. Lewis's comedy is funny—at least, I find it funny—but it is never *just* funny. It always has a disturbing, faintly uncomfortable undertone, a quality that is difficult to articulate verbally because it involves a kind of spectatorial response that one is reluctant even to admit to in oneself. Consider a gag that is repeated obsessively in Lewis's movies: that involving an encounter between the Idiot as spectator and a work of art. In *The Bellboy*, Lewis wanders into an art gallery and feels an irresistible urge to touch a bust representing the face of a young woman. The clay is still wet, however, and he ends up inadvertently remodeling the figure into that of a wizened grotesque smoking a cigarette. In *The Errand Boy*, Lewis tugs at a loose strand of thread coming from the tunic worn by a figure of Samson with his arms around two pillars; he thereby succeeds in unfreezing the statue, so that Samson pulls on the pillars and everything comes crashing down. In *Cracking Up*, the joke is pushed to its most paranoid extreme, as Lewis provokes animate responses from pictures in a museum: he pulls down the pants of a standing male figure in one painting as the result of (again) pulling at a loose thread, he gets pissed upon by a horse in a second painting, and he provokes a charge by a bull—who exits the picture frame and smashes through the opposite wall of the museum—in a third.

How does one respond to such scenes? One is first inclined to dismiss them as puerile or infantile: a horse in a painting pissing on Jerry Lewis represents slapstick of a pretty low order, something we are far too sophisticated to find funny. But there is something defensive in such a dismissive response, something that has to do with the difference of Lewis's gags from traditional comedy. Slapstick can range from the carefully orchestrated looniness of the Marx Brothers to the physical crudeness of the Three Stooges, but in all its forms it is exuberant and guilt free. It provides a carnivalesque release from the usual standards of responsibility, emphasizes grotesque inversions of hierarchical power relations, and directly assaults the icons of social respectability. The transgression of rules of propriety, and the joyous destruction of regulations and norms, is what makes slapstick so pleasurable. But, like all forms of the Bakhtinian carnivalesque, slapstick is deeply ambiguous: it is potentially subversive, but at the same time easily recuperable by power. Creating a socially sanctioned space of spectacle in which values are freely overturned may in fact be an effective way of co-opting any actual pressure for change and preserving hegemonic values from being threatened in other, more effective, ways. A kind of comic catharsis prevents social tensions from accumulating to a dangerous level; a symbolic challenge to the ruling values helps to defuse a real one.

What is strange about Lewis's comedy is that it does not provide such a catharsis. It seems oddly based on an exaggerated respect for social values and norms, rather than on a gleeful defiance of them. In the examples I have just cited, chaos is not desired for its own sake; it results, inadvertently, from Lewis's anxious concern for propriety and his excessive deference before the artifacts of high culture. In *Cracking Up*, Lewis as naive spectator feels inadequate when he is confronted with masterworks on the walls of the museum; he scrutinizes them closely, as if thereby to make up for his own failures of appreciation. His attitude is one of self-abasement before the social prestige of the painting, before what Walter Benjamin (1969) calls the *aura* of the work of art. But as Benjamin remarks, "To perceive the aura of an object we look at means to invest it with the ability to look at us in return" (p. 188). Lewis's respectfulness quickly turns to acute embarrassment, tinged with paranoia, when the object imbued with an aura actually does respond to him. The fetish magically comes alive, but all it can do is humiliate the worshiper whose awe has animated it. The social order is never *directly* disrupted by Lewis's actions; rather, he provokes its self-destruction, precisely as a result of taking it too seriously, too much at its word. He does not subvert the law so much as he masochistically perverts it. Gilles Deleuze (1971) describes the humor of the masochist in terms that could well be applied to Lewis:

> *What we call humour—in contradistinction to the upward movement of irony towards a transcendent higher principle—is a downward movement from the law to its consequences. We all know ways of twisting the law by excess of zeal. By scrupulously applying the law we are able to demonstrate its absurdity and provoke the very disorder that it is intended to prevent or to conjure. (p. 77)*

Lewis's comedy mobilizes all the affects of masochism, but his comic personas never possess the *will* to twist and pervert the law that characterizes the true masochist. Lewis is only an unconscious anarchist. He is not seeking to singularize himself, not trying to legitimate his own deviant pleasures; his only wish is to coincide with what others define as "normal." His quest is to become a proper, obedient employee in *The Bellboy*, *The Errand Boy*, and *Hardly Working*; to be molded into a formulaic media star in *The Patsy*; to be cured of his neuroses in *Cracking Up*; and, most suggestively, to transform himself from the weak, bumbling Julius Kelp into the obnoxious but charismatic and powerful Buddy Love in *The Nutty Professor*. But in all of these films, Lewis's overzealous efforts to obey orders, to mimic models of success, to act pragmatically, and otherwise to accede to the socially defined norm only end in failure and confusion. Lewis is an anarchist not in spite of, but because of, his hyperconformism: he disseminates chaos in the course of earnestly trying to do exactly what bosses, psychoanalysts, media specialists, and other technicians of normalizing power want him to do. In a movement that is very different from that of carnivalesque transgression, order collapses as a result of being fulfilled even to excess. The scene that best epitomizes this is the parade run amok in *The Family Jewels*, where the marchers receive contradictory orders to turn in all directions at once. The attempt at obedience itself generates confusion;

it is only in this backhanded manner that the oppressiveness of social norms and constraints, of the capitalist rationalization of all aspects of life, is revealed.

This implicit critique is not the end of the story, however, for Lewis never experiences the destruction that he unleashes as in any sense a liberation. Take a scene in *The Bellboy*: Lewis is slowly and carefully putting all the hotel's keys in their proper boxes. The boss yells at him to hurry up. He tries to go faster, finds he cannot concentrate, panics, and finally hurls keys about at random. The next shot shows the crowded hotel corridor, with none of the guests able to get into their rooms. Faced with responsibility, Lewis's persona physically and psychologically disintegrates. He experiences chaos in his own body; this chaos is then disseminated in waves around him. He not only creates but magnifies confusion: as in contemporary chaos theory, with its emphasis on "sensitive dependence on initial conditions," so in Lewis's comedy the effect is always wildly disproportionate to the cause. In addition, Lewis's Idiot invariably increases disorder by dint of his very efforts to compensate for whatever disorder he has already created. Good intentions are never sufficient; they often have the most disastrous consequences of all. In another scene in *The Bellboy*, Lewis magically causes a woman to regain all the weight she has lost by leaving her a box of chocolates as a farewell present. The sheer surrealist weirdness of these gags is contradicted by their uncomfortable psychological heaviness. Each incident of disorder is one more thing the Idiot is responsible for, one more cause for him to make endless apologies and excuses, and one more reason these apologies are never sufficient. He reaches a point at which he is forced to acknowledge his own incompetence, but this self-consciousness only makes him all the more unable to function. Such a feedback mechanism is a mainstay of Lewis's comedy: he ties himself into verbal knots, or finds his speech breaking down altogether, as he tries to explain and compensate for his well-meaning but pragmatically disastrous actions.

Conformism and Performance

What is most disturbing in such scenes is that the comic destruction of norms becomes the source of a judgment not against the norm, but against the self. Lewis's characters cannot assert themselves as individuals in opposition to society, for it is only in the stereotypical, hegemonic terms of social order that they can conceive of themselves as individuals at all. This is why Lewis's humor continually threatens to give way, first of all to sentimentality and pathos, but even more to an embarrassing orgy of humiliation and abjection. In the precredit sequences of *Cracking Up*, Lewis's protagonist attempts suicide, but finds that he cannot even accomplish this act successfully. Next, during the credits, we see him in the psychiatrist's office, so nervous that he can neither sit still nor walk peacefully across the room. Instead, he repeatedly slips on the smooth surfaces of the waxed floor and the plastic that covers the chairs and couch. The prospect of confiding his anxieties to Herb Edelman's condescending psychoanalyst terrifies him.

Lewis's protagonists are always trapped in a vicious circle. The self-validation they seek cannot come from within. They can believe in themselves only if they are given permission and encouragement to do so by others. But what gives these others their authority is precisely their self-sufficiency, that is to say, their callous indifference to Lewis's plight. The aura that such authorities project, and to which Lewis pathetically appeals, is the very characteristic that has made Lewis feel inadequate in the first place. Lewis's self-consciousness is given to him from without, and places him in an insurpassable double bind. At the start of Lewis's career, the role of insolent authority was played by Dean Martin. In Lewis's self-directed films, such authority tends to be posed more in social and institutional than in individual terms. But in every case, Lewis's persona can assert his selfhood only at the price of a continuing, humiliating dependency.

The danger, of course, is that in the dramatization of this

pathetic abjection, comedy will disappear altogether. (This may well be the case for Lewis's unreleased film, *The Day the Clown Cried*.) As if to avert this danger, almost all of Lewis's films have the ostensible theme of the protagonist breaking away from dependency and finding his "true" self. Indeed, the simplistic preaching to this effect that crops up now and again in these films is in its own right deeply embarrassing. But strangely enough, the supposedly authentic self that is discovered at the end of Lewis's films is always that of an actor. Lewis can resolve the dilemma of abjection only by having his protagonists turn into "Jerry Lewis": by transforming the Idiot's pain and bumbling incompetence into a self-conscious comic performance. His character in *The Errand Boy* enacts his clumsiness with objects on screen and becomes the studio's next big star; the hero of *Hardly Working* decides to go back to his true vocation as a clown. *The Patsy* poses the problem of abjection entirely in terms of performance: Lewis's character first suffers the ultimate humiliation for a comedian, that of bombing at a nightclub, and succeeds only when he substitutes the comedy of his own impulses for that programmed by his advisers. This transformation of interiority into outer display (performance) is also what motivates Lewis's predilection for weird self-reflexive effects. *The Patsy* ends with the affirmation that the rejection and humiliation we have just witnessed is not real, since it is only a movie, acted on artificial stage sets. *Cracking Up* (originally titled *Smorgasbord*) concludes with the hero, now cured of his neuroses, watching the movie *Smorgasbord*: he has become the spectator (or the maker) of the very film in which we have just seen him, and he can now enjoy the chronicle of his own embarrassing mishaps.

When Lewis's characters turn into performers, they transmute, but they do not escape, their humiliating dependency upon others' judgmental regards. They can "be themselves" only on stage or in film. Their self-regard still needs to be mediated by others, only these others now constitute a mass audience rather than an immediate authority. Self-respect is ironically generated by the very hypocrisies (amply lampooned in *The Errand Boy*, *The Patsy*, and elsewhere) of the entertainment industry. Lewis's sentimentality, his insistence on the pathos of the lowly, unappreciated self, is thus doubled and undone in a kind of schizoid reflection.

The dazzling metafictional leaps and ubiquitous alienation effects in so many of his films work neither to construct a modernist sense of self-referentiality nor to provoke a Brechtian alienation and critical response on the part of the audience. They serve rather to trap actor and audience alike in an escalating, never-ending spiral of inauthenticity. When Lewis's Idiot becomes a self-conscious entertainer he experiences a splitting of the personality that allows him to play the roles of both callous, narcissistic power figure and humiliated victim. This is most evident in the Jekyll/Hyde doubling of *The Nutty Professor*, where the charismatic, manipulative singer Buddy Love is the alter ego of the easily intimidated Professor Julius Kelp. Buddy Love is nothing outside of his public appearances as celebrity and performer; he seems concerned exclusively with maintaining a certain cool in wardrobe and demeanor. In turn, it is by appealing to the hidden exhibitionistic urges in others that he is able simultaneously to flatter and ridicule them (as in the "to be or not to be" scene with the college president). But there is something at once painful and perverse in the way Buddy's flagrant narcissism is presented as a fantasy compensation for Kelp's awkwardness and overwhelming vulnerability.

The hollowness of the performing self is also suggested in Lewis's cameo appearance as "himself" in *The Bellboy*, and in his final appearance as a star at the end of *The Errand Boy*. In both of these films, the character of Lewis-as-star has a baffling encounter with his own incompetent earlier persona. The successful performer at once basks in and is bored and irritated by the adulation he receives, in a manner that disturbingly foreshadows Lewis's grim role as Jerry Langford in *The King of Comedy*.

From Psyche to Socius

So far, I have been psychologizing Lewis's characterizations, in order to get at the way in which his comedy is rooted in a primal experience of masochistic humiliation. This psychological configuration helps to account for both his embarrassing, kitschy sentimentality and his sophisticated, highly self-conscious formalism. Further, it explains Lewis's tendency to resolve his films by appealing to the notion of willed performance, but it also guarantees the continuing inauthenticity of this solution. Such a pattern may even extend beyond Lewis's films to include, for instance, his attempts at self-authentification through tireless philanthropic endeavor and appeals to public sympathy: the combination of absolute sincerity and calculated performance, of total generosity and relentless self-promotion, that so oddly characterizes the muscular dystrophy telethon. Of course, none of this tells us anything about Jerry Lewis the person apart from his performances. Rather, it suggests the way in which comedy in general is driven by the joint impulses of dependency and exhibitionism, with the latter both compensating for and replicating the former. Abjection is not cathartically discharged, but prolonged, sublimated, and displaced by means of spectacle. Lewis's films thus tend to confirm Gaylyn Studlar's (1988) thesis that cinema operates along the lines of a masochistic identification, rather than a sadistic and controlling one.

At this point I need to retrace certain of my steps, however, because psychological considerations alone can neither do justice to the full range of Lewis's comedy nor sufficiently account for its social implications. The configuration I have been tracing comes down to this: the self-definitions of Lewis's characters are entirely generated from without. The more Lewis pathetically strives to be "himself," the more abject and dependent he in fact becomes. But when this movement is carried far enough, it can no longer adequately be described in individualistic, psychologistic terms. It becomes more and more apparent that the subjectivity of Lewis's personas is crudely stereotypical, entirely composed of affects derived from the social realm. And so a point is reached at which the pathos of wounded interiority—which on one level Lewis milks for sympathy—simply ceases to be relevant; instead, the social field of American late capitalism is directly invested by the disintegrative movements of Lewis's physical comedy. In his most striking, intense, and excessive moments, a schizophrenic dislocation of subjectivity is linked to bizarre distortions and topographical transformations of physical, corporeal, and social space.

This process has its roots in Lewis's privileged relation—at once magical and perverse—to physical objects. Straightforward commodity fetishism, in which consumer goods seem to take on a life of their own, is more evident in the films in which Lewis is directed by Frank Tashlin (think of the demonic vacuum cleaner in *Who's Minding the Store?*) than in Lewis's own self-directed works. But the latter are filled with strange moments—more weird than straight-out funny—in which chaos and fragmentation seem to be consequences of the Idiot's special relation to machines and physical objects. Take the moment in *The Bellboy* when Lewis goes outside in the dark to photograph the hotel; at the moment his flashbulb goes off, night is instantaneously transformed into day. Lewis's gags literalize Benjamin's (1969) observation that social space is transformed by "the thoroughgoing permeation of reality with mechanical equipment," the penetration of the world by the camera (p. 234). In this vein, one may also think of scenes in which reality becomes indistinguishable from advertisements, such as when, in *Hardly Working*, Lewis accepts a woman's offer of a cold drink and suddenly finds himself inside a beer commercial. And such scenes find their inverted counterparts in those in which Lewis's dissonant presence inexplicably intrudes upon, and thereby disrupts, an otherwise seamless media spectacle (the TV sequence in *The Ladies' Man*, or several scenes in which Lewis appears in the frame or is heard on the sound tracks of movies being made at the film studio of *The Errand Boy*).

        The social implications of Lewis's comedy are realized more in terms of the movements of his body, and of the articulation of time and space, than in the register of psychology. Lewis does for the late capitalist regime of simulation and technologies of reproduction something analogous to what Buster Keaton does for the earlier regime of capitalist mechanization and production. Keaton is a kind of pragmatic materialist, whose greatest aesthetic affinities, as has frequently been noted, are with Dadaist strategies of subversion and provocation. His comedy triumphantly vindicates Benjamin's (1969) argument that "Dadaism attempted to create by pictorial—and literary—means the effects which the public today seeks in the film" (p. 237). But in accordance with the altered imperatives of an informational age, Lewis pushes Keaton's fascination with machines to an alarming point of disintegration and chaos. Whereas Keaton's physical comedy is based on surprising external connections among discrete and solid objects, Lewis's relies rather on a rush of delirious interpenetrations, in which the separate identities of the initial components are lost. Keaton's body enters into combination with the wheels and levers of a train (*The General*) to form a new and more complex machine. In *The Patsy*, Lewis's voice alone is enough to shatter a roomful of precious objects; the disorganization that he sets off all around him rebounds back on his own body, causing it to lose its integrity in a series of spastic lurches and twitches. It is as if a mechanics of fluids or gases had replaced Keaton's mechanics of solids. Lewis's body is less an integral object than a zone of passive but intensely heightened sensitivity to all the pulls and pressures of the social and political (rather than, as is the case with Keaton, the natural and technological) environment.

In this context, Lewis's experiences of abjection and humiliation are physical postures, elicited in a discontinuous series of comic situations and bizarre gags and stunts, before they are psychological conditions (as expressed and developed by means of narrative). Dependency is the logical consequence of the Idiot's typical position as an unskilled laborer and/or a naive consumer in the American service economy. In such roles, Lewis's personas are induced or compelled to experience physically, and to invest and transform hysterically, the ubiquitous but impalpable, ideological, and superstructural institutions of late capitalism: advertising and conspicuous consumption, the discipline of work and the commodification of leisure time, psychoanalysis, and especially the mass media or entertainment industry. Lewis does not resist these influences: he unleashes and suffers physical turmoil precisely to the extent that he accepts and embodies them. The embarrassing awkwardness of the Idiot's body (poles apart from Keaton's physical grace) is the consequence not of weight or inertia, but of an extreme susceptibility.

It is by virtue of this excessive receptivity, and the coding of his body in terms of labor and consumption, that Lewis experiences the most contradictory dilations and contractions of time and space. At one extreme, physical labor gets done in an impossibly brief amount of time, as when Lewis almost instantaneously sets up an entire roomful of chairs in one scene from *The Bellboy*. At the other extreme, many of Lewis's gags are built around an excruciating slowness of unfulfilled anticipation. Simple physical actions (carrying a heavy suitcase, balancing a heterogeneous group of objects, shutting a door without slamming it, climbing up and down a ladder while holding a large jar of jellybeans) are not only occasions for the display of Lewis's brilliantly choreographed clumsiness, but take painfully long to accomplish. The ultimate tendency of such routines is toward the elimination of any sort of culmination or payoff. Such is the "eluded" gag structure, or elision of punch lines, described by Jean-Pierre Coursodon (1983): "The audience knows exactly how the routine is supposed to unfold. The only surprise lies in the absence of a punch line, either verbal or visual" (p. 197). There is no resolution, positive or negative; Lewis labors on, in a state of perpetual, unresolved disequilibrium. By ostentatiously manipulating duration, both eliminating it entirely and extending it to absurd lengths, Lewis undermines the traditional dramatic and cathartic structure of physical comedy (suspense and relief), and substitutes for it a more properly cinematic presentation of the subjugated body.

The Spastic Body of Simulation

Much recent discussion of postmodern culture has all too readily accepted Jean Baudrillard's notions of hyperreality and simulation. According to Baudrillard (1983), because of the ubiquity of the mass media in our rationalized, late capitalist world, we now live in a situation in which the image "bears no relation to any reality whatever: it is its own pure simulacrum" (p. 11). In consequence, the physical body is completely nullified, replaced by a stream of images without referents. Instantaneous electronic transmission has supposedly replaced the human body as locus and measure of labor power. Now, Lewis's comedy does indeed take place in a space and time of simulation, one in which any concept of authenticity is radically impossible; it evinces no nostalgia for a lost real. Yet, at the same time, this comedy registers the operations of the simulacrum as a corporeal and physical (instead of metaphysical) process. This is behaviorism run amok: Lewis's gestures and comportment are overdetermined, twisted and turned, fragmented and exploded, by the multiplicity of incompatible models, axioms, codes, and sub-liminal suggestions that seem to inhabit him. Push the regime of mass media—of fragmentation, stereotyped images, and rationalized procedures—far enough, and you will encounter Jerry Lewis's disarticulated, deorganicized body. The body is no longer an integral form, but in its inertia and its dense plasticity it still func-tions as an insurpassable reference, a necessary relay. Lewis deconstructs the oppo-sition between the literal insistence of bodies and the impalpability of simulacra. He discovers a materiality inherent to the seemingly weightless, transitory images of film and video.

Lewis's comedy of fragmentation disrupts the traditional struc-tures of cinematic identification. In the first place, it is embarrassing, rather than reassuring, for the spectator to "identify" with Lewis's anxious and incompetent personas. But beyond this, Lewis's own comic routines twist the familiar psycho-logical processes of narcissism and specularization into strange, ungainly shapes. Here again, Lewis can be usefully compared with Buster Keaton. It is difficult to identify with Keaton because we never know what he is thinking; all his thought seems directly realized in physical action, and no pathos of interiority ever disturbs his blank, stoically impassive face. But where Keaton's sublime persona has too lit-tle sentiment, Lewis's Idiot has all too much. Just as his body is decomposed by contradictory movements, so his face is traversed by a ridiculously wide and mobile variety of emotional states, from sheer panic to anxious apology to blissful absorption. According to psychoanalysis, identification is supposed to make the stability of the ego possible; but Lewis's incessant overidentification disrupts this stability. In Tashlin's *The Disorderly Orderly*, Lewis is physically disabled when his "sympathy pains" reproduce the complaints of the hypochondriacal patients he is supposed to be tending. In Lewis's own films, such a pattern is articulated in more complex ways. The Idiot is besieged by the orders and demands of others, and the infinite malleability of his responses is very nearly terrifying. His psyche is affected by everything, but retains nothing. Its only consistency is that of an infantile enthusiasm and an inane desire to please. Identification opens the door not to a solidification, but to a schizophrenic fragmentation and disintegration of the personality. The triumph of mechanical reproduction, its inscription in Lewis's facial expressions and bodily gestures, marks the end of the traditional (Cartesian) model of a unified, originary subjectivity.

In other words, the death of the subject proclaimed in poststructuralist theory has already been discovered by Lewis as a logical consequence of the pressures of the market and the media. Even in *The Nutty Professor*, Kelp's attempt to compensate for his physical humiliation seems motivated less by psychological imperatives than by "98-pound-weakling" advertisements. The ending of the film relegates Kelp's discovery to the category of confidence games: personality change and the restoration of male virility are nothing more than advertising scams.

This parodic revision of the Jekyll/Hyde motif leads to the delirious multiplications of personality in Lewis's subsequent films: the sevenfold impersonations of *The Family Jewels*, the psychoanalytically determined disguises in *Three on a Couch*, and the weird mimicry of a Nazi general in *Which Way to the Front?* But the zenith of this process is reached in *The Big Mouth*. Here, a basic instability of personality affects not just Lewis, but the other characters as well. The film is premised upon a case of mistaken identity, in what is more or less a parody of Hitchcock's *North by Northwest*. Lewis plays an innocent vacationer who looks exactly like a double-crossing gangster. The killers of the latter fall into states of nervous disability when they encounter the former, who appears to have returned from the dead. For his part, Lewis's protagonist can extricate himself from his increasing difficulties only by adopting a Kelp-like disguise (thus neatly inverting the movement of *The Nutty Professor*). Subjectivity is threatened by overly fluid possibilities of identification and recognition. The shock of Lewis's excess of resemblance sets off what is virtually a plague of personality disorders. Identity seems to break down into a series of nervous tics and speech impediments, which proliferate beyond control, migrating from situation to situation and from character to character.

The Big Mouth only carries to an extreme a process that is implicit in all of Lewis's movies. Identification and doubling take the form of a fluid, insidious contagion, rather than that of a normalizing or stabilizing fixation. At the end of *Cracking Up*, similarly, Lewis is "cured" of his fears, incompetencies, and neuroses only because he is able to pass them on to his doctor. In the absence of any positive catharsis, the humiliation of Lewis's persona infects the other characters, and ultimately even the audience.

Precisely because it is infantile and abject, Lewis's comedy disturbs phantasies of subjective plenitude and denies all fixities of identification. As Scott Bukatman (1988) puts it, all we see in the mirror is "an image of motor incapacity, sexual ambiguity, and unfixed identity" (p. 204). Lewis returns himself, and his viewers, to a pre-Oedipal world characterized by a startling mobility and instability of affect. He thus literalizes the movement by which late capitalist culture, even as it promulgates the ideal of individual autonomy, infantilizes the consumer. In his frantic, incoherent responses to an incongruous multitude of advertising admonitions and commands from superiors, Lewis becomes a perpetually neglected or abused child, forever striving, and forever failing, to please his capriciously inscrutable parents.

By masochistically making his own infantilization the very basis of his comedy, Lewis turns the entire process of bourgeois subject formation inside out. He reveals the dark secret of the American family: that it is the parents, and not the children, who are narcissistic. He suggests that "growing up" is not a process of giving up Imaginary phantasies of omnipotence and accepting the lack imposed by castration; on the contrary, it involves assuming the hollowness and rigidity, but thereby also appropriating the power, of a stable and stereotypical ego. This is the commodified form of the self, which can be recognized in the fatuous, overbearing authority figures who populate Lewis's movies (the hotel manager in *The Bellboy*, the college president in *The Nutty Professor*, and so on). Only an adult can indulge in fantasies of plenitude and autonomy, for these fantasies are produced by the commodity form itself. Yet, as Lewis's repeated failure to satisfy his superiors demonstrates, the very forces that demand adult ideals also make them impossible to attain.

Lewis's comedy produces its substantial—if embarrassingly infantile—pleasures, but also acquires a disturbing aftertaste, by pushing the logic of commodified desire to desperate extremes. Against the self-centeredness and capacity to abuse others of the successful adult, Lewis poses a continued abjection, dependency, and maladaptation. In his spastic bodily movements as in his exaggerated facial expressions, he affirms the very nonautonomy that is both presupposed and dissimulated in the regime of the commodity. He lives and moves in a time and space in which all desires are artificially induced, and in which no actions can be extracted from the frenzy of repetitive circulation and brought to a satisfactory conclusion. In thus deriving overt pleasure from the most shameful, inauthentic, and usually unacknowledged aspects of an economy of production and circulation, Lewis wards off or indefinitely postpones the achievement of an adaptive, adult narcissism. By deliriously affirming the *process* of commodification, he subverts the commodified final product. Lewis exhibits his own subjectivity as an empty, reactive form, and founds his comedy on a strangely ecstatic self-abdication before the opinions and demands of others. And in his or her own turn, the spectator is seduced into abandoning the stability of the ego and vicariously participating in a spectacle of self-abandonment and abjection.

Bodies of Fear

David Cronenberg

In the Flesh

DAVID CRONENBERG'S films focus insistently, obsessively, on the body. They relentlessly articulate a politics, a technology, and an aesthetics of the flesh. They are unsparingly visceral; this is what makes them so disturbing.

Cronenberg's explorations of the flesh go against the grain of our most deeply rooted social myths. The body remains the great unknown, the "dark continent" of postmodern thought and culture. We live in a world of ubiquitous, commodified images of sexuality, but one in which the shocks of tactile contact and (in an age of AIDS) of the mingling or transmission of bodily fluids are all the more denied. New electronic technologies, with their clean bits of binarized information, claim to volatilize the flesh. Material needs, Baudrillard tells us, have long since been displaced by simulacra. Desire is described by Lacanian theorists as a linguistic process, and scrupulously detached from any taint of bodily excitation or of affect. Postmodern Western culture is more traditional, more Cartesian, than it is willing to admit; it is still frantically concerned to deny materiality, to keep thought separate from the exigencies of the flesh. As Foucault (1980) suggests, we continue to elaborate the strange "idea that there exists something other than bodies, organs, somatic localizations, functions, anatomo-physiological systems, sensations, and pleasures; something else and something more, with intrinsic properties and laws of its own" (pp. 152–53). This "something else" is the postmodern residue of the Cartesian myth of an autonomous thinking substance. Postmodern ideology has not rejected the notion of absolute subjectivity so much as it has refigured the old fantasy of freedom from the constraints of the body in the new terms of cybernetic information, sexual representation, and social signification. The text is the postmodern equivalent of the soul.

Cronenberg's films display the body in its crude, primordial materiality. They thereby deny the postmodern myth of textual or signifying autonomy. They short-circuit the social logic of information and representation, by collapsing this logic back into its physiological and affective conditions. And they suggest that the new technologies of late capitalism, far from erasing our experience of the body, in fact heighten this experience, by investing that body in novel and particularly intense ways. The machine invented by Seth Brundle (Jeff Goldblum) in *The Fly* is typical in this regard. Its ostensible purpose is teleportation: the quintessential postmodern fantasy of instantaneous transmission, of getting from one point to another without having to endure the inconveniences of bodily movement and the passage of time. "I hate vehicles," Brundle remarks; he perpetually suffers from "motion sickness." But his experiments go awry; the machine quickly reveals its deeper, unintended purpose as a gene splicer. Far from negating the constraints of distance and duration, it implants the difference and delay that they imply directly into Brundle's flesh. Brundle's entire transformation is a kind of "motion sickness": he traverses the enormous gap separating human from insect, not seamlessly and instantaneously but in the slow unfolding of bodily affliction. Similar processes take place in *Scanners*, where ESP—traditionally a figure for the liberation of the mind from space and from the body—instead instances the violent physicality of thought, and in *Videodrome*, where video technology destroys traditional forms of physical presence only in order to incarnate a "new flesh."

Cronenberg's films, then, are violently, literally visceral. They depict the violation and disarticulation of living flesh, and we are spared none of the gruesome anatomical details of the protagonists' physical transformations into flies or living video machines. Seth Brundle's exhibition of an insect's digestive processes blown up to human scale is more troubling than any number of psychopathic murders in a slasher film would be. It is very nearly unwatchable—for the other characters within the film as well as for us—precisely because it is a simple matter of biology, a physical process devoid of symbolic or archetypal resonance. Master narratives of social progress and myths of inherent evil or of spiritual redemption are no longer available to inure us to the excruciating passion of the subjugated body. There is no vision of transcendence in the claustrophobic world of these films. We are left only with affects of despair and rage—embodied in cancers and monstrous births in *The Brood*—or with bafflement and confusion over limits and identities—as in the self-destructive trajectory of the physically identical Mantle twins (Jeremy Irons) in *Dead Ringers*. Passion is anchored in and expressed by the brute facticity of bodily transmutations.

Cronenberg is a literalist of the body. Everything in his films is corporeal, grounded in the monstrous intersection of physiology and technology. Bodily affections are not psychoanalytic symptoms to be deciphered; they actually *are*, in their own right, movements of passion. The body is the site of the most violent alterations and of the most intense affects. It is continually subjugated and remade, and in this process it experiences extremities of pleasure, pain, and horror. The flesh is less rigidly determined, more fluid and open to metamorphosis, than we generally like to think. Cronenberg's science fiction extrapolations of biotechnology register this troubling plasticity and ambiguity. The polymorphousness of living tissue has the capacity to traverse all boundaries, to undo the rigidities of organic function and symbolic articulation. New arrangements of the flesh break down traditional binary oppositions between mind and matter, image and object, self and other, inside and outside, male and female, nature and culture, human and inhuman, organic and mechanical. Indeed, the systematic undoing of these distinctions, on every possible level, is the major structural principle of all of Cronenberg's films. Rose (Marilyn Chambers) acquires a strange and deadly phallic appendage in *Rabid*; a vaginal slit opens in Max Renn's (James Woods's) body in *Videodrome*. The blurring of distinctions between self and other is especially evident in the case of the identical twins in *Dead Ringers*. In *Scanners*, with its telepathic brothers, ESP disrupts the very notions of bodily integrity and of mental privacy, and hence upsets any concept of personal identity based on either of these. This film also refuses to distinguish between natural and artificial intelligence: one scene depicts a violent contest of wills, on nearly equal terms, between human and computer. In *The Fly*, Seth Brundle is first transformed into "Brundlefly," and ultimately finds himself fused with inorganic matter.

But the most important binary opposition that collapses in Cronenberg's films is that between mind and body, or thought and matter. Psychological and physiological processes occur simultaneously, and neither can be said to be the cause or ground of the other. In effect, Cronenberg deconstructs Cartesian dualism by establishing an absolute Spinozistic parallelism between minds and bodies. In *Scanners*, telepathy is "the direct linking of two nervous systems separated by space"; that is why the experience of being "scanned" can culminate in nosebleeds, headaches, and even the brain being violently blown apart. Mental processes—desires and fears, affects and fantasies—are directly registered as bodily alterations. This is the basis for Dr. Hal Raglan's (Oliver Reed's) system of "psychoplasmics" in *The Brood*. Through a series of manipulative psychodramas, he induces his patients to go all the way to the end of their feelings of dependency and rage. The result is a series of grotesque physical deformities. As a former patient, now ravaged with lymphatic cancer, bitterly complains, "Raglan encouraged my body to revolt against me, and it did." Nola Carveth (Samantha Eggar) maternally watches over, and even licks into shape, a "brood" of dwarflike creatures that emerge from external sacs on her body. These beings embody her anger and need for revenge; they are the ultimate product of her own experience of having been abused as a child. They literally enact her rage, murdering her parents and the woman she wrongly suspects of being her estranged husband's lover. The brood is inarticulate (they make gurgling sounds, but lack the organs necessary for comprehensible speech) and self-consuming (they do not eat, but are nourished by an internal food sac and die of starvation once it is depleted). In all these respects, the creatures to which Nola gives birth are the embodiment at once of her victimization and instability and of the way in which she aggressively redirects her pain, perpetuating the cycle of abuse.

Cronenberg thus reverses the popular mythology that would see cancer and other diseases as consequences of repression. The "revolt" of the body is a direct expression of passion, rather than a pathogenic symptom of its denial. Raglan's patients suffer from the very success of his treatment: they become all too capable of venting their rage. Nola literally gives birth to her anger, embodying and reshaping actual social conditions and experiences within the family. Physiological transformations do not symbolize or represent hidden psychological conflicts; they are the arena in which, precisely, these conflicts are no longer hidden. Cronenberg remarks that "the very purpose" of his films is "to show the unshowable, to speak the unspeakable" (in Rodley 1992, 43). Nothing is hidden. These films insist upon the Artaudian imperative that everything be made body, everything be materially and visibly enacted. There can be no recourse to the negative hypotheses of repression and hysterical conversion. Even the miseries and sufferings of Cronenberg's protagonists cannot be defined in terms of lack. Nola Carveth, Max Renn, and Seth Brundle do not perish from ungratified desire, but from bodily fulfillment even to excess. Each in his or her own way is made pregnant with a monstrous birth.

Monstrous Ambivalence

Monstrosity is not the consequence of denial in Cronenberg's films. The reverse is more nearly the case: our ideologies of "health" and "normality" are grounded in the denial or expulsion of monstrosity. Our culture's profound ambivalence toward all forms of birthing and embodiment is the source of the "horror" in these horror films. We feel panic at Cronenberg's vision of the body, its stresses and transformations, the bizarre intensity of its physical sensations. But at the same time, we may also find this vision to be deeply hilarious. Terror and humor alike are rooted in Cronenberg's refusal to idealize: his presentation of the body in its primordial monstrosity and obscenity. In one of Seth Brundle's early, unsuccessful experiments with teleportation in *The Fly*, a baboon is turned inside out, and reappears as a throbbing, bloody mass of bones, hair, and flesh. It has been hideously transformed, but not quite to the point of death. An organic mass continues to pulse and groan imploringly, expressing pain and begging for our assistance. Such a spectacle makes a peculiar claim upon us. It is obscene, and by that very fact it testifies to an extreme vulnerability, something of which we can only be the uncomfortable witnesses. We cannot do anything about this bodily transformation, but we also cannot sit back and view it from a comfortable distance. We are denied the luxuries of objectification and control; fascination is mingled with disgust. Our response is violently ambivalent on every level.

       This monstrous ambivalence has been a frequent source of

critical misunderstanding. Cronenberg's films have been the target of the most violent polemics. The usually perceptive Robin Wood, for instance, regards them with unqualified loathing; he sees them as expressing a hatred of the body and a rabid fear of sexual difference and sexual liberation (Wood 1985, 216–17; to be fair, I must note that Wood eliminated this entire passage when he rewrote the article for his book *Hollywood from Vietnam to Reagan*, 1986). Wood is correct in apprehending that there is no utopian moment, no vision of redemption, no escape from the ambivalent pressures of monstrosity, in these films. But he is wrong in therefore categorizing them as reactionary and defensive. As Cronenberg has said, "I have to tell people that some of the things they think are repulsive in my films are meant to be repulsive, yes, but there's a beautiful aspect to them as well. There's true beauty in some things that others find repulsive" (in Rodley 1992, 66). Wood simply misses this beauty, just as he fails to grasp the political implications of Cronenberg's extreme literalism. To foreground the monstrosity of the body is to refuse the pacifying lures of specular idealization.

By insisting on the gross palpability of the flesh, and by heightening (instead of minimizing) our culture's pervasive discomfort with materiality, Cronenberg opposes the way in which dominant cinema captures, polices, and regulates desire, precisely by providing sanitized models of its fulfillment. *Shivers* (*They Came from Within*), in which a phallic/excremental parasite transforms the inhabitants of a chic condominium into a band of violent, frenzied erotomaniacs, is not (as Wood argues) a paranoid rejection of the sexual revolution of the 1960s. Its mood is one of dark comedy rather than unqualified repulsion. There's a certain "glee," as Cronenberg has put it, in the way in which the film tears apart "bourgeois ideas of morality and sexuality" (in Rodley 1992, 50). It is not Cronenberg but Wood who responds to the sexual monstrosity in which the film revels with phobic disgust, and who regards this monstrosity as an *objection* to the life of the body. *Shivers* does not adopt such a phobic position; its own investments are entirely on the side of shock and spectacle. Everything is at once hideous and hilarious, from the gory apparition of the parasitic creature in the bathtub to the zombielike 1960s orgy in the swimming pool at the end. The film neither idealizes nor condemns these transgressive movements of physical violation and orgiastic excess. If anything, it slyly suggests that the 1960s bourgeois sexual "revolution" in fact merely reproduces the aggressive, hysterical logic of a commodified and competitive society. Transgression is not transcendence.

Cronenberg is thus equally skeptical of "left-Freudian" visions of personal and social liberation through the lifting of repression, and of right-wing claims that desire must always be repressed because it is inherently evil and disruptive. These positions are, in fact, mirror images of one another. They both posit a soul, an originary human essence—whether good or evil—and ignore the shady complicity that always already contaminates desire with the regulation and repression of desire. Humanist visions of unlimited freedom and conservative visions of original sin (or of inevitable limits) both strive to reject monstrosity, to deny the violent ambivalence of bodily passion. Harmonious utopian projections and anxious defenses of the status quo alike betray a continuing need to idealize, a panic in the face of excesses of the flesh. Both ideologies are trying to transcend the anxiety and insecurity implicit in the state of being a body.

Scanners: The Politics of the Body

Conversely, a refusal of these myths of transcendence is at the heart of Cronenberg's politics of the body. His films remind us that everything is implanted directly in the flesh. There is no getting away from the monstrosity of the body, or from the violence with which it is transformed, because there is no essential nature, no spontaneous being, of the body; social forces permeate it right from the beginning. The body is at once a target for new biological and communicational technologies, a site of political conflict, and a limit point at which ideological oppositions collapse. Nobody has gone further than Cronenberg in detailing the ways in which the body is invested and colonized by power mechanisms, how it is both a means and an end of social control. The bodies of Max Renn and Seth Brundle, and of the telepaths Cameron Vale (Stephen Lack) and Darryl Revok (Michael Ironside) in *Scanners*, are zones of intense receptivity; they capture and render visible a wide range of sinister and usually impalpable social forces, from implicit codes of sexual behavior to the financial transactions of multinational corporations. The word of late capitalist power is literally made flesh. The ubiquitous but ungraspable hyperreality of surveillance and domination is materialized and localized in the form of excruciating pains and pleasures. In this subjugated flesh, fantasy and materiality, affect and technology, the circuits of the brain and the circuits of capital, finally coincide.

Corporate power is apparent everywhere in *Scanners*. It is visible in the sets and decors of the film: in the establishing shots of the ugly, anonymous, and yet aggressively self-assertive architecture of corporate buildings, and in the spare, functional interiors of laboratories, interrogation rooms, and corridors that seem to lead nowhere. It is present more subtly in the second-order imagery that runs like a motif throughout the film: the recurring close-ups of corporate logos, the replays of crucial scenes on film and video, the presentation of information on computer terminals, and finally the startling close-ups of the wiring and transistors that constitute the "nervous system" of the computer. The business of ConSec is the invisible activity of security and surveillance; Cronenberg's camera dwells on the hardware, the material base, that makes such a process tangible.

In a film so concerned with the politics of "information," it is appropriate that the main characters should suffer physically from a state of vertiginous epistemological overload. The paranoia and social maladaptation of the "scanners" is a direct consequence of their extraordinary gift of telepathy. They are victims of the extreme permeability of their brains to the ideas and affects of others. Cameron Vale cannot establish his own identity because he cannot shut out the inner "voices" of the people surrounding him; he writhes on a bed in torment under the shock to his nervous system of so many contradictory messages. Vale's role is not so much acted by Stephen Lack as it is walked through; such a character is disturbingly blank and affectless for the ostensible action hero of the narrative. But as one of Vale's fellow scanners pityingly tells him, he is so crippled by his psychic sensitivity as to be "barely human." The other main scanner character, Vale's brother and antitype Darryl Revok, is even more distorted and chillingly inhuman; he drills a hole in his skull in the hope that this will "let the voices out." His ruthlessness and lust for power are merely projections outward of this initial ecstasy of self-laceration. In learning to direct his powers, he becomes "no longer self-destructive, but merely destructive."

For all these characters, as for Artaud, thought is physical agony. *Scanners* is filled with close-ups of faces distorted by a violent tension or effort of concentration: the visible manifestation of the stress felt alike by the scanner and the one being scanned. These shots are usually accompanied by body sounds: breathing and heartbeats. Far from "expressing" or providing insight into the hidden depths of the soul, such distorted physiognomies confront us with a situation in which there no longer is any inner being or soul. Traumatic shock and emotional ambivalence are entirely materialized, and played out on the surfaces of the flesh. Nothing can be held back. Confronted with these contorted faces, the spectators are themselves drawn into the agonizing circuit of telepathic exchanges. Observing the scene, watching the gathering of information—as an audience of businessmen watches a mental duel between Revok and a ConSec scanner in one early sequence—itself becomes a kind of visceral contact. Of course, we cannot actually *know* the thought contents that lie behind another person's facial expression. But when the flesh is pushed to such an extremity, we are affected by a physical shock, touched by the image at a distance, violated in the space of our own mental privacy—and so we no longer need to "know." The violence of communication has priority over the calm registering of information. This is why watching Cronenberg's films can be such an unsettling, or unnerving, experience.

There is a direct link between such extreme affective dislocation and the political implications of *Scanners*. Telepathy is first experienced as a state of radical passivity, a subjection of the body, before it is transformed into a power. The film suggests, therefore, that information gathering and management are by no means calm, neutral processes. A violence like that of "scanning" subtends the technologies of computer data gathering and biofeedback. The vulnerability of the organism is a basic, necessary condition for the mastery of cybernetics. The late capitalist utopia of information flow and control is in fact predicated on the violent extraction of information from, and the inscription of it back upon, the suffering flesh. And this technology of cruelty and domination is the common ground for all the plots and counterplots, the struggles for power, that constitute the convoluted narrative of *Scanners*. At the end, Cameron Vale can see no difference between the megalomaniacal ambitions of his brother Darryl Revok, who wants to set up a dictatorship of scanners, and those of their father/creator Dr. Paul Ruth (Patrick McGoohan), who projects marvelous new scientific frontiers. Both of these visions of autonomy in fact pass through the corporate power and computer circuitry of ConSec. Both also establish their dreams of transparent mastery only by directing violence against — and for that very reason remaining implicated with — the density and opacity of the body in torment.

Videodrome: Uncontrollable Flesh

All of these ambiguous processes are pushed to even further extremes in *Videodrome*. Cronenberg relentlessly materializes not just information systems, but the entire range of referentless media images that are so often said to constitute the postmodern world. Simulation is forced to display its body. The brutally hilarious strategy of *Videodrome* is to take media theorists such as Marshall McLuhan and Jean Baudrillard completely at their word, to overliteralize their claims for the ubiquitous mediatization of the real. Baudrillard (1983) states that television implies not a "society of the spectacle," but rather

the very abolition of the spectacular.... *The medium itself is no longer identifiable as such, and the merging of the medium and the message (McLuhan?) is the first great formula of this new age. There is no longer any medium in the literal sense: it is now intangible, diffuse and diffracted in the real, and it can no longer be said that the latter is distorted by it.* (p. 54)

Media images no longer *refer* to a real that would be (in principle) prior to and independent of them, for they penetrate, volatilize, and thereby (re)constitute that real.

But *Videodrome* suggests that — contrary to McLuhan and Baudrillard — the resultant "hyperreality" is hot, not cool. Far from being "intangible," it is gruesomely physical: the realm of what Dr. Brian O'Blivion (Jack Creley), the McLuhanesque TV theorist in *Videodrome*, calls "the video word made flesh." The body is not erased or evacuated; it is rather so suffused with video technology that it mutates into new forms, and is pushed to new thresholds of intense, masochistic sensation. As it progresses, *Videodrome* moves further and further into the seductive, hallucinatory pleasures of the video-activated body. The key, as Nikki Brand (Deborah Harry) points out early on, is continual, violent overstimulation of the senses. The purpose of the masochistic games into which Nikki initiates Max Renn (cutting herself and sticking burning cigarettes into her naked flesh) is to make bodily sensation more vivid, and therefore more "real." Video technology only further heightens this pleasure. Videocassettes and TV monitors begin to throb like living, breathing flesh; Max embraces Nikki's enormous smile extended in luscious close-up across, and bulging out from, the TV screen. Identities merge and shift; bodies die and come alive again, appear and disappear; it becomes impossible to distinguish between hallucination and objective reality, between what is spontaneous and what is prerecorded. Max doesn't merely lose any point of reference outside of what is imprinted on the video screen, he comes to embody this process directly, as he's transformed into a human video machine.

Brian O'Blivion's categorical, video-recorded pronouncements are repeated like mantras throughout the film: "The television screen is the retina of the mind's eye; therefore the television screen is part of the physical structure of the brain." When experience is absorbed by video technology, then this technology is itself quite palpably "real." To abolish reference and to embrace "virtual reality" is not, as Baudrillard imagines, to reduce desire to a series of weightless and indifferent equivalences. The more images are flattened out and distanced from their representational sources, the more they are inscribed in our nerves, and flash across our synapses. The real is not "lost" so much as it is redescribed in consequence of a radical epistemological break or shift: it is no longer what is referred to, but what suffers and is transformed.

This shift is perfectly expressed by the activities of Spectacular

Optical, the multinational corporation that turns out to be behind the sinister technologies of *Videodrome*. The company's public activity is the manufacture of designer eyeglasses, while behind the scenes it is working to dominate the video market—and therefore the entire social organization—of North America. The trade show (for selling "spectacles," or eyeglasses) over which Barry Convex (Les Carlson) presides is itself an old-fashioned spectacle, a stage show self-consciously organized around the themes of Renaissance perspectivism: "Love comes in at the eyes," and "The eyes are the windows of the soul." But the videodrome experiments target the body, not the soul. Vision is imploded, turned back upon the flesh. Convex gives Max, instead of eyeglasses, a grotesque metal box that entirely encases his head, and that is supposed to record his hallucinations. We have entered a new regime of the image, one in which vision is visceral and intensive instead of representational and extensive.

In this new regime, the body is the common locus of subjectivity and subjection, of inner perception and outer manifestation. O'Blivion claims at one point that his hallucinatory visions are the cause of his brain tumor, and not the reverse. But these visions are themselves physiologically induced by a video signal that directly stimulates the brain. O'Blivion is the first victim, as well as the inventor, of the videodrome project. If cancer in *The Brood* was an articulation of affect, in *Videodrome* it materializes the very act of perception. For his part, Max Renn is first exposed to the videodrome signal in the form of a snuff video, containing harshly realistic scenes of torture—hooded figures beating a naked woman—that fascinate and frighten him. He becomes pornographically addicted to this repetitive vision of violation and death; he wants to show it on his cable TV channel. Yet the program escapes his sensationalistic intentions, for what he has encountered is not the shock of a public spectacle or the transgressive thrill of a novel by Sade, but the secret, anonymous world of state and corporate power, where the most extreme abuses of the body are matters of bureaucratic routine. Vision is rendered to the body in the form of pain; shock is now a chronic condition. Max cannot be just a cynically detached spectator of torture; he must suffer it in his own flesh. This new regime of the image abolishes the distance required either for disinterested aesthetic contemplation or for stupefied absorption in spectacle.

But there is still another twist to this scenario. The videodrome signal, it turns out, is a kind of McLuhanesque joke: it is a function of the medium, not of the message. It is a subliminal stimulus that does not require the extremities of a snuff video, but can function under any kind of program, even in a test pattern. The videodrome project thus marks the end of the primacy traditionally accorded to representation. As vision is technologically rationalized and turned back upon the body, its physiological effects take priority alike over the ideological forms of representation and the contents being represented. The function of vision is no longer to show, but to excite the nerves directly. Sight is not a neutral source of information, but a gaping wound, a violation of the integrity of the body. In this implosive embodiment of vision, spectacle is indeed abolished, but so is the digital coding that Baudrillard sees as taking its place, for there are no more simple images, no more simulation models, no more surfaces. What starts out as a play of impalpable reflections quickly blossoms into a physical metamorphosis: "The visions became flesh, uncontrollable flesh."

By the end of *Videodrome*, the distinction between fantasy and actuality, or between inner bodily excitation and outer objective representation, has entirely collapsed. The point at which subjective reality becomes entirely hallucinatory is also the point at which technology becomes ubiquitous, and is totally melded with and objectified in the human body. When Max is programmed by cassette to be a killer for Spectacular Optical, his gun is incorporated directly into his flesh, first by a series of plugs and cords and then by an odd fusing together of plastic, metal, and skin. Video technology is no longer concerned merely with disembodied images. It reaches directly into the unseen depths, stimulating the ganglia and the viscera, caressing and remolding the interior volume of the body. An enormous slit opens in Max's belly: this is at once an actual slot for inserting prerecorded videocassettes, a link between surface (skin, membrane, retina, image screen) and volume (the thickness and multiple convolutions of the entrails), and a vaginal orifice, indicating the sexualization and "feminization" of Max's body. This is the point of maximum opacity, at which Max's conditioning cannot be separated from his desire. He cannot render himself autonomous from technology; the best he can do is painfully to exchange one programming for another, to replace the "videodrome" tape with the ambiguous lure of "the new flesh."

Cronenberg offers no alternative to a ubiquitous, simulated video reality. He suggests that any promise of utopian transcendence is yet another avatar of manipulative power. In the final scene of *Videodrome*, the television set explodes and burns, but this is only part of a repetitive video loop in which Max is trapped. He shoots himself after seeing himself shoot himself on TV. The quasi-religious doctrine of "the new flesh" pushes Max to a limit, but holds out no promises as to what he will encounter on the other side. The film ends with the sound of his gunshot—perhaps a finality, or perhaps a rewind to one more playback.

Bodies and Genders

All this is not to say that Cronenberg leaves us with a Baudrillardian vision of absolute, totalitarian entrapment. The emphasis, rather, again falls on ambivalence and monstrosity. Max's transformation absurdly, hyperbolically literalizes the ideology that equates femininity with passivity, receptivity, and castration. *Videodrome* makes us obsessively aware that it is cultural and political technology—and not natural necessity—that imposes the restricted economies of organicism, functionalism, and sexual representation. Anatomy is not destiny, precisely in the sense that the corporeal is the realm in which the Symbolic inscription of fixed gender identity reaches its limit, and can be broken down. When a fascistic operative reaches into Max's belly to insert a new program and instead has his entire arm eaten away, this is most obviously a joke on the notion of castration anxiety. But the scene undoes psychoanalytic doctrine in a subtler manner as well. Lacan removes gender and sexuality from the body, interpreting them instead as Symbolic processes. His followers argue that this conceptual distinction—which shows that gender differences are not naturally given—is a necessary first step in criticizing and reversing patriarchy. Cronenberg's supercharged images suggest, to the contrary, that it is only sexist ideology that establishes the distinction (between social constructions and the body) in the first place.

Max's transformations, like the obsessive gynecological displacements of the Mantle twins in *Dead Ringers*, demonstrate that gender isn't a social construction *rather than* a state of the body; it is precisely a social construction *of* the body. To separate desire from the body, or the Symbolic from the Real, is to perpetuate (in inverted form) the myth that sees the body as an essence, outside of history. Power does not work merely on the level of images and ideologies; it directly invests the flesh. Symbolic ascription is not a seamless or conclusive process; it involves continual operations upon the body. The visceral density of the flesh gets in the way of any untrammeled, instantaneous exercise of total power. In *Videodrome*, Spectacular Optical controls all the software, but it still has to depend upon the unreliable materiality of (human or mechanical) hardware. The body is a potential site of resistance, not in spite of but *because* of its being a necessary relay, target, and support of power. The flesh is perpetually monstrous, unstable, out of control.

Cronenberg's films thus exceed the limits of social control to the extent that they locate power and desire directly in an immanent experience of the body. Initially linear plot lines explode in multiple, incompatible directions, following the delirious, paranoid logic of proliferating cancer cells, or of interfaces between biology and technology run amok. Mutations whose original function was to serve corporate or bureaucratic power take on a sinister life of their own once they have been implanted in the bodies of their hosts/victims. Power and authority are swallowed up within the very mechanisms of fear that they themselves have created. Ambiguity, chance, and intense pleasure are unavoidable consequences of embodiment. In *Videodrome*, masochism and "feminization" are instances of this process. Max Renn starts out (thanks to James Woods's consummate performance) as stereotypically "masculine": sleazy, competitive, aggressive, and tough in a self-congratulatory way. But his transformation destroys these pretensions, even as it is a movement not subject to his own control. His body gets penetrated by technology to the very extent that his will is dissolved in passive fascination. He is absorbed by the medium when he no longer possesses the cynicism and detachment necessary to manipulate it. And he is seduced, stimulated, "turned on" by the affective overload of new sensations in new organs. Such a subject position is also that of the viewers of *Videodrome*. Cronenberg's strategy is the perverse opposite of Brecht's; it shatters identification and "alienates" the spectator by virtue of too great a proximity to bliss and horror, and not because of any rational distancing from them. The self-possession of the "male gaze" gives way to the intensely ambivalent—and ambiguously gendered—pleasures of an all-too-vulnerable flesh.

The Fly: Intimacy and Alterity

The relations between power and pleasure in Cronenberg's films are subtle and complex. Max Renn and Seth Brundle experience new forms of affect exactly to the extent that they lose control over what's happening to their own bodies. But it would be too simple to say that their pleasure is therefore a compensation (or a pernicious alibi) for their loss of power. Both of these developments must be seen in conjunction with a mutation in the very form of subjectivity. Passion is imprinted directly in the flesh, prior to any movement of self-conscious reflection. Psychophysiological changes are continually occurring, at a rate that exceeds our ability to assimilate or understand them. In *The Fly*, Seth Brundle's rationalizations of his state always lag far behind the actual, visible changes in his body. He posits a series of ideological explanations—a leap into the plasma pool, a bizarre new form of cancer—each of which is discredited as his physical transformations continue. He is finally compelled to admit that he suffers from "a disease with a purpose" of its own, one to which he cannot himself be privy. He is in effect excluded from the scene of his own metamorphosis. Human subjectivity cannot absorb or "recognize" the being of a fly. And so the movements that turn Brundle into "Brundlefly" are necessarily passive and unwilled. They involve affects and passions of which their ostensible subject is not the master. Sensation and desire are so far from being reducible to self-consciousness that for the most part they are incompatible with it.

There is no stable subject position in Cronenberg's films, just as there is no figure of hypostasized, absolute Otherness. In typical horror films, as Robin Wood (1986) has argued, a socially constructed "normality" is threatened by a Monster that in some sense figures "the return of the repressed." The Monster is the Other, the portion of the self that is "projected outward in order to be hated and disowned" (p. 73); "the true subject of the horror genre is the struggle for recognition of all that our civilization represses or oppresses" (p. 75). But the parasites in Cronenberg's films do not conform to any such dialectical logic. We can say neither that monstrosity is purely extrinsic and has nothing to do with us nor that it is actually internal, really a repressed and projected portion of ourselves. There is no hope of escape, no possibility of separation and expulsion, but there is also no possibility of *recognition*.

Cronenberg's "monsters" are forms of *alterity* that cannot be reduced to the economy of the Same, but that also cannot be identified as purely and simply Other. Autonomy is out of the question. A parasite is neither part of me nor apart from me; it is something from which I cannot separate myself, but that at the same time I cannot integrate into my personality. I do not become cognizant of alterity; rather, it insinuates itself within me, as a new and uncontrollable potentiality of my body. I am passively invested by forces that I cannot recuperate as my own. Boundaries between self and other break down; the festering wound of alterity is incurable. I am affected by, and compelled to "experience," something that remains irreducibly *not-me*: other minds (*Scanners*), media images (*Videodrome*), and even the altogether nonhuman (*The Fly*).

In Cronenberg's films, then, there is a disturbing *intimacy* at the heart of terror. We are not transported to some fantastic realm; everything takes place in the bourgeois privacy of living rooms and bedrooms. Anonymous corporate and professional spaces alternate with the most banal and claustrophobic upper-middle-class decors. There is no escape from this rigidly circumscribed world; a point of explosive, utopian liberation is never reached. Instead, a principle of entropy seems to be at work: the apartments and work spaces of Max Renn, Seth Brundle, and the Mantle twins become increasingly cluttered and strewn with debris. As Brundle turns into Brundlefly, he leaves behind the now useless traces of his former existence: teeth and other body parts, and bits of regurgitated, half-digested food. At one point, he even proposes (with dark humor) to preserve these relics, to turn his loft into a "Brundle museum." The image of increasing disorder, composed of leftover bits and pieces of himself, is entirely apt. Brundle's past existence is not entirely effaced; it remains in the form of discontinuous fragments. He has not been translated from one state of being into another so much as he has been uprooted from the fixity of human identity, and submitted instead to a process of continual flux. It is at the point of greatest intimacy, in his own home and in his own body, that he has become a stranger.

It is this unmooring of subjectivity, its passive immersion in bodily turbulence, that marks the limit of power. The violent metamorphosis of the flesh is fatal alike to the assertion of personal initiative and to the manipulative technologies of social control. Brundlefly is born in the excruciating rigors of an estrangement without hope of return. Such a voyage into the flesh cannot be actively willed, for it approaches precisely that condition in which the will no longer commands. Insofar as Seth can will anything, his need to rehumanize himself is irreducible. But his moving, desperate attempt to preserve his identity from monstrous transformation is *also* a ludicrously literal endeavor to conform to social norms. Seth cannot distinguish his self-preservation from his subjection to socially imposed definitions of what it means to be "human," to be "male," and so on. And so he prevents Veronica (Geena Davis) from aborting her genetically altered fetus, and tries to force her instead to fuse with him, thus creating the ultimate "nuclear family." All this suggests that will and personal identity are inextricably intertwined with forces of domination and social control. And conversely, those movements that exceed Seth's will, that violate the integrity of his body, and that compromise his sense of personal identity also absent themselves from the meshes of normalizing power.

There is nothing utopian or redemptive about this process.

Brundlefly is not a new species or a new identity, but literally a monster, a point of absolute singularity. Seth is free from social control only in the sense that he cannot be part of any society. Yet another of his failed dreams is to balance the two sides of his nature, to become "the first insect politician." But his becoming-fly is an open-ended process, always pulling him further and further away from any community, any identity, any repose. Seth starts out not being able to teleport organic matter, because he doesn't understand the flesh. In the course of the film, he is increasingly compelled to endure the burden of the materiality that he is unable to comprehend or master. His body is traversed by physical forces, and submitted to stresses, that are more and more intolerable. By the end, he is all too acquainted with the flesh: he is even merged with the machinery that alters him, with the telepod itself. This new body, this mass of mingled tissue and metal, is a burden too great to bear. Its sheer weight epitomizes sensory and corporeal overload: an overinvestment of the muscles and the nerves, a sensitivity and vulnerability too great to be endured, and yet that must be endured. Seth crawls forth and gestures imploringly to Veronica; death is the only release from this relentless process, this hell of embodiment. This excruciating materiality cannot be redeemed, this contaminating alterity cannot be assumed or possessed. Yet it is precisely the *untenability* of this position that is most important, and most affirmative. To the extent that the flesh is unbearable, it is irrecuperable. The extremities of agony cannot finally be distinguished from those of pleasure. Bodily intensity is in this sense an *other* to power, an excess that disturbs it, a surplus that it cannot ever control or appropriate.

Fantasy No More

Autonomy and disalienation are empty lures in the postmodern world, in which even the innermost recesses of subjectivity have been commodified by the forces of economic exchange and pigeonholed by normalizing power. Every utopia is already its own reification. But let us not mourn the disappearance of those promises of redemption and transcendence, which were never anything more than pacifying myths, or devices of social control, in the first place. The time for idealization and fantasy is fortunately over. Cronenberg's films desublimate and decondition the affects of fear, anxiety, and mourning; that is to say, they present these feelings positively and literally, as affections and transformations of the flesh, and not as secondary consequences of some originary loss or lack. We are given the experience (an intense physical excitation) without the meaning. Anxiety is not an existential condition, but a churning of the stomach, a throbbing of the arteries, a tension distending the skull, a series of stresses and shocks running the entire length of the body. Fear is not susceptible to phenomenological analysis, for it marks the emptying out of subjectivity and of time. It abolishes all other concerns and feeds only upon itself; it has no external points of reference, no antecedents, and no possibility of cathartic resolution. Cronenberg's films heighten, and indeed celebrate, those extreme situations in which even the intimacy of my own body is an exposure, a vulnerability, and not a refuge.

These films bear witness to the birth of a new form of subjectivity: one that is entirely embodied, that has no sense of privacy, and that can no longer be defined in terms of fantasy. Without fantasy, without the alibis of idealization and transcendence, there is no way to stabilize identity, but also no way to escape from the limits and pressures of corporeality. This is the fundamental double bind of Cronenberg's films. The subject is dispossessed of itself, radically decentered, and yet it remains all the more vulnerable and constrained. It is implicated in processes external to itself, contaminated or diseased beyond all hope of recovery. It cannot free itself from forces that it is unable to control, and that continually threaten to destroy it. These forces are social technologies of power, but they are also passions, obsessions, sensations, and pleasures. And these forces do not exist merely in the imagination; they are visible and tangible, and must be physically endured. Fantasy is extinguished in the radical passivity of visceral anguish.

Dead Ringers: Masculine Embodiment

Nowhere is this movement more powerfully articulated than in *Dead Ringers*; all the more so, in that the film has so little recourse to gory special effects or to the projections of science fiction. Here the monstrosity of the body is insinuated only in the "mutant" shape of Claire Niveau's (Genevieve Bujold's) womb, on the one hand, and in the visual identity of the Mantle twins (the film's one spectacular special effect), on the other. But these minute deviations of the flesh are sufficient to disrupt the workings of fantasy and to unhinge the articulations of self-consciousness. The process is gradual, however. At the start of the film, Elliott and Beverly Mantle maintain a conventional sense of their own identities by objectifying women's bodies. The very first scene shows them, at age 12, intrigued with the idea that fish, who live in the water (as they once lived together in the womb), do not need to engage in physical contact in order to reproduce. As adults with a successful gynecological practice, they maintain the same distance from others, and the same primary attachment to one another. Beverly's voyeuristic probings of women's insides and Elliott's superciliously dry medical school lectures allow them to engage in activities that have a high sexual charge without sacrificing their physical and emotional detachment. They work on problems of female fertility, and steadfastly avoid any questioning of male physiology. ("We don't do husbands," Beverly exasperatedly tells one patient who begs him to treat her husband's sterility, and seems to be implicitly requesting that the doctor take over the role of spouse.) Yet, at the same time, their deepest emotional satisfaction seems to come from mimicking each other, switching their identities in order to fool the outside world. They even share women as sexual partners in this way.

So far, this is a classic pattern of male fantasy. But the film is not content merely to critique the ideology of such an arrangement. *Dead Ringers* does not try to explain the structure of male desire in psychoanalytic terms; rather, it explores the material and corporeal basis of fantasy. Women's bodies are both the target of an objectifying and normalizing technology and the physical support for the Mantle twins' efforts to stabilize their own disincarnate masculine identities. Cronenberg thus assimilates the possessive gaze of dominant cinema to what Foucault calls the "medical gaze" of the male gynecologist examining his patient. Masculine "identity" is not the result of a structuring process involving fears and fantasies of castration; it is the actual product of a concrete articulation of power and knowledge. Such an "identity" is ambivalent and unstable, constituted and traversed as it is by a whole series of forces and resistances. Male subjectivity is a strange affection of the body, articulated in the doubling of the Mantle twins. Their physical resemblance allows them to "pass" for each other; they can share and transfer experiences, and literally be in two places at once. Male fantasy thus separates self-consciousness from the constraints of materiality, purchasing omnipotence by denying embodiment. But this denial is itself rooted in the body. Beverly and Elliott's overresemblance is also a confusing redundancy, an uncomfortable excess of embodiment, that disturbs the freedom of male fantasy. They are too much alike not to suffer from separation.

The uncanniness of this situation is perfectly captured in Jeremy Irons's double performance. The mannerisms of Elliott and Beverly are subtly different, so that we can nearly always tell which one of them is which. But these differences are not enough to negate our awareness that the same actor, the same body, is rendering both. (The film wouldn't work with two actors as the brothers, even if the actors were themselves twins.) Because of their excessive physical similarity, the characters of Beverly and Elliott are more like different performances than like different selves. Neither of them is able convincingly to dislodge his interiority from its reflection in the other; neither can ever be self-sufficient or self-contained. They are unable even to live apart from one another, although Beverly tries at times to escape. Nonetheless, such dependency does not guarantee communion. Because their bodies are two, and separated in space, it is also impossible for them ever fully to coincide. There is no unified identity at the base of their contrasting roles. They are paradoxically too close to one another to be able to resort to the mechanisms of identification. Just as Beverly struggles unsuccessfully to preserve for himself alone the feelings and memories of his relationship with Claire, so Elliott obsesses over his need to become "synchronized" with his brother. These seemingly opposed impulses are in fact mutually cohesive manifestations of the same situation of excessive proximity. The Mantle twins can achieve neither absolute union nor complete differentiation. Near the end of the film, there is a scene in which Beverly and Elliott trudge through their apartment in their underwear. The precise similarity of their appearance, and the perfect correspondence of their physical gestures as they walk, is like something out of silent film comedy; the motions are entirely singular, and yet they give the impression of being robotic or mechanized simply because they are doubled. The Bergsonian absurdity of this otherwise somber scene points up, yet again, the irreducible insistence of the flesh. Just as in Cronenberg's other films, alterity is found within the closest intimacy, at the very heart of the self's relation to itself.

And so Elliott's and Beverly's notion that they are not just identical, but Siamese twins, is something more than a metaphor. What starts out as a fantasy (when Beverly has a nightmare that Claire is tearing apart—with her teeth—the flesh that unites him to Elliott) has to be literalized and enacted by the end of the film. The figure who triggers this movement from fantasy to actuality, from the Mantles' appropriating investment of women's bodies to their ambiguous captivation with their own flesh, is of course Claire herself. Claire doesn't remain safely ensconced in her position as objectified Other, she doesn't play her appointed role in "the Mantle saga," not just because she insists on distinguishing between the brothers, but also because the "mutant" singularity of her sterile, trifurcate womb reminds the twins all too strongly of themselves. Beverly is immediately fascinated by this strangeness in her reproductive system, and Elliott tries to flatter her with his idea of "beauty contests for the insides of bodies." Claire is also an actress, somebody whose profession consists in the simulation of identities; the twins associate the glamour and illusionism of acting with their impersonations of one another. Further, although Claire is quite a capable and powerful figure, her sexual tastes tend toward the masochistic, and she repeatedly makes clear her "need for humiliation." This in turn feeds back into her perception of her own body; she feels "vulnerable, sliced open," and in a position of abject dependency as a result of her inability to have children.

This vulnerability and physical singularity is what attracts the Mantle twins to Claire, but also what allows her to escape them. She frustrates their gynecological gaze because she so aggressively embodies, and claims for herself, those very features that are supposed to demarcate the privileged zone of male fantasy. Beverly and Elliott see Claire—in different ways—as the living realization of their deepest desires and anxieties, but she refuses to be a support for their projections. Beverly's involvement with Claire is the extreme expression, but also the limit, of his and his brother's obsessions. The turning point comes when Beverly calls Claire's hotel suite and, incorrectly assuming that the male secretary who answers the phone is her new lover, launches into an obscene tirade about her anatomical peculiarities. After this, everything collapses. The moment of the most violent male paranoia (jealousy, possessiveness, and dependency compensated for by a need to deny and to control) is also the moment when projection fails, and the reality of the flesh comes most insistently into play. Beverly becomes more and more hysterically misogynous, devising strange new gynecological instruments, complaining that his patients do not have the right sort of bodies, crudely insulting them, and finally even injuring one of them on the operating table. But this only marks his desperation, as the structure of male fantasy implodes. Beverly is no longer able to maintain the distancing equation of femininity, objectified other-ness, and the body. He is brought back, not to any sense of "himself," but to his primordial complicity with Elliott, to the agonizing resemblance of their shared flesh.

Dead Ringers thus emerges as Cronenberg's strangest and sub-tlest study in embodiment. The structure of male fantasy is progressively undone; attention is returned from the objectified female body to the subjectified male one. The Mantle twins end up experiencing in their own flesh the processes they had previously tried to project onto others. Their subjectivity is initially stabilized by its obsessive objectifications of, and hysterical projections upon, women's bodies. But the very excess of these processes ultimately undermines their power. The twins are relentlessly drawn into a spiral of self-disintegration. The hieratic red robes that Beverly dons when performing operations give way to the Caravaggiesque nudity of the two brothers in the final shots of the film. Beverly's bizarre gynecological instruments for treating mutant women find their more inti-mate use as tools for separating Siamese twins. The rituals of medical power and prestige are turned back against the selves that they had previously confirmed and inflated. Elliott reminds us that Chang and Eng, the original Siamese twins, could not stand the shock of separation; when one of them died of natural causes, the other died in turn of sheer fright. The incisions that are supposed to separate

Elliott from Beverly once and for all similarly succeed only in uniting them in the most extreme resemblance there is, that of death. Beverly cannot leave Elliott's body behind and return to Claire, because in killing his brother he has in fact performed a self-canceling ritual of automutilation. Male subjectivity is finally rendered to the flesh, and quietly consumed—and consummated—in abjection.

Shattering Pleasures

The imploding trajectory of *Dead Ringers* is that of all of Cronenberg's films. They reject fantasy and embrace abjection, just as they undermine symbolic and ideological processes in order to affirm the impropriety of the real body. Of course, cinematic experience in general has traditionally been defined in terms of fantasy, idealization, and a dialectic between the pacifying stabilization of identity and the imaginative freeplay of indeterminacy. Cronenberg's films are powerfully disruptive of these norms, even though they depend on the "illusionism" of special effects and observe the formal rules of seamless continuity editing and narrative closure.

When the possibilities of fantasy and appropriative identification are destroyed for the male protagonists of these films, they are equally destroyed for the spectator. The audience cannot be exempted from the processes of contagion. Benjamin (1969) writes that "the shock effect of the film . . . like all shocks, should be cushioned by heightened presence of mind" (p. 238). Cronenberg's strategy is continually to up the ante of shock, in order to anticipate and outstrip any such protective counterheightening. We are pushed to the limits of vision and of representation, compelled to witness what we cannot bear to see. Exploding and multiplied flesh, the violent or insidious violation of bodily integrity, is crucial to Cronenberg's project formally as well as thematically. He doesn't offer a critique of the operations of "suture" or the norms of cinematic representation, for it is from within these very operations and norms that the most perverse and threatening flowers bloom. The imposing plenitude of the image instills in the spectator a heightened sensitivity to the affections of his or her own body. The continuity of character and action binds us to a logic of nonidentity and disintegration. The convincing explicitness of the gore and other special effects makes us feel all the more fragile and insecure, in that our awareness of the fictionality of what we see offers us no comfort, alleviation, or escape. Identification (of the spectator with the protagonist, or with the gaze of the camera) leads to a loss of control, a shattering of the ego. It is the excess of male fantasy, and not a critical reduction of it, that leads to its destruction, just as it is from deep within postmodern technologies of domination, and not at a utopian remove from them, that an irrecuperable *other* to power can be affirmed.

Cronenberg disrupts the power mechanisms normally attributed to classic narrative cinema not by distancing himself from them, but by pushing them as far as they can go. He discovers or produces, at the very heart of these mechanisms, a subject that can no longer be defined in the conventional terms of lack, denial, and fantasy, and whose intense passion cannot be described as a desire for mastery, closure, and self-possession. The viewing subject's most intense pleasures lie rather in the unresolved tensions of vulnerability, ambivalence, and fear. The cinematic gaze is violently embedded in the flesh. I discover, in Cronenberg's films, not a flattering illusion of omnipotence, but the ecstasy and terror of abjection.

v

Masculinity, Spectacle, and the
Body of *Querelle*

Pornographic Ambivalence

BEAUTIFUL MALE bodies are placed ostentatiously on display throughout Rainer Werner Fassbinder's last film, *Querelle*. This aggressive presentation of masculine flesh is a source of both considerable pleasure and considerable anxiety. The combination of pleasure and anxiety, of course, is crucial to the dynamics of sexual tension and play. And *Querelle* has a provocatively pornographic air to it, even though (at least in the cut version released in the United States) the erect penis is never actually shown on screen.

Every aspect of Fassbinder's mise-en-scène—from the fetishistic leather and sailor outfits, to the phallic pillar standing beside the Feria whorehouse, and to the garishly theatrical lighting—is shaped by the signifiers of (post-Stonewall, pre-AIDS) gay male eroticism. The very act of looking is violently sexualized; the languidly posed and lusciously highlighted body of the sailor Querelle (played by Brad Davis) is an obsessive focal point for the gazes of both the other characters and the audience. Fassbinder's film seduces the male viewer, solicits his gaze; it would be futile for me to try to write about it without registering the force of this seduction. I feel powerfully interpolated and implicated by the film; pleasure is always a mark of implication. I am turned on by *Querelle*, cast adrift in its seas of eroticism, caught in its shifting currents of idealization and debasement, identification and objectification. *Querelle* is deliberately "porno-graphic" above all in this, that it cannot be approached with aesthetic disinterest, for it arouses the (male) viewer all the more powerfully in that at the same time it so concertedly alienates and objectifies him.

I am using the word *pornographic* advisedly. *Querelle* is one of the most controversial of Fassbinder's films; and this is the case not exclusively—or in any case, not *simply*—because of its gay content and themes. It is more a question of the *way* the content and themes are broached. Fassbinder's strategy of sexual representation in *Querelle* seems calculated to make well-meaning, liberal viewers and critics—the very ones who turned *The Marriage of Maria Braun* into an art-house hit—intensely uncomfortable. Fassbinder shows obvious contempt not only for the traditional bourgeois notion of redeeming artistic value, but also, and especially, for its more recent equivalent, the demand for a "politically cor-rect"—which is to say, idealized and sanitized—depiction of sexuality. He refuses to provide "positive images" of either gay or straight sex. On the contrary, he will-fully aestheticizes the most troubling moments of his narrative, those when male sexuality is explicitly associated with power and domination, with violence, and with death.

Far from mounting an attack on debasing or oppressive modes of sexual representation, *Querelle* self-consciously foregrounds its own inevitable complicity with pornographic fantasy. Such complicity is, of course, what the cur-rent antipornography movement is most concerned to reject. But as Leo Bersani (1987) suggests, antipornography activists ironically share with "sex radicals" the utopian project of a *"redemptive reinvention of sex,"* a denial of the ways in which sexual desire is unavoidably "anticommunal, antiegalitarian, antinurturing, anti-loving" (p. 215). The fantasy of instantaneous and total self-realization via sexual satisfaction offered alike by sex radicals and by commercial pornography finds its perfect mirror image in the fantasy of an eroticism free of power and oppression purveyed by antipornography crusaders. *Querelle*, to the contrary, does not offer any sort of redemption. All its sexual representations are caught, reflected, and multiplied in an abyss of ambivalence from which there is no hope of escape. The film simultaneously arouses and frustrates the demands of pornographic fantasy, suggesting that we can neither satisfy these demands nor cleanse them of their unpleasant associations with power and violence, with domination and degradation, nor ever become free from them. This pornographic ambivalence is clearly an important reason for my own fascination with *Querelle*.

      Fassbinder's position, in *Querelle* as in other of his films, is politically radical and highly critical of bourgeois society, but also thoroughly nonutopian. *Querelle* mounts a full-fledged assault on our society's (hetero-)sexual norms; at the same time, it links the expression of "transgressive" sexuality not with liberation and transcendence, but with abjection, denial, and ultimately murder. The film's most disturbing and subversive insinuation is that of a complicitous, symbiotic relation between power and sexuality, between desire and the repression of desire, between "perversions" and the norms they claim to violate. Throughout *Querelle*, phallocentric desire is confronted with its own image, one thoroughly imbued with power and violence. "Each man kills the thing he loves," sings Lysiane (Jeanne Moreau) in a song that becomes a leitmotif for the film; every desire is predicated on, and contaminated with, aggression and death. In its pervasive idealization of sexual desire, our culture attempts to deny this fatal ambivalence. But by aestheticizing violence, and by providing such beautiful images of unsatisfied desire, Fassbinder ironically suggests that idealization is itself the source of the aggressivity it refuses to recognize. Every idealization is a violent imposition of power, and cinema is *the* idealizing mechanism *par excellence*. Fassbinder insists on self-consciously locating himself within the very structures he is attacking. *Querelle* does not eschew the idealizations of pornographic fantasy, but overtly mobilizes them, the better to interrupt or suspend them. Every image in the film seems frozen in a kind of visual coitus interruptus. Fantasy is all the more affirmed in that it is denied any outlet in action. Fassbinder's critical politics is inseparable from an ironic, contemplative aestheticism that seeks to intensify affect by heightening the viewer's sense of powerlessness and passivity.

The Question of Style

In order to register the full measure of this passivity and ambivalence, Fassbinder develops a style in his later films, and in *Querelle* above all, that is diametrically opposed to that of his early works. His first films, coming out of his activities in the avant-garde "antitheater," seek to extinguish the mechanisms of visual fascination. They are alienating in form, with their deliberate suppression of camera movement and continuity editing, and oppressively hypernaturalistic in content. They combine a deadpan minimalism with the antibourgeois theater of Brecht and Kroetz. In contrast, the later films revel in their decadent visual opulence. They self-consciously manipulate spectatorial fascination rather than seek to undermine it. These films are dense and fluid, even baroque in their visual style, filled with elaborate manipulations of space, intricate camera movements, and exaggerated, artificial lighting.

Fassbinder's mise-en-scène and cinematographic techniques are reminiscent of Douglas Sirk, of course, and even in a perverse way of Vincente Minnelli. *Querelle* in particular is self-consciously and excessively "cinematic," giving the overwrought impression of a 1950s high-budget Hollywood studio production run amok. (Mark Savitt has suggested that *Querelle*, in its opulent, garish color scheme, as in its treatment of male fantasy figures, is virtually a remake of Minnelli's *The Pirate*; personal communication, 1989.) Even *Querelle*'s most alienating features—the glacial pacing of the action, the deadpan, affectless line readings (Fassbinder turns to his advantage the necessity of dubbing a film that makes use of actors speaking different languages), and the idealized, eroticized posing of male bodies—are the result of Hollywood conventions blown up to monstrous proportions. Narrative and textual codes are exploded, not through the work of critical negation, but by means of a hyperbolic recycling of traditional modes of visual presentation, identification, and objectification.

Fassbinder's love for traditional American genre films is well known. But I do not think the disjunctive, schizophrenic style of *Querelle* and his other late works can be explained, as many critics have suggested, by a supposed conflict between the irreconcilable goals of Hollywood-style audience involvement on the one hand and Brechtian distanciation on the other. (Thomas Elsaesser 1986, 538, characterizes this reading as one of the most common misunderstandings of Fassbinder.) Far from striking an uneasy balance between identification and distance, or foundering on the alleged inconsistency between them, Fassbinder's late films heighten both of these responses simultaneously. Indeed, its refusal to present involvement and alienation as being in contradiction is one of the things that makes *Querelle* an exemplary postmodern work.

The modernist critical paradigm regards involvement or fascination as a state of ideological mystification, and employs the alienation effect as a tool to undo this state. Postmodernism, in contrast, views the very claim to demystification with suspicion. It distrusts the hierarchical privilege implicitly accorded to the negative, critical consciousness. Instead, it regards both involvement and alienation as particular subject positions or modes of implication. *Querelle*, then, does not deploy alienation against identification, but treats them alike as effects of the cinematic apparatus, and pushes them alike to the breaking point. In contrast to the Brechtian paradigm, in *Querelle* and other postmodern works the alienation effect does not free the audience from involvement in the spectacle, but itself functions as a new mode of complicity. For Fassbinder, questions about cinematic form are always also, quite directly, questions about subjectivity, sexuality, and power— and vice versa. But it is for this very reason that he strives to inhabit the norms and conventions of the Hollywood film, rather than simply and categorically rejecting them. It is by exploring the workings of visual fascination in the cinema from the inside, and by acknowledging his own continuing implication with them, that Fassbinder is also able to address such issues as the construction of male sexuality in our society. This immanent, always complicitous, questioning of power relations may be contrasted to the more traditionally modernist critical practice of Kluge, Straub and Huillet, and Syberberg. From Fassbinder's point of view, when such filmmakers claim to maintain a rigorous critical distance from illusionistic Hollywood techniques, they are laying claim to a spurious radical purism and refusing to come to grips with their own complicity, their inevitable positionality within late capitalist culture.

Fassbinder and Genet

There is yet another level of complication that needs to be acknowledged. Fassbinder's film announces itself in the opening titles as "a film about Jean Genet's *Querelle de Brest*." Any account of the film must try to capture the force of this "about." A film *about* a novel is not the same thing as a film *of* a novel; *Querelle* is not in the conventional sense a literary adaptation. In his introductory notes to the screenplay, Fassbinder (1983) insists that *cinematic transformation of a literary work should never assume that its purpose is simply the maximal realization of the images which literature evokes in the minds of its readers. Such an assumption would, in any case, be preposterous, since any given reader reads any given book with his own sense of reality, and therefore any book evokes as many different fantasies and images as it has readers. (p. 11)*

There can therefore be no "realization of the author's world of images in some fixed and final consensus of separate and contrary fantasies" (p. 11).

        Fassbinder's film *inscribes* Genet's language in various ways—sometimes literally, by means of intertitles—but it does not seek directly to *translate* that language into visual or cinematic terms. The last image of *Querelle* is the most literal of these inscriptions: the signature of the novel's author. Genet's handwritten words, visible on the screen, are read verbatim by the narrator: "apart from his books we know nothing about him; not even the date of his death, which to him seems near. Jean Genet." (These words also, inevitably, resonate with the contingency of Fassbinder's own untimely death, making *Querelle* his final film, his unintended last will and testament.) Many critics have complained that Fassbinder's campy, kitschy rendering constitutes a betrayal of Genet's novel; they have forgotten that the inevitability of betrayal is already one of Genet's main preoccupations. Fassbinder includes within the film his oppressive awareness that the imminent, yet inscrutable, "death of the author" ruins in advance any project of adaptation, translation, or appropriation.

        Death and debasement are the ultimate, unreachable limits of the film's images, because they are also the defining conditions for their genesis. As the narrator states at the very beginning of the film (in what is also a version of the opening lines of the novel), "the thought of murder often evokes thoughts of the sea and of sailors. What naturally follows thoughts of the sea and murder is the thought of love or sexuality." One thought, one image, is evoked by another, not along a straightforward path, but through the intricate detours of sexuality and death. Fassbinder (1983) speaks of the radical "discrepancy between objective plot and subjective fantasy" (p. 11) that characterizes Genet's novel; his film is similarly predicated on a violent disjunction between text and image. Genet is fascinated by the beautiful and aberrant ways in which images are evoked and sustained; his prose is intimately concerned with describing and interpreting the most minute poses and gestures of the male body. Fassbinder refuses to provide a direct visual equivalent of Genet's text, for his film seeks to evoke images in its own aberrant fashion, to generate its own processes of idealization and debasement. It seeks to articulate its own sense of how "Querelle, already inside our flesh, was growing, developing in our soul, feeding off the best within us." And so, rather than a direct replication of the novel on screen, there is an intricate series of disjunctions, displacements, and interchanges: between fiction and cinema; among nonverbal sounds, words, and images; and between Genet and Fassbinder. Fassbinder does not combine text and image, but plays them off against one another. Where Genet's writing is charged with visual detail, Fassbinder's images seem to contradict the spoken or written text, and to grow and multiply in an autonomous dimension of their own.

Imitations of Life

The typically postmodern self-consciousness of Fassbinder's images—their blatant sound-stage artificiality, their continual doublings and reflections, our sense that they are always already "in quotation marks"—indicates that they cannot be regarded as (more or less adequate) representations: not of Genet's novel, and still less of "real life." Fassbinder's Sirkian fondness for mirrors and for overly ornate visual tableaux has never been more in evidence. We quickly come to recognize the play of simulacra: since everything in the film is a reflection, an "imitation of life," "reality" and "life" are entirely exhausted and consumed by artifice, or by commodification. There is no outside reality left to be imitated and reflected. Everything is on the surface, posed for the cameras, bathed in an artificial glow, processed through orange or blue filters. There is no truth behind these images; they are neither primary phenomenological intuitions nor signs of some hidden, deeper level of meaning.

And yet, if the images of *Querelle* are irreal and devoid of external reference, they still possess a compelling weight and density. Fassbinder's sets are intensely claustrophobic; even at their most brightly lit, they do not seem to radiate heat and light, but rather to absorb all energy within themselves. Everything is delimited and confined. The multiplication of images in mirrors seems only to take away all breathing room. There are no suggestions of the sublime, and no lines of escape. The images of this film are not windows onto infinity, but abysses of reflection, insidious traps for the gaze. In Baudrillard's terms, they are not simulations after all, but instances of seduction. These images do not show anything, but merely demand to be seen. They are so hyperbolically visible, so flat and vacuous, so aggressively superficial and stereotypical, that they develop a violently intensive force. They are no longer illustrative; they do not depict action, but arrest it. Again and again, it is the voice-over narration that informs us of what is happening, of the relationships between characters, and even of who is looking at whom, while none of these events is actually depicted on screen. *Querelle*'s static images rupture the continuity of the narrative, to manifest instead only the passive, fetishistic quality of what Laura Mulvey (1988) famously calls "to-be-looked-at-ness" (p. 62).

One might say that in *Querelle* vision itself is rendered visible. The image is not just something to be seen; in its icy beauty it captures the very process of seeing. Kaja Silverman (1992) describes this process in Lacanian vocabulary as one of "the non-coincidence of the look and the gaze"; the gaze makes the individual's act of looking possible, but also continually exceeds it. The gaze must be located "at the site of ... the *object* of vision"; this implies "the conflation of gaze and spectacle, a conflation which is made on the basis of what might be called the spectacle's 'lit up' quality." The gaze must then be compared "not to the male look, but to woman-as-spectacle" (p. 151). By foregrounding this process, Silverman concludes, it becomes possible to push further the argument of feminist film theory, by "exposing the impossibility of anyone ever owning that visual agency [the gaze], or of him or herself escaping specularity" (p. 152).

As is so often the case when I read Silverman, I find her distinctions powerfully suggestive but her insistence upon coding such processes in terms of "lack" and "the recognition of castration" deeply problematic. When Silverman opposes the delusion of fullness that comes from specular misrecognition to the stance that takes up the burden of castration by overtly recognizing that nobody owns the gaze and that insufficiency is insurpassable, she is still working within the modernist and Brechtian logic that I have criticized above. I think it is more useful to read Fassbinder's play with the passivity of image and gaze affirmatively, to see the nonownership of vision in terms of a process of accretion and multiplication. A primordial ambiguity is repeated unto infinity. The overt action of *Querelle* is doubled and suspended by the passion of looking (just as Fassbinder says that Genet's creation of a subjective "world of images" revitalizes what would otherwise be a "third-class" crime story; 1983, 11). The gaze is swallowed up within its object.

As Casy McNeese (1989) points out, everything in the film has its reflection or double. There are mirrors placed throughout the brothel; especially in the scenes between Lysiane and one or the other of the brothers, the camera moves back and forth, slowly but relentlessly, between image and reflection. The invisible, but continually verbally asserted, resemblance between Robert and Querelle is doubled by the unspoken visual resemblance between Robert and Gil, both of whom are played by the same actor (Hanno Pöschl); when Querelle prepares Gil for the robbery, he even disguises him (with a suit and a false moustache) to look exactly like Robert. Doubling is also a principle in the placement of subsidiary characters and props. When Lieutenant Seblon (Franco Nero) addresses Querelle blackened with coal dust, we see another officer with another soot-bestrewn sailor in the background. The final shot of the film (aside from Genet's signature) is a repeat of the opening one—the germinal image of sailors toiling on the deck of the ship—except that it is run backward. Every image in the film must be duplicated in some way, because it incorporates the traces of the gazes that it attracts. It is as if our eyeballs were turned inside out, as if the virtual images in our retinas were themselves exteriorized and imprinted on the screen, alongside the images that originally stimulated them. The gaze thus replicates, and extends to infinity, the workings of the camera. To look at an image is to lose oneself within it, to be oneself transformed into an image.

Voyeuristic Passivity

Fassbinder's heavily ironized use of the Hollywood convention of shot and reverse shot also reflects this logic of endless duplication. The shot/reverse shot structure, as it is generally understood, serves not only to establish continuity, but, more important, to enforce the possession of the gaze. We identify with the (generically male) protagonist's act of looking in the first shot, and objectify what is being looked at in the reverse shot. The reaction shot, or return to the initial point of view, then closes the sequence, confirms the protagonist's perspective, solidifies the controlling (male) power of his look, and heightens the "suturing" identification between that look and those of the spectator, on the one hand, and of the camera, on the other.

One may doubt whether this conventional system is ever as absolute and totalizing, even in classic Hollywood cinema, as many recent theorists have made it out to be, but in any case, it is important to note just how Fassbinder works through this convention. He undermines the authority of the gaze not by rejecting the shot/reverse shot structure, but by extending it to infinity. Every image in *Querelle* exists to be looked at, and nearly every shot is framed or interrupted by another shot in which somebody is engaged in looking at the scene of the first shot. But this expanded network of gazes does not permit closure, and leaves no room for the stability of an active and controlling subject position. Looking is instead a movement of decentering, alienation, and dispossession. Often the voyeur is a character who is explicitly marked by passivity and isolation: Seblon staring longingly from the other side of the windowpane, or Lysiane compelled to endure the humiliation of witnessing the ritual activity between males from which she is so pointedly excluded. At other times, reaction shots function like extradiegetic inserts: they focus on characters, such as the hoodlums and garishly made-up transvestites who are patrons of La Feria, but otherwise not involved in the action at all. These characters gaze languidly and affectlessly at the scene before them; they seem to be looking only in order that they may become objectified images, to be looked at in their own turn. The reaction shot does not close off the scene being viewed, but rather initiates an infinite relay of glances. Voyeurism cannot be celebrated as a state of sadistic mastery, but neither is it frustrated in the denial of that mastery. Voyeurism is invoked and affirmed precisely to the extent that it is a passion of powerlessness and separation. The gaze loses itself in an abyss of mirrors and stagnant fixations, drawn ever more deeply into its own abnegation and abjection, without hope or desire of return. The play of multiple looks leads neither to a suturing identification nor to the simple denial of identification, but rather to the cold, hyperbolic frenzy of duplication and fragmentation.

The hierarchical relation between the gaze and the field of its vision is thus turned upside down. In Fassbinder's antiphenomenological cinema, "to-be-looked-at-ness" cannot be defined as the mere complement of a primary, intentional act of looking. Fassbinder rejects the traditional model of vision as a form of active appropriation; in doing so, he also rejects the standard philosophical account that sees power operating in the manner of a sovereign subject, and that in turn equates subjectivity with spontaneity, with the capacity for self-initiated, or at least self-conscious, activity. Everything in *Querelle* is defined in terms of a primordial passivity. Querelle is not objectified, or defined in terms of visual display, because he is subjected to a dominating gaze; it is rather his unconscious, but provocatively stylized, objectification that initially incites the gaze. Seblon is helplessly seduced by Querelle's sublime indifference and seeming self-containment: "Querelle's great passion is his own body in repose. It is as if he is reflecting himself in his own image.... But how shining is his body in the glory of his proud movements." This glorious body is an image that attracts the gaze of Seblon, and of the spectator, precisely because it does not *need* to be looked at; it arouses desire by virtue of its apparent absence of desire. The image forever escapes the act that strives to appropriate it; it lures the gaze beyond itself, outside of itself. Seblon's gaze cannot penetrate Querelle's "terrible body"; it can only lust impotently after the sailor's image, which is something as impalpable and evasive, as removed from concrete possession, as are the photographs of statues of naked men in the book whose pages Seblon idly turns.

In his impotent distance from the events of the narrative, the passively voyeuristic Seblon is a stand-in for the audience, the one figure with whom the spectator is forced to "identify." Overwhelmed and incapacitated by his desire for "boys with big cocks," Seblon is nothing but a pure gaze. He watches every scene of sexual interaction between men, but is able to participate in none. The more avidly he looks, the more he is seduced, but also the more he is separated from what he sees, and consumed by the emptiness of his dispossession. His incessant verbal commentary—the crude words scrawled on urinal walls and the flowery yearnings and laments dictated into and played back from his tape recorder—all this language marks his futile effort to bridge the distance inherent to the gaze, to supplement (in Derrida's sense) the passivity of looking. Yet this flow of words serves only to accentuate his isolation.

   Seblon's powerless detachment might be regarded either as a state of aesthetic contemplation or as a fascination proper to commodity fetishism. But in either case, the passion of looking implies both the paralysis of radical separation and the vulnerability of utter absorption. This double entrapment is the inverted *cogito* of Fassbinder's film, the point of reflection at which the spectator becomes conscious of himself as a subject. Subjectivity is produced not in an intentional act of seeing and grasping what one sees, but in a radical passivity that encompasses and undoes that act. Seblon is an exemplary figure of subjectification in *Querelle*, because he is petrified by his impossible burden of desire, and because he seems to have a boundless, but ever-unfulfilled, appetite for abjection. He accurately defines himself as the bearer of the "humility" that "can only be born of humiliation." Sexual excitement and humiliation are united in the infinite powerlessness of the gaze.

   Ronald Hayman (1984) regards Fassbinder's strategy of voyeuristic excess in *Querelle* as a kind of exhibitionism; he cites Sartre's analysis of Genet's development as "self-realization that bases itself on being an object for other people" (p. 133). But for Fassbinder, this formulation doesn't go far enough, since it still implies that "other people" are normative, conventionally active subjects. Sartre's Genet is expelled from bourgeois society by the condemning glances of socially "right-thinking" Others; he defines and realizes himself as literally an outlaw, a criminal and a pederast, by deliberately choosing to ground his being in the very negations and exclusions that have been projected upon him. But this logic cannot survive the relegation of the voyeur to a state of impotence and exclusion. In Fassbinder's version of Genet, such projections and such a choice are impossible. How can one define oneself as an outlaw when the traditional position of the Law, that of the master appropriating and controlling the world through the force of his look, has itself ceased to exist? There is nobody left *for whom* Querelle's exhibitionistic display could take place, or *under whose regard* he could define himself, by choosing to assume the condition of objecthood and of Evil. When everything exists merely to be looked at, everything is equally co-optable, and the line separating Good from Evil, or bourgeois norms from transgressive revolt, entirely disappears. Self-realization cannot take the path of negativity when there is nothing to negate. This is the deepest sense of Fassbinder's betrayal or debasement of Genet's text. As Christopher Sharrett (1989) argues, Querelle's self-objectification no longer has any subversive force, since it has been absorbed into "the commodity status of the image" (p. 124). The master/slave dialectic that underlies Sartre's description of the gaze, and the sadistic thrust that dominates Mulvey's, are neutralized, or frozen into passivity.

The Masculine Image

Querelle almost programatically demonstrates how postmodern power functions on the side of the object, rather than on that of the subject: it explores the shift of power away from the gaze, and toward the image itself. But this shift is not a simple reversal of the traditional intrication of vision with power; it bespeaks a radically different account of subjectivity and visual experience. When power is invested in the image, this does not mean that the image in its turn acts like a subject, and actively wields power. Nothing acts in *Querelle*; everything is static and artificial, tending toward the condition of scenery and decor. It is the distance and impassivity of the image, its very failure to be active, that gives it a force of fascination. The spectator's gaze is arrested as a result of the utter impossibility of engagement or response. The state of being looked at, of being an image, is a state in which one provokes desire without reciprocating it, and perhaps even without being aware of provoking it. Querelle arouses Seblon's (and the spectator's) desiring glances to the precise extent that he remains unaffected by them, indifferent and inaccessible. Thus, being desired, while himself not experiencing desire, invests Querelle with an aura of intense erotic power. But since this power is a function of unawareness and indifference, it is not something that its bearer can wield or possess. Querelle's insolent swagger is a sign not of self-conscious negativity, but of inner blankness. His erotic aura is all the more splendid and seductive in that it cannot be used or touched. Querelle is not an active, self-conscious subject, but a "monster," a sacred figure who "might be compared with the Angel of the Apocalypse" (Fassbinder 1983, 76), a fetishized incarnation of phallic impassivity. In his sterile perfection, his intense, magical to-be-looked-at-ness, he approaches a mythologized social ideal of masculinity, of virile power and grace.

Lysiane remarks at one point that "there is a masculine passivity which is expressed in the indifference towards courtship; the completely relaxed anticipation of the body concerning its role in the taking or giving of passion." Querelle's idealized body is passive in this way; it is magical and alluring because it has assumed the objectivity, artificiality, and emptiness of a mere image. It is this blankness that allows it to serve as a focus and support for everyone else's fantasies and projections. But Querelle's apotheosis, the transubstantiation of his body into pure image, is also a form of subjection. If he is an image of the sacred, figuring a phallic power that he does not in his own person possess, this also means that he is banalized, transformed into a commodity, imagined in terms of the most obvious and clichéd stereotypes of late 1970s gay male sexuality. The "glorious" and "terrible" body of the sailor is also a body that has been defined, contained, and sexualized precisely to the extent that it has been made to conform to preestablished canons of virility, power, and perfection. It is captivating to others only because it has itself been captured within the mechanisms of what Foucault calls "the deployment of sexuality." This body turned image is not an object fantasized or produced by masculine desire so much as it is the lure that arouses and shapes such desire in the first place. As Querelle grows "within us," he imposes himself upon us as the very definition of our desire, the image of what we would like ourselves to have (possession of the image) and to be (identification with the image). The spectator is interpellated as a subject, and gendered male, in the course of his encounter with and seduction by this banal image. The film traces a double dependency, a double passivity: the process by which the male body is imaged and objectified is concomitant with that by which it is captivated and subjectified. Both the subject and the object of the gaze are submitted to the absorptive, derealizing play of the image.

Fassbinder's images of masculine beauty are compelling and vacuous, fascinating and factitious, unique and stereotypical, all at once. They *are* extremely desirable, so much so that they confirm our own subjection to the idealizing demands of a regime of hypervisibility. The commodified image simultaneously arouses desire and exhausts it: its sheer perfection is matched by its insubstantiality and pointless proliferation. In the postmodern world of simulations and seductions, the opposition postulated by Benjamin in his discussion of the image collapses: the establishment of the aura and its disintegration are now one and the same event. According to Benjamin, mechanical reproduction destroys the aura by

undermining the uniqueness that was essential to the cult value of the aesthetic object. Fassbinder's film, with its vaguely sacramental music and its bathetic, kitschy
evocations of Jesus' Passion, suggests rather that the aura is itself merely a cinematic "special effect," created after the fact by the normalizing power of mass culture and mechanical reproduction. The postmodern images of *Querelle* are thus
stereotypes of uniqueness, ironic forms of individuation. For Fassbinder as for
Genet (and as also for Bataille), the sacred or auratic object immediately deconstructs itself: it points not to transcendence but to self-annihilation. The elevation
and isolation that give it birth are inseparable from the movement of humiliation
in which it is extinguished. *Querelle* thus narrates the social production of masculinity, in a double register of idealization and demystification, of exaltation and
debasement. Querelle's objectification—his exaltation when he is sanctified in the
eyes of Seblon—is doubled by his subjectification, which is accomplished through
his "execution" or "death sentence" (as he first thinks of being fucked by Nono)
and ultimate abjection. The irreducible ambivalence of this process marks the extreme limit of the sexualizing power described by Foucault: at once its most complete expression and the point at which it begins to fall apart.

      Querelle, we are told by Lysiane at the start of the film, is in
great danger: the danger of "finding himself." But what is this danger? First of all,
Querelle's "finding himself" involves the stabilization and consolidation of his
identity in conformity with socially imposed norms. *Querelle* traces the tortuous
process by which the title character evolves into the generic figure of the masculine hero: "Pursuing his destiny, his development within us, we shall see how he
goes about realizing one single end, which seems to be his own will and his own
destiny." This "single end" is Querelle's consciousness of himself as male. But it is
only in a very ironic sense that Querelle gradually becomes self-aware, that (as
Fassbinder says in his introductory notes) he begins to be "identified with [his]

own self" (1983, 11), for masculinity is not a fixed state or a self-conscious activity, just as it is not an anatomical given. It is rather an image that must be taken from outside, imprinted upon or burned into the flesh. The self that Querelle discovers is not an authentic, singular identity, but an extrinsically defined and regulated stereotype. What seem to be his "own" will and destiny are in fact generated in the course of a long series of events: simulations, seductions, metamorphoses of the image. Querelle is a product of the projection of sexual fantasies and of idealized images of the body, a projection that Fassbinder equates with Hollywood techniques. Fassbinder traces the engenderment of masculinity, and its being endowed with power and prestige, in the course of the unconscious bodily assumption of an image.

Rituals of Subjection

This projection and this assumption are not *just* processes of ideological misrecognition. They involve actual operations upon, and actual cravings of, the flesh. The spectacular figure of male fantasy that we recognize as Querelle is the product not so much of a mode of representation as of a literal investment and subjugation of the body. The structures of visual identification and gender identity (of what Lacan calls the Imaginary and Symbolic orders) are anchored directly in the agitated and violated body of Querelle. As is nearly always the case in Fassbinder's films, impalpable images give way to the living flesh: the ideality and artificiality of the former find their condition in the latter's seemingly endless capacity for suffering. Silverman (1992) suggests that Fassbinder's films "make the male body the point at which economic, social, and sexual oppression are registered" (p. 154). I would put the point even more strongly; in *Querelle*, as in *In a Year of Thirteen Moons* and many other films, power relations are not just registered or allegorized in terms of the male body, but concretely function through their operations upon,

Masc.

and their construction of, this body. Querelle quite literally "finds himself" in the process of having sex with other men. He must passively endure being gendered male, just as he must endure being fucked by Nono. I become male only through a long initiation: a violent, ascetic process of being-affected, a subjection and passion of my body. The hierarchy and authority that define my position as a man are themselves generated in the gestures and rituals through which men challenge and fight one another, touch one another, physically interact with one another. Think of the precisely, absurdly choreographed duel between Querelle and Robert; or of the torments that Theo inflicts upon Gil in order to incite the profoundly sexual response that is Gil's murder of him. This interplay of bodies is the material base for the production and transmission of masculine subjectivity. These games of dominance and submission are the rough ground upon which the most idealized images are grown.

There is a painful ambiguity at the heart of this process. Masculinity is formed in a process of ritualized subjugation; it must be imposed from outside, and suffered as an aggression, before it can be internalized and actively assumed. It is only at the price of self-laceration that I gain access to the authority and stability of a unified masculine self. This is why every move Querelle makes is doubled and negated by defensive rituals of denial, disavowal, and betrayal. He initially arranges to be fucked by Nono as a self-willed punishment for his murder of Vic. His symbolic "execution" is supposed to bring with it a kind of absolution: by enduring it, he will be magically exempted from the danger of any further feeling, as of any further punishment. Abjection cannot be avoided, but it comes to be regarded merely as the price to be paid for masculinity, an ascesis of desire whose ultimate reward is virile mastery and a stabilized sense of self. The male subject must pass through these abysses of weakness and dependency, but only because they are the obstacles he must overcome in order to prove himself, to become a real man, to accede to phallic power. Invulnerability is purchased at the cost of momentary pain. In return for this self-willed subjugation, the danger (or possibility) of giving way to passion is warded off and suppressed.

Nono (Gunther Kaufmann) and Mario (Burckhard Driest) are the characters who exemplify the superlative endpoint of this production of masculinity. They exude supreme masculine authority as the result of having subjected their wills to a harsh, impersonal discipline. They attain perfect manhood by negating their own desires and identifying instead with an ideal, transcendent phallic order. Nono enjoys fucking Querelle and other males (except for Robert, who alone remains inaccessible to him, and who—despite his denials—he therefore still desires), but claims, "I never understood how anybody could fall in love with a man." He maintains control by indulging in a pleasure with "absolutely no emotion" attached; his credo—stated as he directly faces the camera and repeated in a title card—is "They knew they were risking nothing, that nothing was muddying the purity of their games. No passion." As for Mario, he even more perfectly embodies phallic authority and prestige. Mario conflates the glamour of the outlaw with the authority of the cop; he exists at the ironic point where (homosexual) transgression becomes complicit with dominant (heterosexual) power. He represents the Law by profession; his virility, toughness, and impassivity—guaranteed by his position in the police—are the very qualities that make him an alluring image of homoerotic fantasy. Sitting motionless on a bar stool, in his leathers, Mario's arrogant display of the image of police power is a provocative sexual turn-on.

This posture of authoritative self-possession, this refusal of passion, represents the *ne plus ultra* of socially constituted and sanctioned masculinity. The ritual, ascetic disavowal of "weakness," and the concomitant establishment of virile power—as embodied in masterful figures like Mario and

Nono—is clearly not a movement peculiar to, or intrinsic to, male homosexuality. On the contrary, it is the normative process enacted in fraternity initiations and masculine rites of passage, in the psychoanalytic narrative of (male hetero-)sexual maturation (and perhaps in teleological narrative in general), and in the mechanisms of cinematic identification as they are usually understood to operate in Hollywood films. To the extent that desire is referred back to a fixed self and is defined and regulated in terms of idealizing fantasy (for these always go together), all its modes of expression—looking and wanting, voyeurism and sexual excitement—are implicated in normalizing mechanisms of social control. And Fassbinder never lets us forget this; he disturbingly suggests that idealization—whether in the form of individual projection or of collective utopian imagining—is always complicit with power. The unrelenting "pessimism" of *Querelle*, as of most of Fassbinder's films—what Silverman (1992) aptly calls "his aversion to the fictions which make psychic and social existence tolerable" (p. 126)—comes from an exacerbated awareness of the identity between ego-satisfaction and political oppression (including self-denial and self-oppression). When sexual desire is recuperated in terms of self-autonomy, the anxious instability of passion—its seductive unpredictability, its violent heightening of sensation and affect, its opening onto otherness—is irretrievably lost. The endpoint of idealizing homoerotic fantasy in *Querelle* thus turns out (ironically? or all too predictably?) to be one of conformity to bourgeois norms, to the laws of the phallus and the commodity.

Power and Vulnerability

Querelle remains perturbingly equivocal. The film is all at once a seductive, erotically charged allegory of homosexual initiation *and* an ironic, distanced, critical account of the social construction of normative masculinity. These two directions do not qualify one another and cannot be adequated to one another, but they exist simultaneously in every movement of the film. The singularity of male homosexual desire, as Fassbinder articulates it, lies not in the forms of virility that it posits, or even in the processes of discipline and training by which it produces figures who conform to these forms, but rather in the ambivalent way in which it invests and eroticizes such figures. The to-be-looked-at-ness of Fassbinder's perfect male bodies partakes both of Hollywood's traditional fetishization of the vulnerable female body and (as Sharrett notes) of its presentation of iconic male figures of rebellion such as Brando and Dean. This ambiguity is one indication of the troubling way in which power communicates with vulnerability, or virile impassivity with the passivity of the victim, throughout the film. The pornographic brutality of *Querelle*—its relentless eroticization of violence, and its insistence on portraying sexual acts as forms of physical violation—is a necessary condition for its (equally pornographic) idealizations. Fassbinder makes the viewer complicit in this process; my pleasure is all too explicitly predicated upon a willing engagement in processes of abasement and subjugation. My own self-aggrandizement (or pornographic gratification) fatally leads me to the point at which my vulnerability is exposed.

This insidious complicity makes any sort of moral judgment radically impossible. When Querelle is sodomized by Nono, and then by Mario, he discovers his deepest desires in the very movement by which he endures the violation of his body. Everything is violently overdetermined; Querelle at once experiences intense pleasure and submits to the discipline of phallic power. Is he giving way before uncontrollable sexual excitement? Or has he chosen Nono to punish him, to represent conscience and Law, to be his executioner? Does he find ecstasy and release in Mario's grip? Or is he bowing down in worship of the cop's "objectivity," which he regards as "the companion of total power," holding "unchallengeable moral authority," and representing the "perfect social organization" of fascism? The answer can only be: both at once. Every event in *Querelle* must be registered doubly: as an instance of power and domination, but at the same time as a deeply arousing experience of passion and excitement, a heightening and quickening of life. Desire is most enticing, most ambiguous, most dangerous, when it is rooted in passivity and subjugation. Mario seduces Querelle by boasting to him about the size of his hard-on; when Querelle responds by giving him a hand job, Mario cocks his gun and opens his switchblade knife, only to drop them both on the ground. Mario's aggressive assertion of phallic power is transformed into a gesture of self-abandonment. Virility is undone by the very excitement it provokes. Structures of domination are not overthrown, but a *supplemental* pleasure, abject and anonymous, coexists with them, and cannot be reduced to their measure.

And so Querelle is torn apart by the very processes that *also* stabilize his identity, defining him as male and endowing him with the power and prestige of masculinity. His "finding himself" also involves the risk of his becoming disidentified, of losing control. He is in danger of no longer being able to regulate his own identity and the manner in which he presents himself to others; of abandoning all self-possession and giving way to violent, involuntary sexual arousal. Against the normative masculine self whose impassivity and virile self-possession is both an effect of and a support for social circuits of power and domination, Fassbinder posits an ecstatic, empty, masochistic subjectivity whose form is not that of a self-enclosed ego. This subjectivity must be equated not with active mastery, but with an extended capacity for suffering and with a paralysis of the will. Throughout the film, such paralysis spreads like a plague from character to character, and from the characters to the audience, along the inverted pathways of the impotent gaze. The icy beauty of masculine display is immediately echoed and undone in the vulnerability and helpless fascination of the gaze that such beauty attracts.

If to be looked at is to manifest erotic power, then to be the one looking is to be exposed, to be made accessible to pain and loss. This is the burden of subjectivity: I feel desire, I am touched and moved, to such an extent that I am frozen, unable to act, unable to do anything that might resolve or realize my desire, for desire is not freedom, but a compulsion so all-embracing that it simply leaves no alternative. My seemingly active, self-conscious identity reposes on a deeper, preoriginary passivity. This is the real "danger" involved in "finding oneself": a continuing potential for abjection subtends every act of self-identification and self-aggrandizement. It is bad enough that I must suffer; even worse, I must entertain the possibility that I profoundly desire, and take pleasure in, this suffering. When Querelle offers his ass to Nono, he expects to be hurt; he is perplexed by his discovery that he enjoys being in the passive position, and being physically penetrated. Querelle's "danger" is finally his vulnerability, both to passion and to power. He is passively exposed, violently subjected not just to the social forces that define masculinity, but—even worse—to the intractability and impersonality of desire.

When Querelle first visits La Feria, he falls under the spell of Mario's rigidly congealed impassivity: "Querelle was frozen by Mario's gaze. More than indifferent, Mario's gaze and stance were glacial." Mario's posture is erotically compelling because it suggests absolute invulnerability. Querelle feels a disturbing sense of masculine rivalry, for Mario's indifference to him is greater even than his own indifference to Seblon. He is seduced by Mario's gaze, because that gaze sees nothing; Mario seems to be looking right through him, and scarcely condescends so much as to acknowledge his presence. The cop's stance and gaze exist only to be looked at; Querelle is in the weaker position, since he is now, for the first time, the one impelled to look. He "finds himself," at the price of losing his magical invulnerability, of being himself drawn into the play of impotent voyeurism and unsatisfied desire. At the end of the scene, the camera moves in from Querelle's fascinated stare to a close-up of Mario's powerful hand, with its numerous rings, as the narrator informs us of Querelle's admiration for the cop's beauty and "terrestrial" power. Subjectivity is born in suffering, as the gaze falls back into its primordial passivity, troubled before the impassive beauty, and therefore the power, of an object it can never hope to possess. The more fetishistic and sexually charged the image, the more the gaze is drawn into an abyss of passion and subjectivity, into its own abjection.

Querelle moves, in the course of the film, from the display of virility to the unveiling of vulnerability. His initial position of erotic power and indifferent, highly stylized masculine objectivity gives way to—or reveals its hidden dependency upon—an indefinable Passion of subjectivity, expressed in humiliation and suffering, and in his involuntary submission to the force of his own homosexual desire. Querelle becomes increasingly subject to pleasures and passions that he does not have the strength to master. His perturbation in the presence of Nono and Mario; his ambivalent identification with—and aggressive rivalry toward—his brother Robert; his passionate tutelage of—and consequent betrayal of—Gil; his final passive acquiescence in Seblon's guardianship: these are so many Stations of the Cross, stages in Querelle's Passion, moments in his assumption of a "destiny" and a desire that cannot be those of his conscious self.

Virility is shadowed by vulnerability throughout the film; power secretly communicates with, and continually nourishes, the very weakness that it is overtly concerned to master, suppress, or deny. The erotic aura is efficacious only so long as it is held in reserve; any actual, open display of erotic power leads to an irresistible temptation to sacrifice or abdicate that power. And so the film dwells relentlessly, indeed pornographically, on its numerous moments of abjection. The more it presents beautiful images of masculinity, the more it insists on their vulnerability, and on their eventual betrayal and debasement. Narrative is suspended for the purposes of fetishistic display; the spectator is given time to dwell on idealized images of masculine beauty. But these carefully composed tableaux are transformed, in the course of the film, into exaggerated displays of defeat, suffering, and entrapment. We see Robert drunk and passed out at a table in the bar, and Querelle himself collapsing at Seblon's side. This debasing movement is the other side of spectacle, the underside of Fassbinder's demonstration of the normative power of masculinization. Abjection is always already presupposed, as the unacknowledged ground of idealization. Every posture of male self-possession is mirrored by, or metamorphosed into, one of debasement and humiliation; visual fascination is resolved into the intense sexual pleasure that can be felt in such humiliation.

Abject Identification

Abjection provides the link between visual fascination and physical sensation, as well as between the image as a normative model of masculinity and the image insofar as it is invested with homoerotic desire. Everything hinges on the paradoxical, passive role of identification in the inverted visual regime of Fassbinder's cinema. Identification is necessary to produce masculine identity, but it always also implies distance and dissociation. The idealized masculine self with which I identify is only an image, apparently belonging to somebody else, in any case remaining forever beyond my grasp. In normative masculine development (as in the conventional visual regime of Hollywood cinema), the virile subject is identified and empowered through a play of visual captivation. More fundamentally, however, such play refers the subject outside of itself, and back to an experience which contradicts its autonomy. Narcissistic self-recognition is then inseparable from a heightened vulnerability to, or even an abject dependency upon, forces outside the self: forces which the self cannot help responding to, but which it also cannot appropriate or control. The self is ruptured even before it can be unified: its humiliation is prior to, and serves as a necessary condition for, its constitution. The contradictions of Lacan's "mirror stage," which are evoked as latent, threatening possibilities in discussions of conventional Hollywood cinema, are instead obsessively foregrounded and actively affirmed in Fassbinder's films. Identification no longer works to shore up the illusion of the virile ego; rather, it is the path that leads from the assertion of virility to its sacrificial expenditure or self-destruction.

But further, as Genet's obsessive, pseudoreligious more-than-metaphors (retained and amplified by Fassbinder) of incarnation and transubstantiation indicate, this hyperbolic identification is rooted in the body, and is something more than the mirror stage's play of disembodied images. Querelle is indeed first attracted to Mario because Mario seems to be an idealized reflection, an even more rigidly impassive version of himself. It is as if he were coming under the sway of his own erotically charged aura, of himself objectified and externalized. But in a later scene, as Mario fucks Querelle, while Seblon watches from the distance, a title card reads: "For the first time in his life Querelle kissed a man on the mouth. It seemed to him as if he were pushing his face against a mirror which reflected his own image, as if he were thrusting his tongue into the rigid interior of a granite head." Here the narcissistic play of reflections is heightened into a harsh, physical contact. There is no reciprocity, no answering tenderness, to accompany the shock of recognition.

It is significant that this initial, momentous kiss is recounted only on the title card, and not explicitly shown. (Much later, we will actually see Querelle kiss Gil on the mouth; this scene is directly followed by the one in which Querelle betrays Gil by giving the tip that leads to his capture.) We are given not a shot of Mario and Querelle together (which would imply communion), but two separate close-ups: first Mario's face as he spits into his hand in order to lubricate his cock, and then Querelle's strained and ecstatic face as he is penetrated from behind. What begins as a game of images and reflections, a play between men supposedly untroubled by passion, culminates in a violent frenzy reaching directly into the body. The movement toward orgasm shatters any form of mirroring visual representation. The sexual act does not unify the two partners, and does not identify them with each other; Querelle experiences his unbridgeable separation from Mario at the very instant of their most intense physical contact. Identification with the erotic aura can take place only in the form of loss, at the very point of the violent, physical destruction of the aura.

When I am "identified"—or subjected and subjectified—in this way, my desire is no longer articulated through fantasmatic projections, but rather is intensely grounded in the violation and penetration of my body. Querelle's subjectivity is physically engendered in spasms of ecstatic self-annihilation. This is an intimate, subjective experience that is yet not that of a phenomenological (active, masterful, normatively masculine) self: affects violently flood the body, and exceed its powers of reception. My fantasies of power and control in sexuality give way, in anticipatory excitement or in the orgasmic shuddering of the body, to a humiliating self-abandonment. As Leo Bersani (1987) puts it, sexual experience, when pushed far enough, or to a point of sufficient intensity, implies a violent, ecstatic "self-shattering": a movement "in which the opposition between pleasure and pain becomes irrelevant, in which the sexual emerges as the *jouissance* of exploded limits, as the ecstatic suffering into which the human organism momentarily plunges when it is 'pressed' beyond a certain threshold of endurance" (p. 217). This continual, repetitive experience of "self-shattering" can occur in many forms, and under many relations of power. But it is at its most intense, Bersani suggests, in the "passive" position in anal intercourse, a position commonly regarded as one of shame and degradation because, according to the mores of patriarchal society, "to be penetrated is to abdicate power" (p. 212). Fassbinder, following and expanding upon Genet, hysterically hyperbolizes—rather than simply rejects—the stereotypical binary opposition of active and passive. The film pushes this opposition to the point of paradox and absurdity, which is a way of both acknowledging Fassbinder's (and our own) complicity with dominant power relations and questioning the limits of these relations. Fassbinder insists that there is no utopian escape from power and oppression. It is only from within structures of domination that we can discover the "lines of flight" that may be able to undo them. The subjective experience of powerlessness, abjection, or "self-shattering" is at one and the same time the product and consequence of being subjected to virile power, and the sole point that in a radical sense (precisely because it is "powerless") remains "outside" of this power, irreducible to its logic and to its control.

To Invent the Woman

The opposition of active and passive, of course, is also at the heart of our culture's hierarchical coding of the difference between male and female. The passive position is nearly always represented as "feminine," and Fassbinder's own films frequently appropriate female figures to stand in for the passive underside of masculine desire. (I am thinking particularly of *The Bitter Tears of Petra von Kant*, in which an all-female cast plays out what is really a campy male melodrama in drag, and of *In a Year of Thirteen Moons*, with Volker Spengler's transvestite depiction of a transsexual.) But these films also go out of their way to foreground their own complicity in such an exploitative mode of representation.

The figure of Lysiane, the sole female character in *Querelle*, similarly supports the burden, and designates the outer limit, of the masculine drama of power and abjection. Todd Haynes (1985), whose own film *Poison* is among other things a powerful reading of the ambiguous interplay of power and desire in Genet, points out that Fassbinder—following Genet—explicitly calls attention to the exclusion of women from the scene of male homoerotic fantasy, an exclusion that actively works to structure and to empower that fantasy: "Lysiane represents the mark of exclusion within *Querelle*, designating, as remainder to, the condition which makes possible this freeplay among men" (p. 97). As the narrator of *Querelle* says at one point: "Between such men and for them alone, a universe is established from which the idea of woman is banished. The absence of woman forces the two males to draw a little femininity from within each other, to invent the woman." It is typical, and telling, that the camera focuses on Lysiane during this statement, for the masculine project of "invent[ing] the woman," by expelling actual women and yet appropriating their images, is perturbed by Lysiane's insistent presence throughout *Querelle*. She remains visible even—or especially—in her banishment; the film obsessively narrates the process by which she is frozen out of the action, culminating literally in a freeze-frame on her anguished, isolated figure. Her progressive rejection from the erotic world of men is accompanied by her continuing, pathetic dependence, for her own self-definition, upon this very world of powerful gestures and splendid appearances. The more she puts on makeup, wears jewelry, and strikes seductive poses, the more her role of desperate, male-oriented display—the only position open to her—is itself usurped by men.

The female body thus serves as an actual physical prop, as well as a negative reference point, for male fantasy. "Femininity" must first be imposed or projected upon Lysiane in order that subsequently it can be drained from her. This is how virility finds the terms with which to designate its "other." Masculine "identification" depends upon the appropriation of female bodies—even when it is explicitly homoerotic, and all the more so when it is not—even though it provides absolutely no terms for women's own pleasures. Through the conflation of passivity and femininity, even the most radical experiences of "self-shattering" can be reinvested within the dominant, virile economy. For the male characters in the film, the delirious rush of abjection propels them "outside" of power; but this "outside" is not a tenable position, and is not itself subject to representation. To the extent that, inevitably, representations are projected and positions are marked out, the question of "femininity" reasserts itself. The rapture of Querelle is doubled by the entrapment and decline of Lysiane. There is no utopia of male sexuality in *Querelle*—not even in the negative form of the pleasures of degradation—because there is no escape from complicity in fresh processes of subjugation.

Disavowal, Passion, Erotic Play

It is then not sheer negativity (as Silverman 1992, 55, suggests) so much as it is radical ambivalence that Fassbinder pushes to an almost unbearable extreme. Abjection must always be read doubly, both as victimization by power and as an ecstatic rupturing of power. Fassbinder simultaneously insists that these two conditions be kept radically distinct, and does his best to make them utterly indistinguishable. One can say, alternatively, that masochistic desire collaborates in its own subjugation, and that it unleashes a pleasure that ruptures the boundaries of subjugation. Again, one can say both that homoerotic idealization projects and posits the phallic norms of masculine identity and power, and that the destabilizing play of homosexual passion perpetually troubles and undermines those norms. The fetishistic images that crystallize masculine desire are undone by fresh irruptions of that desire; every ideal is profaned and debased by the very passions it provokes. Virility continually runs the risk of being seduced into vulnerability. Desire is forever divided against itself; Fassbinder never allows us to untie the knots of this complicity.

Because this ambivalence is intolerable, because giving way to homoerotic passion constitutes a betrayal (or a sacrificial debasement) of the virility and impassivity that are the object and guarantee of that passion, and above all because passivity and abjection are both seductive and shameful, at once ardently desired and literally insupportable, every instance of "self-shattering" identification in *Querelle* is doubled by a movement of disavowal. We have already seen how disavowal can function as a reactive, defensive movement, maintaining the state of virile self-possession by negating and mastering the disruptive tensions of desire. But in a deeper sense, disavowal is an active, affirmative process: a constitutive element of passion, rather than a force directed against it. In *Querelle*, the disconcerting bodily expression of homosexual desire is always accompanied—amplified and protected—by verbal denial. Most of the male characters in the film must adamantly deny that they are gay, in order to gain access to the pleasures of actually being so. Again and again, they construct elaborate rationalizations in order to affirm their manhood, even as they are being seduced into the "feminine" position of passively submitting themselves to other, more powerful, men. Querelle in particular is afraid of being considered a "fairy," for such an admission would compromise his virility. He can be seduced by Mario only after the cop reassures him on this score: "I've met plenty of sailors who were into that. That didn't stop them from being real men.... You don't have to prove to me that you're a man. We know. We're both men.... You see, if it's fun there's nothing wrong with it." Again, Gil explains that he had to kill Theo because Theo had insulted his "honor"; this murder, as a disavowal (and therefore a disguised admission) of homoerotic attraction, is an all-too-appropriate response to Theo's own desire for Gil, disavowed and disguised in the form of fag-baiting. Similarly, Querelle is impelled to betray Gil to the police precisely because he has learned to love him, because he has been forced to assume the vulnerability and dependency that such a love implies. In the end, this betrayal is really a masochistically disavowed act of recognition: it is more the seal of Querelle's passion for Gil than it is a defense against it.

The deferral or momentary denial of passion is of course often the most effective means of provoking and intensifying it. As Haynes (1985) notes, "Disavowal in *Querelle*, far from disabling desire, seems rather to facilitate it" (p. 87). Disavowal is a way of self-consciously playing with and arousing erotic tension; such teasing duplicity is part of the dynamics of male homosexual seduction. The male characters in *Querelle* are never more highly charged with sexuality than when they deny being so. Gil makes love to Roger under cover of wanting to possess his sister; and Querelle is clearly not the only man who asks to have sex with Lysiane in order to have an excuse for being buggered by Nono. The search for pleasure without consequences, for "fun," serves throughout the film as an alibi for being drawn into the deeper and more abject implications of passion. Poses of impassivity and disinterest serve not so much to ward off desire and perpetuate mastery as to heighten the pleasures of ultimate submission. Fassbinder beautifully hyperbolizes this flux and reflux of erotic play: it is the underside of, and the countermovement to, his ceaseless demonstrations of the horrors of power and domination. In its continual evocation of evanescent sexual pleasures, *Querelle* is much less alienated and negative a film—and much more playful and "pornographic" (in the legal sense of seeking deliberately to arouse sexual excitement)—than has generally been acknowledged.

I think that it is finally this affirmative sense of erotic play (rather than any degree of alienating negativity) that has been most troubling to certain viewers of *Querelle*—especially to many male heterosexual viewers. For example, in a review that overtly proclaims its sympathy to the goals of gay liberation, but that is covertly (or unconsciously) homophobic, James Roy MacBean (1984) complains that "in the way both Fassbinder and Pasolini depict and privilege male homosexuality, one senses almost a smug proselytizing. Fassbinder, especially, seems to toss out a heavy macho 'dare' to the audience, as if to say 'try it, you'll like it'" (p. 15). The trite, bigoted complaint that Fassbinder is "proselytizing" for homosexuality is of course the index of a deeper, uneasy feeling of implication. Even though everything in *Querelle* is clearly marked in terms of (pre-AIDS) gay subculture, it is *also* unavoidably addressed to a normative—which is to say male heterosexual—spectator. Such a spectator identifies with the masculine icons on the screen, but at the same time needs to deny the erotic dimension of such an identification. He does not want to admit that the very process that allows him to appropriate the aura of virility also implicates him in sexual desire for other men.

Fassbinder's inverted strategies of identification and disavowal address just such a response, for in *Querelle*, identification affirmatively shatters identity, rather than reactively consolidating it; and disavowal actively constructs and enables desire, instead of defensively disguising or repressing it. Thus, Fassbinder reminds us that every formation of masculinity in our culture must have its element of disavowed homoerotic desire. A normative subject position can maintain itself only by exploiting (feeding upon, or extracting surplus value from) all the other potential arrangements of desire that it circumscribes and rejects. Masculine self-representation is grounded simultaneously in a primordial homosexual desire articulated through passive visual display, and in the verbal denial or displacement of this desire. The normative spectator at once idealizes the representations with which he identifies, and disavows the desires aroused by these identifications. But *Querelle* turns the process of identification back upon the body of the spectator, and emphasizes the solidarity between illicit desires and the rituals and verbal formulas that claim to dispel them. It programmatically deidealizes desire, by suggesting that experiences of self-abandonment and self-debasement (or what the heterosexual viewer phobically perceives as such) are potentially charged with extreme pleasure. And it subverts virility by so insistently displaying the similarity between giving way to passion and being subjected to power. A mounting homosexual excitement undermines every effort to appropriate erotic energy as phallic power, as a means of staying in control. In all these ways, the male heterosexual viewer is implicated—even against his will—in *Querelle*'s homosexual scenario. As he watches the film, it is his masculine privilege that is put into question, and his vulnerability and capacity for abjection that are exposed. There is no point of escape for this spectator, no way he can regard *Querelle*'s spectacle of passion as merely exotic, as something that remains safely other than himself.

A Masochistic Aesthetics

Everything in *Querelle* arises out of spectacle and returns to spectacle. By forcing the normative male viewer to acknowledge his own implication in the machinery of spectacle, in the ambiguous interplay of identification and disavowal, Fassbinder produces a film of hyperreal, hyperbolic mimicry. The norms of phallic masculinity are traced with fatal accuracy, and yet violated beyond all hope of repair. Fassbinder locates the social construction of masculinity at the intersection of incompatible—yet inextricably connected—movements of pleasure and power, of debasement and idealization, and in the gap between the proximity of physical embodiment and the infinite distance of fascination with the image. Yet if these are the lines along which normative male subjectivity is constructed, they are also those along which it can be dismantled or "deconstructed." Fassbinder's strategy is to restage—in all its excess—the spectacle of masculinity: to present masculine embodiment *as* a spectacle, and fetishistically to arrest the process of its formation.

With its self-conscious artifice and its intensifying suspension and deferral of desire, spectacle serves the purposes of seduction; it is built upon the playful posturings—sometimes exaggeratedly virile, sometimes self-deflatingly campy—of homosexual fantasy. But such erotic play is dangerous: if on the one hand it refers back to the reified satisfactions of the fixed ego, then on the other it paves the slippery slope that leads to the most humiliating (and secretly desirable) self-abandonment. Querelle finds his final release and satisfaction in the impotent arms of Seblon: "I'm on the brink of a shame from which no man ever rises; but only in that shame will I find my everlasting peace. I'm so weak; I've been conquered, totally conquered." None of the males in the film is exempt from this humiliating "weakness": at the end of the film, Querelle smirks that if he is a "fairy," then for all his virile attitudes, "that makes Nono a fairy too." There is a continuity, and not an opposition, between seduction and "self-shattering," between the relaxed enticements of self-conscious erotic play and the self-annihilating violence of sacrificial expenditure. In these rites of male sexuality, power exerts itself only in order to disable itself. The postures of insolent virility so ostentatiously displayed throughout *Querelle* are finally nothing more than lures and signposts on the road to abjection.

In the light of this drive toward abjection, normative masculinity is deprivileged and denaturalized: it is displayed as a reactive, mimetic consolidation of spectacle, a countereffect or counterproduction of (disavowed, but all the more ubiquitous) homoerotic desire. For Fassbinder, as for Genet, virility is finally an *imposture*: a simulation that imposes itself upon the flesh and insinuates itself within an otherwise chaotic play of images and reflections. The norms of masculinity are based upon a systematic misconstruction: the seeming "error" of shifting the burden of shame onto others, of overlooking the pull of seduction upon the body, of bracketing the passion and excitement that always accompany identification, and of forgetting the ontological instability of spectacle.

Of course, virile power is no less real, and no less effectual, for being an imposture. The "error" of virility is an operation both grounded in and directed against the sexualized body. But when Fassbinder displays this body under the conditions of suspension and hypervisibility, and when he pornographically spectacularizes and fetishizes the operations of power, he performs a mock-Nietzschean reversal of perspective: power is now seen from the point of view of weakness. Just as the authority of the gaze is questioned when it is resituated within a visual regime centered upon the image, so too the dominant model of masculinity is contested when it is regarded from the position of the homosexuality that it spurns and disavows, but secretly mobilizes. Power and mastery are not overturned, but they are *compromised* by being contemplated, and secondarily defined, in terms of powerlessness and passivity. Abjection is an impossible, radically inauthentic postion; yet in *Querelle* it is valued for its own sake, indefensibly, as an extreme form of pleasure and passion. It is scandalously affirmed *against* the norms of narrative and of identification that alone have the authority to justify or legitimate it. It is from within the very heart of domination that I am drawn into this debasement and this ecstasy.

Silverman (1992) appreciates Fassbinder's "aesthetics of pessimism," his apparent valorization of suffering, "the masochism which alone makes [his] negativity endurable," but she also worries that this masochistic stance becomes "most politically dangerous" even as it becomes "most libidinally complex" (pp. 155–56). I am trying to suggest that a filmmaking practice that actively embraces these dangers and ambivalent complexities is more politically incisive than one that averts them. It is precisely *because* Fassbinder's position is evidently *compromised* on every conceivable level that in his films the mechanisms of normalizing power—embodied in the apparatuses of sexuality and of the cinema—have the potential to be "perverted," or turned away from power.

Through this inversion, the politics of radical contestation is joined to a passive, contemplative aestheticism. *Querelle* revels in the very beauty that it also shows to be a lure and a product of power. The alienating distance that makes room for detached critical response is *also* the enabling condition for a masochistic heightening of affect. Critical rationality, like every other discourse of power and authority, is infected with and transmuted by passion. The film's apparent retreat into contemplation, its turn toward Querelle's final abject contentment in "that heaven of heavens where beauty unites with beauty," is not *merely* ironic. Or rather, Fassbinder's most complex and most compelling irony is precisely the absence of irony in the last analysis. Because everything is political, there can be no refuge of interiority that is not invested by power, and there can be no escape from complicity. Fassbinder's aesthetic of pain and humiliation marks the exact point of this implication, the point at which power confronts and traverses the body. *Querelle* makes an embarrassing public disclosure of the shame of complicity, giving voice to a dangerous ambivalence that usually dares not speak its name.

The masochistic enjoyment of beauty, born in one's own suffering, is not (as is so often said) an internalization of oppression. On the contrary, it reflects an exacerbated awareness that there is nothing to internalize, that the outside is always already inside, and that the utopian fiction of a space free from power and domination is itself an insidious manifestation of normalizing power. The masochistic stylizations of *Querelle* take up—rather than avert—the unspeakable burdens of complicity and victimization, and twist them into ungainly forms of pleasure and desire. In this way, the most marginalized and neglected corners of "personal experience" can give birth to a nonutopian politics of resistance. And this is why, watching *Querelle*, we are seduced and initiated into the secret pleasures of abjection.

VI

Warhol's Bodies

Living the Hyperreal

ANDY WARHOL remarks, in a 1967 interview with Gretchen Berg, that "all my films are artificial but then everything is sort of artificial, I don't know where the artificial stops and the real starts" (Berg 1989, 60). One may find Warhol's offhand vacuousness, his peculiarly blank manner, alternately charming and chilling. But in his deadpan and slyly paradoxical way, Warhol raises, and weirdly inflects, all the issues that I have been grappling with throughout this book. Culture theorists such as Baudrillard and Jameson have defined postmodernism in terms of an eclipse of the real, a proliferation of simulacra, a freeing of the sign from its referent. Capitalist commodity production culminates in a regime of unlimited artificiality, first expressed by mechanical reproduction and by the cinema, but brought to its highest pitch through the ubiquity of electronic media (TV, video, computers). Baudrillard (1983) defines the *hyperreal* as a condition in which the "contradiction between the real and the imaginary is effaced. The unreal is no longer that of dream or of fantasy, of a beyond or a within, it is that of a *hallucinatory resemblance of the real with itself*" (p. 142).

Nobody has done more than Warhol to make such definitions seem inescapable. Already in the mid-1960s, long before *postmodernism* became a term of critical debate, his works explored, embodied, and affirmed this strange condition. His films, his plastic art, and his construction of a social persona all assume a world of media-drenched simulations, in which nothing can be regarded as authentic because everything is always already "sort of artificial." Warhol erases the critical standpoint from which one could talk of a *loss* of history, or a *loss* of the real, for there is no prior condition for him: "I have no memory. Every day is a new day because I don't remember the day before. Every minute is like the first minute of my life" (Warhol 1975, 199). In this eternal present, the "real" is not absent so much as it is coextensive with artifice, and hence radically indefinable. The nuance is important: Hollywood hasn't displaced nature, because Hollywood is already one with nature.

Warhol thus *lives* the enigmatic condition of hyperreality, rather than defining or critiquing it. His most characteristic gesture is his unqualified embrace of static materiality, of all that is untransformable and undialectizable. He's fascinated by blankness and insignificance, to a point of paradoxical overload. In his work, we are drenched in the brute evidence of inert matter to such an extent that we can no longer fix the point "where the artificial stops and the real starts." Warhol uncritically celebrates our culture's accretion of inauthentic, defunct, and alienated productions and reifications: he affirms everything that Sartre disparagingly terms the "practico-inert." His films, like his paintings and other works, continually confound boundaries and erase conventional distinctions, yet they do this in the name of a bland acceptance of things as they are, rather than any utopian transcendence of the real. They present transgression not as a heroic or radical act, but as a mindless and banal self-evidence.

Another way to put this would be to say that for Warhol, the simulacrum is physical before it is metaphysical. Simulation is a social process to be sure, an aspect of mechanical reproduction under late capitalism; but it is an event of the body and not of the spirit, a superficial (in the sense of having to do with surfaces) affection of the flesh rather than a structural determination of language and consciousness. Where Baudrillard and Jameson define postmodern simulation in terms of the ubiquity and precedence of the code, the freeing of the sign from referential meaning, Warhol sees it rather as a detaching of the body from signification: "If you look at something long enough, I've discovered, the meaning goes away" (in Berg 1989, 61).

The mechanical reproduction of commodities, itself reproduced in Warhol's silkscreens and films, effaces the duality of essence and appearance, of signifier and signified, of presence and meaning. The physical body does not signify beyond the silent, obsessive evidence of its own image, and images and words are radically incommensurable. As Warhol asserts over and over again, "There's nothing really to understand in my work" (in Berg 1989, 61). Why, then, photograph the Empire State Building for eight hours? Why paint an interminable series of Campbell's soup can labels? Foucault (1983b) suggests one answer: "A day will come when, by means of similitude relayed indefinitely along the length of a series, the image itself, along with the name it bears, will lose its identity. Campbell, Campbell, Campbell, Campbell" (p. 54). Warhol repeats images *in order to* drain them of pathos, meaning, and memory. When the name is effaced by meaningless repetition, and identity is swallowed up in self-resemblance, then only the physical trace remains. There is nothing but a body, nothing but an image:

How terrible things are, when they come out of themselves, into a resemblance in which they have neither the time to corrupt themselves nor the origin to find themselves and where, eternally their own likenesses, they do not affirm themselves but rather, beyond the dark flux and reflux of repetition, affirm the absolute power of this resemblance, which is no one's and which has no name and no face. (Blanchot 1985, 71)

Warhol is haunted by the facelessness of resemblances: "I'm sure I'm going to look into the mirror and see nothing. People are always calling me a mirror and if a mirror looks into a mirror, what is there to see?... I'm still obsessed with the idea of looking into the mirror and seeing no one, nothing" (Warhol 1975, 7). It's not that Andy won't be able to see anything at all in the mirror; it's rather that "no one, nothing" is precisely the image of "himself" that he expects (fears? hopes?) to see. The object is not "lost" or distorted when it passes through the defile of the signifier or submits to the canons of representation; these devices serve rather to anchor and specify it, to bind it to itself. On the contrary, the object is altered, deprived of its identity, and emptied of itself when it is repeated exactly. The most powerful mirror is one that so entirely submits to the object being reflected, so passively and literally repeats it, that it absorbs it and renders only the pure play of reflection itself. Isn't the movie camera such a mirror, a device for drawing bodies into the anonymity and multiplicity of appearances? Promiscuously recording everyone, it transforms this "everyone" into a "no one." Strictly speaking, then, Warhol's films do not *represent* the real. Rather, passively and casually, these films actually *enter into* the real: they trace it, embrace it, amplify it, multiply it, and thereby empty it out. What you see is what you get, since the reality of the image is precisely equal to the reality of the object of which it is an image. It is only "lack" that has been removed, only the unfathomable depths of signification, representation, and interiority that have been "lost."

Nothing Is Hidden

What might it mean to accept Warhol's notorious claim that he is interested only in "the surface of things" (in Berg 1989, 54), and that there is nothing behind those ostentatious surfaces? One may distinguish between modernist and postmodernist readings of Warholian superficiality and emptiness. The modernist reading applies a hermeneutics of suspicion to Warhol's blankness. Thus Carter Ratcliff (1983) asserts that Warhol's mysteriousness arises from our search for "what stays hidden" in his work; even as we are faced with "the seemingly absolute impenetrability of Warhol's surfaces," we still "tend to believe that the more an individual, an art form, even a culture insists on its outward image, the more there is going on beyond it" (p. 9). The modernist approach assumes that there is a hidden dimension to Warhol's work, that his inner life is somehow expressed in it, if only by its absence: in short, that he has something to hide. It looks for indications of depth, denial, or struggle. It tries to *decipher* the work, interpreting symptoms, searching for signs of repression, uncovering latent meanings. But when this effort fails—as it inevitably does with Warhol—the last resort of the hermeneutics of suspicion is to jump to a metalevel: to decipher the very fact of the work's indecipherability. Warhol's art is then made to signify the hidden conditions of its own production and reception: it is taken to reveal the ubiquity of the commodity form (in a Marxist reading); or the enigmatic self-withholding of Being (in a Heideggerian reading); or the anxieties of the spectator, upon whom the burden of interpretation is now placed (in a performative reading); or the neurotic affectlessness and detachment of contemporary culture (in a liberal humanist reading); or even the "pathological remoteness" and narcissism of Warhol himself (as in Stephen Koch's psychologizing, more or less Sartrean reading; 1973, 29).

The problem with all these modernist readings is that they discover only levels of meaning that they have themselves first assumed and imposed. They laboriously reinvent the very *depth* that Warhol has gone to such great pains to eliminate. I want to argue, instead, for an aggressively postmodern reading of Warhol, one that takes quite literally his claim to present nothing but surfaces. For Warhol, as for Wittgenstein (1968), "nothing is hidden": "Since everything lies open to view there is nothing to explain" (secs. 435, 126). This immediately disqualifies any hermeneutics. What is scary and uncanny about Warhol's art and films is that *it has no latent content at all*. His surfaces are impenetrable precisely because there is nothing beneath them, no depth into which one could penetrate. It would be equally accurate to say that these surfaces are completely porous, since they are so blandly and passively open to whatever constructions we try to impose upon them. All possible interpretations of Warhol, no matter how much they contradict one another, are thus equally plausible and equally unfounded. The "real" Warhol never appears; all we see is a mask, but there is nothing behind the mask.

　　　　Warhol is mysterious and charismatic not because he is so good at keeping his inner life a secret, but because he has no secrets to keep. His offhand blankness is more disturbingly enigmatic, in and of itself, than anything concealed behind it could possibly be. The greatest mystery of all is the utter absence of mystery: the flatness and self-evidence of what is only an image, without interiority, without emotions, without "lack." William Flesch (1984) writes suggestively of the sublime charisma that results from indifference: "Those figures tend to be charismatic who are beyond loving . . . invulnerable, desireless and affectless figures" (p. 13). Or as Warhol (1975) himself puts it: "As soon as you stop wanting something you get it. I've found that to be absolutely axiomatic" (p. 23). We are desperate for Andy's interest and approval exactly because he seems to have no need for us. Warhol's greatest work of art was himself; he transformed himself into a blank and glamorous—and hence charismatic—figure of pure appearance. His cinematic and visual art then consists in the transfiguration of the entire world into this at once sublime and banal state, a transfiguration that is all the more strange for being boring, unrevelatory, and nonredemptive. Warhol is less a mirror than he is a kind of black hole, democratically seducing everything and everyone into the same grace of emptiness that he has discovered or fabricated for himself. As he sort of boasts, "When *I'm* there, they tell me, nothing happens. I make nothing happen" (Warhol 1975, 50).

It is very difficult to "make nothing happen": it requires a lot of work, even if part of Warhol's accomplishment is to give us a sense that "nothing" is easy and obvious. The banality and self-evidence of Warhol's surfaces seem to be simplicity itself; but this blankness and "hallucinatory resemblance" is a "look" that needs to be carefully, deliberately produced. Warhol always emphasizes his devotion to the American work ethic, even as he continually searches for the most facile and effortless method to attain his goals. Indeed, Warhol's famous desire to be a machine could be realized only through a long process of hard work and experiment. He recalls that, at the beginning of his Pop career, "I still wasn't sure if you could completely remove all the hand gesture from art and become noncommittal, anonymous" (Warhol and Hackett 1990, 7).

Where a modernist critique would read personal pathology back into Warhol's anonymity, or would see his desire to be a machine as a symptom and reflection of social constraints, a postmodern approach will rather regard this machinelike anonymity as what Deleuze and Guattari (1987) call a "motor program of experimentation" (p. 151). A program is a kind of *work on the body*, an actual physical and conceptual transformation, and not just an interpretation. It arises out of, and ruptures, a given social context: it *produces effects*. Deleuze and Guattari oppose the program to the psychoanalytic notion of phantasy, an interpretation that always needs to be interpreted in its own turn, and which refers back to a social or subjective context as its underlying cause. Warhol's studio was of course called the Factory, and the miming of industrial and advertising procedures in his art has been much commented upon; but it's important to see this depersonalization as a program of mimicry and not as a phantasy, a hyperbolic, hypermimetic generation of ambiguous effects rather than a mere mimesis (reflection, representation, replication, or parody) of late capitalist market structures. Warhol's greatest joke is that he so painstakingly employs artisanal means to produce, on his own account, things that have already been mechanically reproduced. Warhol, then, doesn't simply regard simulation as a ubiquitous social process; if anything, he suggests that simulation isn't ubiquitous enough, since he expends all his effort to produce it, extend and multiply it, saturate the world with it. He isn't commenting—either critically or acquiescently—on the supposed vacuity and superficiality of the contemporary, commodity-drenched world; he is appropriating and diverting the techniques of mass production and publicity precisely in order to achieve vacuity and superficiality in a world that is never empty, flat, or stupid enough.

Bodies Are Stupid

There is a certain primordial *stupidity* of the body, a weird inertness and passivity, something that freely offers itself to all the categories of thought and representation, allows them to invest it and pass through it, yet somehow always effortlessly evades them. Stupidity is the key to Foucault's (1977) incisive discussion of Warhol:

Stupidity is contemplated; sight penetrates its domain and becomes fascinated; it carries one gently along and its action is mimed in the abandonment of oneself; we support ourselves upon its amorphous fluidity. . . . we accept stupidity—we see it, we repeat it, and softly, we call for total immersion. (p. 189)

The body is "stupid" in the sense that it is overly passive and indifferent, affected by everything but responsive to nothing, so plastically open to every force, every stress, and every stimulus that it is ultimately determined by none. This is why the body's stupidity is *seductive*: we are incited to keep on looking, again and again, precisely because our desire for comprehension and control is never satiated. The more we look, the less we are able to make anything of what we see; we can only abandon ourselves to it. As I discussed in chapter I, voyeuristic fascination is at work in Warhol's films before, and even altogether without, the presence of an actively looking subject. It is not necessary that there be a viewer, only that there be a body to be viewed. Voyeuristic fascination implies neither mastery over what is seen nor even exactly the frustration of a drive for mastery. It takes hold only when the drive for mastery is metamorphosed into something radically different: into the dumbness of infinite acceptance, an absorption or distraction nearly indistinguishable from boredom, the passive bliss with which Warhol is reported to have watched his own films: "a perfect contentment that could just go on, and, I realized, could go on for hours and hours like that unless he was interrupted" (Ronald Tavel, quoted in Smith 1986, 153). Voyeuristic fascination is thus a "miming" of stupidity; it arises when vision is seduced by the turgidity of its object, and enticed in its own turn to assume the stillness and weightiness of an inert body.

Indeed, the seductive stupidity of the body obsesses Warhol; it is his greatest discovery, and it is what facilitates his bland erasure of boundaries. Many accounts of Warhol emphasize his extreme dislike of being touched, his need to create buffers between himself and reality, his professed preference for fantasy sex over real sex (see especially Koch 1973, 21–32). Yet this willed distance cannot really be coded (as Koch tries to do) as a gap between self and other, an existential alienation or a self-protective retreat, for Warhol also absents himself from himself in the very gesture by which he absents himself from others: "I don't want to get too close.... I don't like to touch things ... that's why my work is so distant from myself" (in Berg 1989, 61). Once again, Warhol's avoidance of tactile contact must be read affirmatively: it is not a sign (a symptom of some prior existential inadequacy), but a positive expression (a machine for producing certain subsequent experiential effects). In his voyeuristic remoteness, his suspension of tactility, Warhol doesn't avoid the body so much as he encounters (discovers or produces) a new state of the body. Corporeal stupidity is dissociated at long last from the impertinencies of the critical intelligence.

Warhol's paintings and silkscreens are often discussed as paradoxical explorations of commodification and stereotyping in late capitalist culture. But his films go even further, for only they directly grasp and present the body in its radical externality, as commodity and stereotype. As Ratcliff (1983) puts it, the Superstars of Warhol's films "strike us as personalities so utterly externalized, so completely given over to the moment, that they—like Brillo boxes or Campbell's soup cans—exist sheerly as images" (p. 52). By abstaining from touch, Warhol reduces the body to the status of an image, a mere surface appearance; but thereby he affirms the image as an intrinsic property of the body, even as its unique "expression." All of Warhol's films, from the most rigorously structural and conceptual (*Sleep*, *Kiss*, *Empire*) to the most lax, content-filled, and ostensibly commercial (specifically including such works as *Flesh*, *Trash*, and *Heat*, made in Warhol's name by Paul Morrissey), are marked by the *literalism* with which they evacuate all other significance and content in order thereby to capture, record, and display the sheer, stupid, inert presence of bodies. Perhaps only Robert Bresson has gone as far as Warhol in emptying out representation and directly equating cinematic presentation with the stupidity and passivity of the flesh. (I elaborate this seemingly strange comparison, and discuss Bresson at greater length, in Chapter 7.)

Film Portraits

Consider, for instance, Warhol's interminable series of film portraits. Visitors to Warhol's Factory were routinely asked to sit in front of the camera for about three minutes, enough time for Warhol's assistant Billy Linich to shoot a silent, 100-foot reel. The "portrait" was completed when the roll of film ran out. That was it; there was no subsequent editing or elision. Some of these reels were later spliced together to make films titled *The Thirteen Most Beautiful Women*, *The Thirteen Most Beautiful Boys*, and *Fifty Fantasticks and Fifty Personalities*; many more remained unseen in Warhol's vaults. What is the aesthetic effect, what is the *point*, of such films? Nothing *happens* in the course of their duration, nothing anecdotal or psychological is revealed. And that is of course itself the point. The sitters remain motionless, isolated in the frame. Three minutes may not seem like much, but it is a very long time to have to sit still, frozen, without making any gestures, trying not even to blink. Sitting for these films thus "requires endurance" (Smith 1986, 154). The (seeming) candor and immediacy of a snapshot are out of the question; there's no way to avoid the rigidity and bad faith of a formal pose. And the camera, with its mechanical gaze, offers no compensation for this cadaverous stiffness; it does not pretend, like a painter—or even a great still photographer—to make visible an inner dimension of the sitter. The appearance on screen doesn't point to anything beyond itself; specifically, it doesn't "stand for" (represent) the personality of the subject, as would be the case in traditional portraiture. This effect of surreal vapidity is only heightened by the fact that the films are run in slow motion (like all of Warhol's silent films, they were shot at 24 fps, but are projected at the silent speed of 16 fps). In the alien temporality of the film, in its remorseless scrutiny of a face, subjectivity is suspended, emptied out, put under erasure.

In this way, Warhol's film portraits are indistinguishably "artificial" and "real." Real because of the films' unflinching literalness—nothing is given beyond immediate appearance, the physical trace of bodily presence. Artificial because of course this immediacy is itself produced as an effect of the cinematic apparatus. And indistinguishably so, because the literal reality of the image is *not* an illusion; it is mechanically produced, to be sure, but it is no less "present" and actual than are the camera, the projector, and the screen. Using the most outrageously reductive and artless of means, Warhol equates the literal with the fictional and the indubitable presence of the body with the intangible proximity of the image. Representation is short-circuited—or subversively transformed into simulation—when the image does not reproduce an object or refer to a prior original, but simply repeats what is already an image. And such is precisely the case with Warhol's portrait films: the body of the sitter, the object of the camera's gaze, has already become an image at the moment of the profilmic event. The body before the camera is a mute appearance, devoid of consciousness, will, or interiority. Warhol's "subjects" are emptied out, distanced and absented from themselves, drained of their subjectivity, and reduced to a silent (yet insistent) spectacle of bodily presence. To be photographed is to be transformed, to exist in a new way: as an object, an image, an appearance solely for others. Flesh is at once degraded and exalted, diminished to mere, unsignifying matter and yet heightened with the mystique of an ungraspable aura. The film camera, that mechanical recording device, does not reproduce or represent its subjects so much as it draws them into its own insidious realm of stupid, automatous materiality.

The Marriage of the Artificial and the Real

Warhol's films at once perform and testify to a perverse, parasitic marriage of the real and the artificial. Mechanical reproduction becomes immanent to lived experience, appearance to essence, objecthood to subjectivity, performance to self-expression, the cinematic apparatus to the scenes that it records and reproduces. Recording devices aren't just a screen or buffer between Andy and the outside world; they actually transform the nature of what is "real." Warhol (1975) thus hilariously recounts his own "marriage" to the apparatus:

I didn't get married until 1964 when I got my first tape recorder. My wife.... Nothing was ever a problem again, because a problem just meant a good tape, and when a problem transforms itself into a good tape it's not a problem any more.... Everybody knew that and performed for the tape. You couldn't tell which problems were real and which problems were exaggerated for the tape. Better yet, the people telling you the problems couldn't decide any more if they were really having the problems or if they were just performing. (pp. 26–27)

Self-expression is thus radically compromised from the beginning, because it always implies the artificiality of performance, the priority of display for others, something that is staged before the mechanical ear of the tape recorder or the mechanical eye of the camera. We are always already acting, even if our performance is usually unconscious or involuntary. David James (1989) shows how this logic informs Warhol's film portraits: "Rather than documenting the ability of the subject to manifest an autonomous, unified self, these portraits narrate the sitter's response to the process of being photographed" (p. 139). "Narrate" may be something of an overstatement; James goes on to speak of the sitter being impelled self-consciously to "construct himself" before the camera's gaze, whereas I would emphasize rather the sitter's passive, unconscious entrapment. These portraits aren't legible as fictional characterizations any more than as signs of a preexisting interiority, for there is no process of construction to be narrated, only a series of already-artificial presences, of constrained postures and inscrutable expressions. Self-conscious reflection is evacuated before the camera, to be replaced by the unfettered display, in strange slow-motion suspension, of carnal stupidity.

High modernist critics tend to value Warhol's early, silent films above all: they see in them a deconstruction of the cinematic apparatus, a reflexive focus on the ontological paradoxes of filmmaking and film viewing. But

Warhol never really was a self-referential or modernist filmmaker, not even in the most formal and most unwatchable of his early works. Films like *Kiss*, *Sleep*, and *Empire* indeed touch on such matters as the temporal duration of film, the nature of perception, the materiality of the film stock and of the mechanisms of recording and projection; but, in striking contrast to avant-garde cinema, their treatment of such matters is always contextual and external. Warhol is concerned not with the inner nature of cinema, but only with its most blatant and superficial effects. His approach to filmmaking is physiological and behavioristic rather than ontological or phenomenological. Even the earliest films deliberately highlight a crude logic of stimulus and response. In a kind of perverse behaviorism, they patiently, mindlessly record the body's negative responses to deviated stimuli. Hence, the frequent sadism of these films: by immobilizing not just his camera but also his sitters, Warhol gets the chance both to make the sitters squirm and (ultimately) to reduce them to a state of disarticulated stillness. Close-ups without prior establishing shots literally fragment the physical organism: this is done most powerfully in *Blow Job*, where the unseen activity is radically severed from the visible responses it provokes. The distances between living beings and inert objects are reduced to a minimum: the leaps are not all that great from the isolated face of one of the "most beautiful boys," to the fragmented body of John Giorno asleep, to the distant, motionless "body" of the Empire State Building—which Warhol boasted of making into a "star!" (Smith 1986, 153).

What I have been calling these films' literalism and stupidity thus leads to a radical desublimation and dehierarchization. Everything is on the same level: everything is a body and nothing more than a body, and every body is presented as it "is," in its artifice, insofar as it is reduced to—or captured as—an image. There are no metalevels in Warhol's films: they don't privilege form over content, and they don't reflect upon themselves any more than—or any differently from how—they reflect upon the outside world. Where avant-garde cinema tends toward a sublimation of content into form, the exclusion of all contents other than those pertaining to the formal processes of filmmaking and film viewing, Warhol's films move in precisely the opposite direction. They refuse to privilege form, treating it instead as just another content, alongside all the others.

Warhol sees the movie camera as a machine that is already immanent to the world, rather than as a device standing at the transcendental threshold of the world, and mediating our perceptions and representations of it. The film stock itself is present as an image—captured through the simple, lazy expedient of leaving in the white leader at the beginning and end of each reel—in exactly the same way that the human face or body is present as an image. Everything is located on the same immanent plane, the same level of simulacral actuality. The self-referential devices associated with experimental film thus turn out to be surprisingly flat, naturalistic, and unrevelatory when they are appropriated or reinvented by Warhol.

In these films where "nothing" happens, even the minimalist aesthetic is undermined. Our usual response to minimalism is to pay more concerted attention, since the minutest gestures take on an immense weight. But Warhol frustrates this expectation as well, since whatever minuscule changes we do observe are random and do not signify. In the wake of mechanical reproduction, all alternatives are rendered undecidable, all boundaries indiscernible. Whether we watch with heightened attention or turn away from the screen in boredom, our ability to make distinctions is paralyzed. "The image is the moment of passivity, having no value either significative or affective, being the passion of indifference" (Blanchot 1981, 89).

The Aesthetics of Indifference

Indifference is the secret behind what Peter Wollen (1989) aptly defines as Warhol's major achievement: "to bring together the apparent contraries of 'minimalism' and 'camp' in a paradoxical and perverse new combination" (p. 14). The passive capture of being by the camera and tape recorder, the hypervisibility of surfaces, the stupid, meaningless insistence of the flesh: this is the common condition for the close-up, serial presentation of a sleeping body or of couples kissing at excruciating length, and for the undisciplined, campy performances, the haphazard zooms and pans, and the bad sound of the later sex films. The excessive stillness and immobility of the silent works seduces us into contemplation, only to frustrate our voyeuristic expectations and deny us any hope of transcending the mute passivity and inertness of the flesh. The later, sound films achieve an analogous result by a multitude of other means. Now a desultory hyperactivity, together with an overly casual depiction of behavior that in other contexts would be considered outrageous (sex, drug-taking, etc.), at once solicits and scatters our attention.

Films such as *Kiss*, *Sleep*, and the silent portraits are analytic: they decompose the body by isolating particular gestures and expressions. Sound films such as *Beauty #2* and *The Chelsea Girls*, and also *Lonesome Cowboys* and Morrissey's *Flesh* and *Trash*, are, in contrast, synthetic: they exhibit whole bodies over long stretches of time in order to display the charismatic personalities of their Superstars, to reconstitute their gestures, talk, habits, and routines into coherent wholes. But early and late alike, Warhol's films collapse the ontological into the anecdotal. They focus on the hyperbolic presence and artificial staging of the body; and they provoke a consequent withdrawal of affect on the part of both the actor and the viewer.

Critics oriented toward the aesthetics of high modernism and experimental cinema resent what seems to them to be the descent in the later works to a bland comedic mannerism. Annette Michaelson (1991), championing Stan Brakhage against Warhol, objects to the latter's reinvention of culture-industry styles of narrative. She argues that Warhol, by moving from part objects to whole bodies, and at the same time maintaining a suspended temporality by means of long, unedited takes, insidiously restores "the narrative syntagma" of Hollywood, "and with it the space of the whole body as erotic object of narrative desire" (p. 62). Stephen Koch (1973), so perceptive about the earlier films, is even more violent in dismissing Warhol's more accessible later ones as uninteresting capitulations to commercialism, or worse. He regards films such as *Nude Restaurant* and *Lonesome Cowboys* as "degrading and degraded works," implying not just "pornographic spectacle," but Warhol's "violation of his own artistic sensibility, which is far more shocking and repellent than any imaginable violation of sexual taboo" (p. 100).

Even leaving aside the homophobia possibly implicit in such responses — and the exquisite irony of encountering critics who accuse Warhol (of all people!) of abandoning his inner aesthetic integrity by taking too strong an interest in popular culture — it is striking how deftly Warhol evades the theoretical categories that have been used to define and contain his work. The offense to modernist taste of Warhol's campy and frankly exploitative later films has less to do with their conflation of high and low culture, or even of "normal" and "perverse" sexuality, than with the fact that their transgressive effacement of boundaries occurs so carelessly and casually. Warhol deconstructs the oppositions dear to avant-garde cineastes and Frankfurt school critics. He breaks down modernist distinctions between avant-garde and commercial cinema, between elegance and crassness, between critical distance and naive, uncritical absorption, and between the purity of self-reflexive filmmaking and the vulgar narrative thrust of "the movies." It is perhaps by an unconscious replication-cum-inversion of this logic of indifference that the very critics who privilege Warhol's early over his later films are bizarrely incapable of distinguishing such works as *Lonesome Cowboys* and Morrissey's *Flesh* and *Trash* from mainstream Hollywood fare.

Bad Performance

Still, it's important to be more precise about what happens when Warhol focuses, in his later films, on whole bodies engaged in a wide range of self-conscious behaviors. The characteristic procedures of Warhol's sound films have been catalogued in every account of the old Factory (see Koch 1973; O'Pray 1989; Smith 1986). The films are unstructured, casual, and anecdotal; their concern is "not plot, but incident" (as Warhol instructed his screenwriter Ronald Tavel; Koch 1973, 63). Sometimes they solicit their subjects to perform before, and in full awareness of, the camera; at other times they invent fictive situations of egregious ridiculousness, incoherence, and improbability; at yet other times they track the banalities of day-to-day existence. In any case, the actors were not allowed to rehearse beforehand; they picked up and read their scripts on screen, stared ostentatiously at cue cards, or acted in response to audible off-screen prompting and suggestions; their attention was distracted by the presence of the press and other outsiders at the shooting. Either the camera's gaze was entirely fixed or else it moved nonfunctionally, gratuitously zooming in on irrelevant details or panning away from the action to focus on a blank wall. The field of vision often included extradiegetic elements, such as people doing things in other corners of the Factory. There were no retakes: mistakes and accidental occurrences were incorporated into the completed film. With a kind of offhand sadism, actors were baited and provoked, goaded into "freaking out" or "acting out" on screen; the point was to make their carefully constructed personas decompose, giving way to behavior that, because of embarrassment, would be even more awkward and ostentatious.

These devices don't "alienate" us from the spectacle so much as they compel us to accept its actuality and immediacy *as* spectacle. Yet more complexly and disorientingly than before, they scramble our habitual distinctions between the artificial and the real. It's equally plausible to claim on one hand that Warhol's strategies interfere with the artificiality of representational performance by inserting bits of raw and unmediated reality, and on the other hand that they disrupt the cinema's reality effect, its claim directly to capture and reproduce the real, by forcing us to recognize the ubiquity of artifice. Everything is trapped in an impure, disconcertingly *in-between* state. As David James (1989) notes:

Any such polarization of reality and appearance cannot be maintained, but it does provide the basis for a more or less consistent and recognizable acting style in which the actor neither fully inhabits the role nor creates any constant distance from it, for example by quoting as in Brechtian theory. The role is engaged fitfully and often tangentially in such a way that its authority is constantly on the point of disintegrating even as the actor that is thus revealed can never be fully independent of the persona. (p. 142)

Warhol's most startling innovation is not to differentiate between the persona assumed by the actor and the actuality of the person who is acting, but to treat these two in precisely the same way. Warhol recalls:

Everybody went right on doing what they'd always done—being themselves (or doing one of their routines, which was usually the same thing) in front of the camera.... Their lives became part of my movies, and of course the movies became part of their lives; they'd get so into them that pretty soon you couldn't really separate the two, you couldn't tell the difference—and sometimes neither could they. (Warhol and Hackett 1990, 180)

Since everything is always already a performance, the "actual" and assumed "identities" of the performers are equally fictive, equally shallow, and equally problematic. It scarcely matters whether the people photographed by Warhol's camera are sincerely "being themselves" or deliberately "doing one of their routines," trying to project a persona. In either case, character is reduced to an objectified image, to a repertoire of tics, affectations, postures, and gestures. Interiority and critical distance are dissipated in favor of a stupid, flamboyant display of the body in its spatial extension and temporal duration.

Warhol (1975) charmingly remarks: "I can only understand really amateur performers or really bad performers, because whatever they do never really comes off, so therefore it can't be phoney." He complains that, to the contrary, "every professional performer I've ever seen always does exactly the same thing at exactly the same moment in every show they do" (p. 82). "Good" or professional performance (whether in life or on the stage) is the calculated attempt to project a consistent and substantial self, one identical to itself at every moment. Bad or amateurish performance subverts this art of projection, reminding us that "no person is ever completely right for any part, because a part is a role is never real" (p. 83).

Traditional theater's claim to reality or to realism and avant-garde theater's demystifying confession of its own artifice are equally "phoney"; indeed, the latter is yet more treacherous and disingenuous than the former, insofar as it raises its pretension to authenticity to a reflexive metalevel. Only a stupid performance, or a willfully incoherent one, escapes this ubiquitous truth claim. Bad acting can be opposed equally to the authenticity effect of (for instance) method acting, and to the alienation effect of Brechtian acting. In either case, "good" acting is dialectical: it expresses the inner through the outer, deploys absolute artifice in order to arrive at absolute reality, moves between the extremes of surface appearance and underlying truth. But bad performance disempowers this entire dialectic: it continually affirms the immanence (what Hegel disparagingly calls the "bad infinity") of the undecidable, the indifferent, and the in between. It undoes the movement by which the performer is either identified with or distanced from his or her role. It isn't "phoney," precisely because it doesn't embody a deeper truth: in its infinite acquiescence and superficial evidence, it cannot pretend to any sort of authenticity or authority (even a negative, demystifying one). Bad acting is unable to project beyond its own immediate presence; it continually fails in its attempt to move from shallow, moment-to-moment appearances to something more substantial. It interminably suspends the process by which a stable "self" could be constructed.

The Aura

The inauthenticity of the self and the immediacy of bad performance: these are the keys to Warhol's paradoxical interest in the superficial observation of human character and temperament. "I still care about people but it would be so much easier not to care . . . it's too hard to care" (in Berg 1989, 61). The camera explores other people in a distant and uninvolved way: it's a prosthesis for caring or, better, it enables Warhol to care and not to care all at once. Other people are alluring and mysterious because of their very remoteness, because we haven't yet gotten to know them. Warhol's (1975) remarks on the notion of aura supplement and update Benjamin's: "I think 'aura' is something that only somebody else can see. . . . You can only see an aura on people you don't know very well or don't know at all" (p. 77). The aura is an otherness conterminous with my very self, a superficial radiance, a dimension of my presence in the world that pertains uniquely to me even as it is radically distinct from—and inaccessible to—my "I." My aura is an "it," something that I cannot experience for myself, but that other people seem to perceive in me, and that therefore can be marketed. Warhol reasons that "if somebody was willing to pay that much for my it, I should try to figure out what it is" (p. 77). His advice to artists and performers is therefore that "you should always have a product that's not just 'you' " (p. 86).

But even as he insists that the aura is not the real "I," but only a commodity, Warhol takes the radical step of locating "personality" precisely in this aura, rather than in intimacy or interiority or self-consciousness. His films are people centered in the strange sense that they seek obsessively to expose the aura of his Superstars: "That screen magnetism is something secret. . . . You can't even tell if someone has it until you actually see them up there on the screen. You have to give screen tests to find out" (p. 63). Star presence is a bizarre tautology: the mysterious quality revealed by the movie camera is something that the camera itself has first brought into being. Aura doesn't exist independent of the distance embodied in the cinematic apparatus. Warhol (1975) claims that "the only people I can ever pick out as unequivocal beauties are from the movies, and then when you meet them, they're not really beauties either, so your standards don't even really exist. In life, the movie stars can't even come up to the standards they set on film" (p. 68).

And so Warhol's films give people their beauty by confronting them with the presence of the camera. If the only beautiful people are those in the movies, then for Warhol the inverse is also true: that anyone who appears in the movies is automatically made beautiful. The camera invariably captures beauty, since it exclusively reveals the epiphenomenal and trivial, and beauty for its part is only skin deep. Warhol's filmmaking credo is consequently "I've never met a person I couldn't call a beauty" (1975, 61), and "It's so easy to make movies, you can just shoot and every picture comes out right" (in Berg 1989, 61). No matter how desultorily and indifferently, Warhol's camera (and Morrissey's) continually interacts with, and magically invests, faces and bodies. It lingers over, or else passes idly by, the beautiful languor of Joe Dallesandro; the antics of gay men camping it up; the hysteria, bitchiness, and self-absorption of the female Superstars; and the elaborate artifices of drag display.

Poor Little Rich Girl foregrounds the charisma of Edie Sedgwick, even as it "reverses the rigid control of the studio system in Edie's random actions, the out-of-focus shooting, off-screen sound and the noise of the running camera motor" (Rees 1989, 134). More ostentatiously, Screen Test #2 at once produces, reveals, and "deconstructs" the beauty of Mario Montez, in his hyperreal drag impersonation of what is already a pure cinematic fabrication: the ultrafeminine Hollywood star. In all the later films, from Chelsea Girls to Flesh and Trash, individual singularities and eccentricities, the minutiae that constitute the personality, are separated from their causes and contexts, isolated and magnified, foregrounded as perhaps never before in the history of cinema. Warhol exalts his subjects' auratic beauty in the very process of using the camera to uncover their behavioral peculiarities and to reduce them to objects.

Benjamin (1969) seems to suggest that there's something secondary and factitious about the aura of the movie star, in contrast to the aura associated with the "ritual value" of works of art made before the advent of mechanical reproduction:

The film responds to the shriveling of the aura with an artificial build-up of the "personality" outside the studio. The cult of the movie star, fostered by the money of the film industry, preserves not the unique aura of the person but the "spell of the personality," the phony spell of a commodity. (p. 231)

Warhol undermines this distinction: his films sardonically demonstrate that the "unique aura" of the person is always already artificial, that it is never anything more or other than the factitious, commodified "spell of the personality." Benjamin doesn't pursue his own insights about mechanical reproduction radically enough when he subordinates them to a narrative in which the aura gradually de-cays, as "cult value" is replaced by "exhibition value" and as an aristocratic society gives way to a capitalist one. The problem with such a narrative is that our notions of precapitalist social and economic formations are themselves back-projected from the perspective of commodity capitalism. Aura, which Benjamin (1969) beau-tifully defines as "the unique phenomenon of a distance, however close it may be" (p. 222), is itself a category derived from and pertaining to commodity production. The aura's distance derives first and foremost from what Marx describes as the "mysterious," "enigmatic," and "mystical" character of the commodity-as-fetish. The aura is not the vestige of an older form of social relations, as Benjamin seems to imagine. On the contrary, it is a commodity, only thinkable under the regime of generalized commodity production, for it is a *product*, an image produced for and exchanged with others, something that cannot be experienced or enjoyed by and for oneself.

The aura always implies a certain *pastness*. But this sense of the past is itself created in the present: it is the temporal expression of the aura's dis-tance. Nostalgia—as Warhol, with his camp aesthetic, knows all too well—is a phenomenon of the moment in which it is savored, and not of the time to which it ostensibly refers. The pastness that I yearningly reach for has nothing to do with the actual past; it is rather the obsession of a past time that never was present, and that therefore cannot be remembered or recovered. Warhol is fascinated by *left-overs*, "things that were discarded, that everybody knew were no good" (1975, 93). Something out of style or obsolete is invested with what might be called signifi-cance-in-the-past-tense: it acquires a "lost" meaning that it never had in the first place. A camp object is enjoyed in the decadent splendor of its having already vanished. But Warhol's "recycling" of "leftovers" is finally just a self-conscious ap-propriation of something that Hollywood does all the time. The aura—of an object or of a person—is a retrospective formation that needs to be fabricated in the film studio, precisely in order that it may be destroyed; it comes into being, *nachträglich*, as a consequence of its very disintegration. This is why I claim, in Chapter 1, that cinema involves the repeated shattering of the aura, and not just its simple absence. There is no dialectic of estrangement and recuperation, but only the paradoxical proximity of distance itself: "a distance, however close it may be."

Warhol plays brilliantly with this infinitely ambiguous and strangely intimate distance. His voyeuristic remoteness behind the camera—from which he would often simply walk away, if he had not already left the actual task of filming to others—is matched by a cinematically fabricated distance that becomes intrinsic to the very worldly presence of the people he portrays. His films are not remote from their subjects so much as they explore a remoteness that is manufactured, and that subsists, at the very heart of postmodern subjectivity. By placing everyone and everything, indifferently and casually, before the eye of the camera, Warhol demonstrates that the production and destruction of the aura cannot be separated, that this ambivalent, duplicitous process is at the heart of the mystique of the film star's personality, and that the "spell of the personality," thus objectified or reduced to an effect of pure visibility, can be equated with late capitalist subjectivity *tout court*. This is the real reason everybody will be famous for fifteen minutes. Someone is interesting or noteworthy because he or she is famous, rather than the reverse; subjectivity is an effect of celebrity, which in turn is a mechanically (re)produced hyperbole of appearance.

Warhol at once makes us conscious of his subjects' casual and contingent beauty and makes it impossible for us to imagine anything beyond this beauty. The soul is an effect of the body, and psychology is lodged in the evidence of the epidermis. The people exposed in Warhol's movies are thus pure creatures of the aura, of its projection and its shattering: they remain as empty and remote as they are perversely fascinating. Warhol's camera at once exalts its subjects and debases them; it accords them fame and glamour, but at the price of embarrassment and humiliation. In Warhol's media-drenched world, to be is to be perceived by the camera. My existence is confirmed only at a remove from myself; my self-presence is a state without privacy, one in which I am excessively visible, and therefore abjectly vulnerable to exposure (in all the senses of this word). The seductive distance of the Superstar that constitutes his or her aura and the sadistic violation or obscene penetration of that distance are simultaneous effects of this dependence upon the cinematic apparatus.

Drag

Personality, then, is a pure image, the most transitory and superficial layer of the body: it is something that needs to be put on each day, just like clothing and makeup, the hypervisible accoutrements of fashionable socialites and drag queens. And indeed, drag queens occupy a privileged position in the world of Warhol's films. They carry the logic of pure appearance, of selfhood as artifice, and of existence as an image solely for the camera and for others, to its most extreme and powerful—and perhaps also most subversive—point. Ronald Tavel (1989), writing of Mario Montez's performance in Warhol's first sound film, *Harlot*, notes that female Hollywood stars are themselves already virtually in drag: "Jean Harlow is a transvestite, as are Mae West and Marilyn Monroe, in the sense that their feminineness is so exaggerated that it becomes a commentary on womanhood rather than the real thing or representation of realness" (p. 66).

But is "feminineness" ever anything "real"? Hyperbolic exaggeration ruptures the logic by which we accept as "real" whatever conforms to a standardized "representation of realness." Drag is akin to Warhol's notion of "bad performance," in that it is so spectacular and so immediate that it cannot pretend to the authenticity of a "true" representation: it ruins the very notion of representation. Severo Sarduy (1989) thus describes the simulacral logic of drag:

The transvestite does not imitate woman. For him, à la limite, there is no woman; he knows—and paradoxically he may be the only one who knows this—that she is just appearance. . . . The transvestite does not copy; he simulates, since there is no norm to invite and magnetize his transformation, to determine his metaphor; instead, it is the non-existence of the worshipped being that constitutes the space, the region, or the support of his simulation, of his methodical imposture between laughter and death. (p. 93)

By foregrounding the constructed and always clichéd nature of personal identity, and by lodging that identity so insistently and so exclusively in outward appearance, the transvestite upsets the norms and models that generate and regulate our gendered, and supposedly interior, selves.

I don't mean by this that the drag queen reveals, in a kind of Brechtian alienation effect, the falsity of (his own) femininity, and thereby of all gender constructions. On the contrary, a drag queen's greatest triumph is often that of "naturalizing" his artifice, of successfully "passing" as a woman. But even when the "imposture" is obvious, as when a drag performer explicitly displays himself as a-man-posing-as-a-woman, the effect is less to deconstruct the self-evidence of appearances than it is to project a new and heightened mode of appearance, and therefore of sexual personality—one that doesn't conform to the prevalent binary coding of gender. In drag, then, something more profound—or, strictly speaking, more superficial—than ideological unmasking is at stake. When they change clothes, drag queens perform an actual corporeal transformation, rather than merely mirror a situation for the benefit of critical consciousness. They grasp the social mechanism by which identity is ascribed on the basis of appearance, and they divert or hijack this mechanism for their own ends. They don't expose and discredit the social construction of gender; quite the opposite, they appropriate it, they revel in it, and they push it to new extremes. It is for this reason that, as Robert Thomas argues, drag has been a crucial mode of empowerment, especially for working-class gay men (personal communication, 1991). Drag performers exteriorize themselves so completely, they exalt visibility and artificiality so ostentatiously, they enact the cinematic fiction of "femininity" so precisely, they so utterly give themselves over to the mystique of the aura, that they disrupt the very models (of appearance and behavior, and ultimately of sexual "identity") that they are ostensibly imitating. If power functions in our society, as Foucault argues, by assigning a deep "truth" to sexuality, then drag subverts this power, insofar as it brings all the expressions of sex and gender to the surface, freeing them from essence and from signification.

   Warhol admires drag queens for the particularly "hard work" (1975, 54) that their appearance requires. He slyly remarks that for everybody, "being sexed is ... hard work," but he immediately adds that drag queens "do double-time. They do all the double things: they think about shaving and not shaving, of primping and not primping, of buying men's clothes and women's clothes" (p. 98). Like everybody else in our society, but more intensely than anybody else, drag queens work at "being sexed," at producing and displaying themselves as gendered beings. They push this forced labor even to excess, until they reach a point where there is "no norm" any longer, but "just appearance."

   Subjectivity is lodged in the body, and not in any presumed interiority. But the body is a flat surface of inscription and reflection, comprising all the image layers that are incised or overlaid upon it. It is composed or imposed from the outside in; it is a matter of dress and cosmetics as much as it is one of skin, genitals, and hair. This is why Warhol (1975) "believe[s] in low lights and trick mirrors" (p. 51), and why he declares that "nudity is a threat to my existence"

(p. 11). The body (like the cinema screen) becomes in postmodern practice a "flatbed," rather than a window of the soul (I borrow the term from Leo Steinberg 1972, 82–91, who applies it to the paintings of Rauschenberg, and then Warhol). Drag queens don't "originate" their own images; ambiguous, they both subvert and reinforce traditional stereotypes of gender when they provide "living testimony to the way women used to want to be, the way some people still want them to be, and the way some women still actually want to be" (Warhol 1975, 54). But in any case, drag queens grasp the fictiveness of this "want to be"; they know that "there is no woman." They understand the constructivist logic of the body better than anybody else, which makes them perfect Warholian Superstars. They shine in the immediacy of their presence, which is identical to their performance. Paradoxically, it can be said more truthfully of transvestites than of anybody else that they are exactly as — and *only* as — they *appear*.

Fabricating the Real

As it is with drag queens, so it is with all of Warhol's performers in *Chelsea Girls* and the later films. Sometimes the Superstars are shooting drugs, masturbating, or engaging in hysterical tirades; at other times they may just be eating a banana, talking on the telephone, or sitting on the toilet. In any case, the subjectivity displayed in these performances is always imposed from outside: it is unstable and supplemental, a mode of behavioristic reactivity, at best a shifting pragmatic response to unavoidable social stimuli. Warhol's films demonstrate and document every aspect of this reactivity, of the coerced and/or resistant construction of bodies as selves. Simon Watney (1989) rightly observes that "no artist has ever undermined notions of Self more thoroughly or insistently than Warhol. No artist has ever explored more exhaustively the implication that the Self is merely 'a practical convenience,' as Leo Bersani puts it" (p. 120).

Warhol sometimes likes to claim that his films are "like actual sociological 'For Instances' ... like documentaries" (1975, 48), providing audiences with a sensationalistic "look at real people" and at "realistic scenes of modern life" (Warhol and Hackett 1990, 280). And these films are indeed "realistic" in precisely the sense that drag queens are: they fabricate their reality rather than merely re-present it. They bury the myth of the authentic self beneath a delirious proliferation of willfully excessive, eccentric "personalities." Warhol's Superstars multiply the *effects* of subjective identity, sometimes by their unconscious assumption, but more often through a deliberate, gleefully campy reenactment, of the processes by which personal identity is socially produced and enforced. As Deleuze (1990) says of the simulacrum, performance in this sense "produces an *effect* of resemblance" by means of an initial "disparity," "difference," or "dissimilarity" (p. 258).

Again and again, Warhol's actors and camera discover points at which the banal, unconscious gestures of everyday life, the signs of those behaviors that are socially defined as nonnormative (homosexuality, sadomasochism, and drug addiction), and the self-conscious posturing of Hollywood clichés all seamlessly intersect. Moving between the imperceptible and the ultratheatrical, between the unconscious and the hyperconscious, between the uncoded and the overdetermined, these films at once "naturalize" or "normalize" the "aberrant" and imply the sheer contingency and potential deviance of all processes of social normalization. Warhol never seeks to undo or to unmask the mechanisms of normalization, of subjectification, of ideology, and of cinematic illusion; but by hyperbolically assuming and incorporating these mechanisms, by subsuming subjective self-presentation and cinematic process within them, his films coolly foreground the ways in which such mechanisms are always already at work, unsurpassable, immanent to the real. Warhol puts all of American society into drag, as it were; he grasps social life, on the level of the body, as a simulacral and superficial product.

Even passively viewing Warhol's films, we aren't spared the effects of such transformations. These performances disrupt our inveterate habit of inferring identity from appearance and behavior, of taking the latter as signs of the former. As Paul Arthur (1989) notes, Warhol's films provoke a "hyperawareness of our own corporeality," since as we watch "the desire to substitute affect for physical gesture is mobilized only to be rendered absurd" (p. 150). We are thrown back upon the evidence of the flesh, and nothing but the flesh. Visible and physical surfaces resist translation into psychological depth. We find ourselves unable to penetrate appearances, to interpret expressions, to ascribe interiority and sentiment to the bodies exposed to our gaze. We cannot read their postures, gestures, and countenances as indications of inner emotional states. We are made oppressively aware that corporeal appearance and behavior in fact precede identity, that they are the "quasi-causes" (to use Deleuze's term for the action of the simulacrum; 1990, 142–53) of which identity is a transitory effect, and that such quasi-causes are themselves incited and relayed by the presence of the movie camera, and by all the codes of cinematic display.

And so, the more fascinated we get, the more our voyeurism is deprived of an anchor. That strange internal distance, that remoteness from oneself as much as from others, that characterizes both Warhol behind the camera and the Superstars in front of the camera is extended to us as well. The position of the spectator becomes interchangeable with those of the filmmaker and performers, not because these positions "identify" with one another, as orthodox film theory would have it, but because they share or suffer from a common inability to perform any act of identification, because they are seduced alike into a hysterical paralysis of the faculty that judges and makes distinctions. In the throes of this paralysis, in the blank distance of the camera's indifferent, insufferable gaze, the poles of self and other, reality and artifice, sincerity and affectation, normality and eccentricity, activity and passivity, voyeurism and exhibitionism, all become infinitely reversible, and endlessly, mutually substitutable.

Immerse Yourself!

And so we immerse ourselves, as Foucault suggests, in this stupidity; we abjectly enjoy this passivity, this hysteria, this suspension of the intelligence. "Because the more you look at the same exact thing, the more the meaning goes away, and the better and emptier you feel" (Warhol and Hackett 1990, 50). It is as if the sheer quantitative accumulation of images made up for—supplemented—the absence of intellectual commentary. A gratuitous redundancy takes over the place once reserved (in the long-obsolete era of high modernist art and Frankfurt school theory) for strategic deferral, for critical negativity, and for utopian speculation. There is something unavoidably affirmative about Warhol's very indifference: in Blanchot's (1981) words, something "like an inexorable affirmation, without beginning or end" (p. 47). One film after another, one Marilyn canvas after another: images are incessantly repeated, accumulated, magnified. Warhol yearns only for emptiness, but he knows that the very project of emptying out entails an addition, not a subtraction. His reductions only increase the clutter: "I really believe in empty spaces, but on the other hand, because I'm still making some art, I'm still making junk for people to put in their spaces that I believe should be empty. . . . I can't even empty my own spaces" (Warhol 1975, 144).

Biographical accounts tell us that Warhol could never throw

anything away; he put everything he had used up or no longer needed into boxes, and then left the boxes in storage, carefully dated, never to be opened again. Images are pieces of "junk" in precisely this way: obsessive, obtrusive, inexpungeable physical traces. Hyperreality is not the death of the real, but its supplement and its embellishment, for you actually add something to a face when you reduce it to its image, preserving its trace in a Polaroid snapshot and then transferring the photograph via silkscreen onto canvas, just as you adorn that same face by leaving out the pimples and blemishes when you paint it. Less is more, not in the purist sense of a minimalist aesthetic, but in the literal sense that the more you get rid of, the more leftovers, detritus, and bizarre odds and ends you are stuck with. Warhol embraces anything and everything in the same weirdly unreflective affirmation: "The world fascinates me. It's so nice, whatever it is. I approve of what everybody does. . . . I wouldn't judge anybody" (in Berg 1989, 60). Or again: "Anything a person really wants is okay with me" (1975, 194). Every desire is equally singular and equally stereotypical, equal to every other desire. Such mindless, ludicrously infinite approbation is of course undecidably subversive *or* conformist: it coolly effaces hierarchies of value just as much as it recalls the relentless cheerfulness of TV advertising campaigns.

This ambiguous affirmation, or affirmation of ambiguity, is the great postmodern lesson of Warhol and his art. Baudrillard (1983) describes postmodern simulation as an endeavor "to empty out the real, extirpate all psychology, all subjectivity, to move the real back to pure objectivity. In fact, this objectivity is only that of the pure look—objectivity at last liberated from the object, that is nothing more than the blind relay station of the look which sweeps over it" (pp. 142–43). In a certain sense, this is an extremely accurate description of Warhol's aims and procedure. But Baudrillard's *tone* (the effect of his style, which is of course more important than his substance) is totally at odds with the Warholian sensibility. Baudrillard always portrays simulation as an act of radical negation, as the nihilistic "extermination" of the real. Beneath all the layers of irony, it seems that a nostalgia for concreteness, the last echo of lament for a vanished and irretrievable reality, oddly haunts the French master of cool. This kind of hidden nostalgia is utterly foreign to Warhol. With his bland humor, American pragmatism, and acute sense of camp, Warhol has no rage for negativity, and no regrets for a (supposedly) lost presence and immediacy. He searches out and busily disseminates those very signs, images, and traces that Baudrillard depicts under the colors of inexorable fatality, and secretly deplores. Warhol remarks that to see, reproduced on the movie screen, scenes at which he had been present in actual life "somehow made it seem more real to me (I mean, more *un*real, which was actually more real) than it had when it was happening" (Warhol and Hackett 1990, 251). This is a vision of hyperreality without Baudrillard's apocalyptic sense of closure. The event is swallowed up in its own replication, but this replication is only one event the more, contingent and superfluous. (Warhol is referring to the unique showing of his 25-hour film ****, in which images from two projectors were continually superimposed. This event encompasses the entire trajectory of postmodern vision: the processes of the construction and shattering of the aura, of mechanical reproduction and destructive consumption, of the delirious proliferation of images and of their instantaneous obsolescence.)

The real is not abolished when it is interpenetrated with artifice or reduced to its own resemblance so much as it is affirmed in its residual subsistence (the image as trace) and in its irreducible surplus (the image as embellishment). The cinema's icy exaltation of surfaces, its capture of people in a state of "pure objectivity," and its subjection of all images equally to the indifference of the "pure look"—all this precludes any radical destruction or negation. Warhol's formula for hyperreality—more unreal and *therefore* more real—involves an ever-open series of accidents and happenings. Nothing could be further from Baudrillard's scenario of the suppression of all events and contingencies in the absolute reign of a master binary code. In Warholian simulation, images and traces rise repeatedly from below, rather than being imposed once and for all from above. The evacuation of meanings and identities, the surfeit of images, the plethora of recording devices, the ubiquity of mirrors: all this implies a multiplication of physical presence, rather than its effacement.

Transforming himself into a machine, reducing expression to its visible inherence in the body, Warhol explores the neutral positivity of "what remains when you take everything away," which is how Deleuze and Guattari (1987) define the "Body without Organs" (p. 151). He confronts what Blanchot (1981) calls "the stubbornness of what remains when everything vanishes and the dumbfoundedness of what appears when nothing exists" (p. 47). He approaches Wittgenstein's sense of a world in which descriptions and language games are forever ramifying and forever changing, precisely because there cannot be such a thing as a private sensation or a private language. All these thinkers grasp theoretically what Warhol experiences and produces practically: the positivity and untotalizable plenitude of what's come to be known as the postmodern condition. They affirm this condition, refusing to see it as a phenomenon of belatedness and loss. Conservative elitists, liberal humanists, Marxist critics of the "culture industry," and hip theorists of media saturation unite to deplore the waning and flattening of affect, the paralysis of will and agency, that they see as intrinsic to contemporary culture. But Warhol, like the theorists mentioned above, can help us to view things otherwise, to grasp *affirmatively* the affects and perceptions, and even the implicit politics, of postmodern culture. Warhol (1975) summarizes his artistic and personal trajectory in the 1960s thus:

I think that once you see emotions from a certain angle you can never think of them as real again. That's what more or less has happened to me. I don't really know if I was ever capable of love, but after the 60s I never thought in terms of "love" again. However, I became what you might call fascinated *by certain people. (p. 27)*

Warhol's films aren't only *about*, but they *embody*, they produce and reproduce, this emotionless coolness, this strangely impersonal fascination. Hence their frequently sadomasochistic ambiance, which is a style, an attitude, more than it is a theme or subject matter. From a reservoir of almost infinite indifference, these films reveal bodies in the throes of ecstasy and torment. They indeed explore states of insensibility, but in this insensibility they discover infinite gradations of pleasure, and even more of pain. They wallow in shamelessness and embarrassment, in the abjection of willful exhibitionism and in the still greater abjection of unintended exposure. They destroy "emotion" only in order to heighten and intensify different forms of experience, new modes of affect and feeling. American film and media culture today, from David Lynch to Arnold Schwarzenegger to Madonna, emulates Warhol by exalting the media fabrication of selfhood, by indulging in the kitschy display of ostentatiously fake sentiment, and by placing emotions "in quotation marks" (or, as one might say, under erasure). We should not be too quick to see these procedures as symptoms of narcissistic withdrawal, as ironic reserve and refusal to be implicated, as repressive desublimation, or as a smug display of hipness. The repetition of stereotypes may be a way of unleashing singularity, even as the blankness and willed dumbness of quotation at a distance may be a means for inciting and magnifying passion. Simulacral artifice and inauthenticity become ways of affirming the life of the body; the passively voyeuristic dispersion of our attention and the exhibitionistic compulsion always to perform before the camera help to liberate subjective experience from the confining armor of the self.

Conceptual Pornography

Finally, Warhol's art and films can be described as a kind of conceptual pornography. I mean this as a term of praise, not opprobrium; and I think it applies whether or not a given work is explicitly sexual. Just like pornography, Warhol's films at once provide titillation and provoke boredom. They render everything visible, and they bring everything back to the visible evidence of the body. They portray eerily blank personalities, devoid of interiority, of warmth or emotional resonance, or of any capacity for empathy. They incite reactions in their audiences that are immediately physiological much more than they are intellectual or reflective, and that in any case cannot be described as psychological states. (As Wittgenstein, Warhol, and pornographers all know so well, disinterest, expectation, and arousal are not psychological states.)

In their voyeuristic distance, Warhol's films, like pornographic ones, crassly exploit the exhibitionism of their actors. The frivolity of these works wipes out any pretension to redeeming social value. Their obviousness and overt idiocy disarms intellectual commentary in advance; if you try to approach them on such terms—as I have been doing for so many pages—you've already missed the point. And as is also the case with pornography, the political implications of Warhol's films cannot be circumscribed in terms of a binary alternative between complicity and resistance, or between advocacy and critique. *Of course* Warhol is complicit with the commodified world of fashion, publicity, and the culture industry; it was logical that he would eventually seek to make films (though with only limited success) that would actually earn money in the porn market. But such complicity, to the limit of total coincidence, is beside the point. It is precisely *because* Warhol's movies—like pornographic films in general—extinguish critical consciousness that they are so scandalously able to render the mechanisms of power *explicit*. Warhol's films calmly, unprotestingly mimic not only commodification, but also the processes of normalization and sexualization that Foucault has shown to be ubiquitous in our society. They do not ever oppose these forms of power, but by taking "deviance" for granted—which, among other things, was a way of articulating a gay style in those pre-Stonewall days—they drown the postmodern technologies of power in a sea of limitless approbation, in the perverse excesses of their own exercise.

My own words are swept up in this redundancy effect. They become drained of sense, even as they proliferate indefinitely. Warhol's surfaces invite endless commentary, yet in the end they leave us with nothing to say. Warhol's art arises out of the radical disjunction between language and appearance; words can provide no equivalent for, can give no sense to, Warhol's endless accumulation of images, of objects, and of bodies. As Warhol remarks, "The whole idea behind making these movies in the first place was to be ridiculous. I mean, Edie and I both knew they were a joke—that's why we were doing them!" (Warhol and Hackett 1990, 124). And again: "That's what so many people never understood about us. They expected us to take the things we believed in seriously, which we never did—we weren't intellectuals" (p. 169).

Warhol's films lure us toward a ridiculous, drugged-out, nonjudgmental, noncritical point: one at which the elucidations of the intellectual critic are even more ridiculous. Yet even as I recognize this, the stupidity of Warhol's bodies continues to exert an insidious and beautiful fascination. I can only get involved in the spectacle in my own turn. Warhol is a faceless mirror; like everybody else who has written on him, in expounding on his peculiarities I have succeeded only in exposing myself. I have tried to *use* him, but he has ended up using me, just as he did everybody else. The critic can either praise Warhol's works or condemn them, can continue looking at them or can walk away, or can even attempt—typically and unavoidably—to transform the distance of their indifference into the very different distance of critical estrangement and judgment. Yet all these strategies ultimately fail, because all of them only add to the interminable flood of words, which mimics but never corresponds to Warhol's equally interminable flood of images. Warhol gives me no choice, finally, other than to go along with him. Perhaps for this reason, my fascination and delight are tinged with the peculiar feeling of an avidly desired, yet disturbingly inescapable, embarrassment and abjection.

VII

A Note on Bresson

Warhol and Bresson

ANDY WARHOL and Robert Bresson—at first glance, no pairing seems more perverse and inappropriate. These two directors are worlds apart aesthetically; the differences between them are immense and immediately obvious. Bresson is usually regarded as a religious and reflective filmmaker: he is the master of what Paul Schrader (1988) calls "transcendental style in film," someone whose art—as Susan Sontag (1983) puts it—"detaches, provokes reflection" and "appeals to the feelings through the route of the intelligence" (p. 121). What common ground could there be between Bresson's severe intelligence and Jansenist austerity and the campiness, permissiveness, and overall laxness of Warhol's films? It even seems that Bresson and Warhol can be opposed point by point. Bresson is an *auteur* in the classic style, an artisan controlling every aspect of the film; Warhol usually left the decisions, as well as the work, to others. Bresson is a scrupulously careful director who made only thirteen laboriously perfected films in more than forty years; Warhol is a passive and negligent one, who at the peak of his activity in the Factory turned out virtually a film a week. Bresson explores intense interior states, and Warhol sticks to externals; Bresson is a mystic and a moralist, and Warhol is a materialist and an aesthete. Bresson hates the theatrical falsity of "cinema" as much as Warhol loves the mystique and artifice of the "movies."

Bresson's films are composed of short takes, which are then rigorously and severely edited; Warhol's films use long, uninterrupted takes, and eschew editing almost completely. The actors' words and gestures are always carefully choreographed in Bresson's films, but they are unrehearsed, improvised, or left to chance in Warhol's. Bresson continually fragments and reconstructs cinematic space, while Warhol casually accepts the space in front of the camera as an unchanging given; Bresson compresses time, and Warhol dilates it. Bresson's art is impersonal, essentialist, hermetic, formalist, and opposed to any sort of popular culture: it is quintessentially modernist. Warhol's films, on the other hand, are decidedly postmodernist: they are facile, formally slack, content and experience centered, knowingly inauthentic, aggressively superficial, blatantly obvious, obsessed with tackiness and glamor, and filled with bizarre personalities. Indeed, I argue in chapter VI that even Warhol's earliest and most minimal films reject the premises of any modernist aesthetic.

Nonetheless, Bresson and Warhol *do* share a certain attitude toward personal experience, and toward the presentation of that experience in the cinematic apparatus. Even Paul Schrader (1988), who goes further than anyone else in making the case for Bresson as a spiritual filmmaker, timeless in his concerns and alienated from secular culture, concedes that Bresson and Warhol share a "surface aesthetics" of the "everyday" (p. 62), a powerful drive toward "stasis" (pp. 82–86, 166–68), and so great a refusal of "emotional involvement" that they risk boring the viewer (p. 70). Schrader is careful to differentiate Bresson's project to go beyond the immediate and *"express* the Transcendent" (p. 6) from what he regards as Warhol's "parody of the Transcendent" (p. 112) and nihilistic vision of "life as totally deprived of meaning, expression, drama or cathartic" (p. 42); but I want to argue that the affinities between the two are sufficiently deep to problematize and deconstruct Schrader's oppositions, or those that I have stated above.

Bresson and Warhol are both literalists of the body: they both foreground the immediate actions and reactions of the flesh itself, at the expense of any depth or interiority that these movements might be taken to signify. They both record the
minutest details of bodily repose and movement; they both present (often nonpro-
fessional) actors who don't "act" in any conventional way, who do not manifest or
project emotion, and with whom the audience consequently cannot identify. The
radical styles of Warhol and Bresson, however different in inspiration and in aim,
have at least one thing in common: they are both concerned to produce the *effect*
of evacuating subjectivity and of subverting canons of representation.

Focus on the Body

It is only through an intense and precise attention to the body that Bresson
broaches his ultimate religious themes of loss and redemption: "Unusual approaches to bodies. On the watch for the most imperceptible, the most inward
movements" (Bresson 1986, 35). No filmmaker has ever given so crucial a role to
bodily postures and gestures, to physical comportments and to the motions of
hands and feet. Think of the famous scene in the railway station in *Pickpocket*,
where the camera follows the passage of the stolen objects from hand to hand. But
this effect is not limited to such bravura action sequences. All of Bresson's films
are filled with unsignifying details, such as close-ups of somebody's feet as he or
she crosses a room or climbs the stairs; violent and climactic actions are frequently
elided, but these weary, quotidian expenditures of effort never are. Bresson always
shows us the efforts and fatigue of the body, rather than the alienation and anguish
of the spirit; even if the latter is supposedly his theme. His resolve is always to
"apply myself to insignificant (non-significant) images" (p. 11).

Hands and feet are not conventionally taken to signify inner
states: this is why Bresson gives us close-ups of these appendages' "inward move-

ments," in violation of the editing convention that reserves the close-up for the task of emphasizing significant details of plot and action, and (especially) for underlining psychology by presenting an empathic and expressive vision of the human face. Even the faces of Bresson's actors, of course, are blank and devoid of sentiment; the films insistently focus on gestural and behavioral details, to the exclusion of any facial, vocal, and tonal expression. There is no correspondence between inner and outer, between visible surface and emotional or spiritual state. And the spectator is drawn into this state of inexpressive stasis as well, thanks to Bresson's dry, minimalist stylization of both mise-en-scène and editing. Bresson (1986) remarks that he avoids "obvious *travelling* or *panning* shots," because such shots "do not correspond to the movements of the eye," and hence work "to separate the eye from the body" (p. 89). Spectatorial vision is always something *embodied* for Bresson, even as his characters live exclusively as bodies. Sontag (1983) writes that Bresson's later films "refuse[e] the visual" and "renounce the beautiful" (p. 134). But this ascetic neutralization (and de-eroticization) of seeing is not an expression of formalist purism (though of course there is much of that in Bresson) so much as it implies a rejection of anything extravisual and a radical corporealization of vision itself. In Bresson's films, sight cannot be panoptical or omnivoyeuristic, precisely because it is so insistently, immediately tactile.

Bresson is notorious for his hatred of professional actors, and for his disdain for any sort of psychological explanation or motivation. He prefers to work with "models," nonprofessionals who have never acted before and whom he rehearses in their roles entirely by rote. His aim is to "radically suppress *intentions* in your models" (Bresson 1986, 15). The deadpan, affectless acting style of his films is attained only through a long process of wearing down and emptying out the performers. And so Bresson instructs his "models": "Don't think what you're saying, don't think what you're doing.... Don't think *about* what you say, don't think *about* what you do.... One must not act either somebody else or oneself. One must not act *anybody*" (pp. 15, 57). The Hollywood star is always doubly acting: Bogart plays both the role of Bogart and that of whatever character he is supposed to be in a given film. But Bresson's models do not act; they are neither themselves nor somebody else. They do not project themselves in either of the senses that a Hollywood actor does. The models *are* exactly as, and only as, they *appear*. They are literally present in their empty and repetitive gestures, in their vacuous images on the screen. They have been turned into mindless automatons, voided alike of inner being and outer expression.

Bresson (1986) continually reminds us that "nine-tenths of our movements obey habit and automatism. It is anti-nature to subordinate them to will and to thought" (p. 22). His films endeavor to free automatism from the distorting lenses of will and thought, to put it into motion, to seize its movements in the models as they appear on screen, and finally to transmit these movements to the audience as well. In their silences and ellipses, Bresson's films thus destroy all our myths of depth, interiority, and psychological integrity. We cannot attribute identity to either the actors or the characters, just as we cannot read their blankness psychologically, as a sign of reticence, despair, or alienation. Bresson confronts us with "involuntarily expressive models (not willfully inexpressive ones)" (p. 71), figures entirely coincident with, and having no existence beyond, their flat and barely perceptible gestures on the screen. Bresson's anonymous models extinguish subjective inwardness by means of this minimal yet absolute presence, just as radically as Warhol's Superstars do through their campily stereotyped and exaggerated acting, their ostentatious displays of non-self-coincidence.

Bresson's antipsychological treatment of his actors goes together with his elliptical editing style. Bresson's editing is "elliptical" both in the sense that it is so conventional and so unostentatious that it approaches a condition of invisibility and in the more usual sense that it is highly compressed, operating mostly through omission. The narrator of Michael Brodsky's (1985) novel *Detour* muses over "the ambiguity of a cut" at the end of *Mouchette*, the juxtaposition of the girl's suicide with the shot of a tractor: "Did the turn of her head bring the tractor into being. Or was the vision of the tractor imposed on her sight, on her cloud of unseeing.... Did the tractor express her, did the tractor cut her off, did the tractor have nothing to do with her" (p. 61). These questions are unanswerable; it is impossible to reduce the alternatives. We respond automatically to the sequence of shots, accepting the connection between the tractor and the suicide; but we are paralyzed by our very response, and find ourselves unable to explain just in what—beyond simple contiguity—the connection consists. Our reactions, like those of the characters in the film, become so immediate and unconscious that we cannot (re)construct the usual chains of causal or psychological explanation. This is what makes Bresson's films seem so fatalistic and preordained, yet so enigmatic and inscrutable, all at once. Absolute necessity and sheer contingency are conjoined, as when the counterfeit money passes from hand to hand, generating an ever-escalating series of catastrophes, in *L'Argent*. Shot is linked to shot, and action to action, all the more rigorously and inexorably in that no justification or rationalization of these links is available. There is no choice and no explanation; the middle terms provided by will and thought simply drop out. The chain of epiphenomenal effects is divorced from any notion of an underlying or sufficient cause, and directly equated instead with the linear chain of images on celluloid. Gesture answers gesture and body joins to body, without the intervention of the spirit.

Affirming the Real

This automatism, this refusal of depth, and this obsessive focus on the body are Bresson's means for attaining and affirming the real. Ordinary or "natural" perception—enmeshed in a metaphysics of theatrical presence—never encounters the real in its primordial nakedness: "The real, when it has reached the mind, is already not real any more. Our too thoughtful, too intelligent eye" (Bresson 1986, 69). Even the most immediate and phenomenologically pure perception is already caught up in a drama of imitation and recognition, a re-presentation in the theater of the mind. Ordinary perception, precisely like the art of theater, "suppresses [nature] in favor of a naturalness that is learned and maintained by exercises" (p. 8). In order actually to attain the real, it is necessary to extinguish thought and consciousness, to reject canons of naturalness and verisimilitude, and to break down pregiven structures and hierarchies of representation.

Bresson regards cinematography, without contradiction, both as an unmediated tracing of the real and as an arbitrary process of construction (I have already argued this point in chapter 1). The camera captures "the crude real" (p. 69), immediately and passively, "with a machine's scrupulous indifference" (p. 26). But "the crude real will not by itself yield truth" (p. 96). A rigorous composition and construction, the *writing* of cinematography, is required in order to affirm the power of the real, to keep it from degenerating into mere real*ism*, to avoid the trap of turning images into clichés by "display[ing] things as everyone is in the habit of seeing them" (p. 84). Only the exact, careful juxtaposition of sounds and images allows us to attain the real as it is, without or before the intervention of consciousness, for "to create is not to deform or invent persons and things. It is to tie new relationships between persons and things which are, and *as they are*" (p. 14). The cinematographer discovers the real precisely by constructing it. Bresson orchestrates new relationships between sounds and images in order to force us to perceive persons and things apart from the meanings we customarily project upon them. A compulsive automatism ruptures, and replaces, our usual habits of association and interpretation. We encounter the real only when we are forcibly and violently propelled into it, riveted to it, after having been uprooted from ourselves. "Your film is not made for a stroll with the eyes, but for going right into, for being totally absorbed in" (pp. 85–86); and again, "To set up a film is to bind persons to each other and to objects by looks" (p. 12).

Editing must impel the viewer into the real; it must force objects and images into new connections, while at the same time leaving them exactly *"as they are,"* without deforming or newly inventing them. The "crude real" is raw material for Bresson's radical constructivism: things are grasped by the camera in their absolute, asignifying immanence, before they have been organized into stratified structures or organic wholes. Editing therefore presupposes a prior movement of pulverization or atomization, the resolution of bodies into their constituent elements. Bresson (1986) insists that "fragmentation . . . is indispensable if one does not want to fall into REPRESENTATION" (p. 84). His films are composed of part-objects that never combine into representational totalities, fragments that remain fragments even as they are inexorably linked one to another. These sounds and these images are not representations or metonymies of integral, previously existing entities; they are themselves autonomous, like elementary particles, material components of an actual new construction (and not a mere representation) of the body. The compositional logic of Bresson's films is that of what Deleuze and Guattari (1987) call the *plane of consistency*: a space-time in which "there is no structure, any more than there is genesis. There are only relations of movement and rest, speed and slowness between unformed elements, or at least between elements that are relatively unformed, molecules and particles of all kinds" (p. 266).

How does this work concretely? In many sequences of *Pickpocket*, for example, Bresson minimizes or eschews establishing shots, cutting rather between medium shots (e.g., Michel standing motionless in a crowd at the racetrack) and extreme close-ups (e.g., Michel's hand reaching into the other man's vest and removing the money). The effect is not to present the hand as a part of which Michel's body is a whole, but quite the contrary: it seems as if the hand moving slowly and the motionless torso and face (the body from the waist up) are independent vectors that must be conjoined to create the figure of Michel. The protagonist's character is thus constructed and defined by his physical apprenticeship as a thief, the ways in which he learns to move his hands, to avert his eyes, to jostle his victims, to escape unperceived through crowds. Michel's capture and ultimate transformation are similarly expressed through details (nearly autonomous close-ups or tight medium shots) of visual and physical contact: the shock of the cuffs closing around his wrist, the kisses through the prison bars at the end. Thus, the human body is never an organic whole in Bresson's films, but rather a repertory of disconnected, autonomic functions. And this fragmented body does not exist in a pregiven milieu; cinematic space and time are themselves articulated as extensions or constraints of bodily rest and motion. The relative paucity of establishing shots forces us to enter into the spaces of the films, to explore them only as the characters do by physically traversing them, in accordance with the rhythms of Bresson's editing. Thus, Deleuze (1986) writes of the "tactile space" of *Pickpocket*, of "vast fragmented spaces" constructed piece by piece in "rhythmic continuity shots" following the motions of the thieves' hands (pp. 108–9).

The evacuation of psychology and sentiment, the fragmentation of spaces, persons, and things, the hyperbolic accentuation of the blank materiality of the body: these are Bresson's most distinctive strategies as a filmmaker. I have been trying to suggest that such practices should not be regarded merely, or primarily, as forms of negation, deprivation, and destruction. For Bresson, every emptying out implies a positive attainment, a new accession to and affirmation of the real. Bresson seeks to extinguish what we already know and recognize, in order thereby to put us "face to face with the real" (Bresson 1986, 95) and "make visible what, without you, might perhaps never have been seen" (p. 72). In this sense, Bresson's films demand an *immanent* reading, supplementing or opposing the transcendent one put forth by the majority of his commentators, and most comprehensively by Schrader. Schrader (1988) describes Bresson's style in terms reminiscent of negative theology: he argues that the films express the ineffable, the totally Other and Transcendent, by emptying out the everyday to the point where a "disparity" emerges, where the experience of privation leads to a radical rupture with phenomenal existence (pp. 70–82). Emotion is repressed in the alienating quotidian world, but this ultimately leads it to burst forth in a spiritual dimension (the action of grace).

Now, such a reading may indeed correspond on one level to Bresson's intentions. But the quick recourse to an allegory of salvation doesn't really explain how Bresson produces the *effects* of affective dislocation, especially in the later films, which end not with redemption but with suicide or slaughter. Everything turns on the allegorical discontinuity between the deliberate banality of concrete expression (gestures, movements, words) and the ineffability of what is being expressed. There is no participatory movement, no direct and ready passage, linking one realm to the other. In Bresson's peculiar version of Roman Catholicism, the very logic of salvation demands that it be infinitely deferred. Everything is thrown back upon the everyday and upon the body. The radical incompossibility of worldly and spiritual existence is what must be incarnated and materialized, made actual and given flesh. An immanent reading of Bresson thus focuses on the strange literalness, the positivity and intensity, of his films' embodiments of abjection and humiliation, of despair and emptiness. There is no lack or negativity in the world of Bresson's films—not because the everyday is in any way redeemed, but precisely because nonredemption or deprivation, even to the point of death, is given full actuality, endowed with a tenacious corporeal subsistence.

Literal Images

It is here that I return to my initial suggestion of a parallel between Warhol and Bresson. Both directors are concerned exclusively with surfaces, with the literalness and immediacy of flattened images. Both deny any intrinsic value or meaning to these images, but affirm and mobilize them precisely on account of their blankness. Both directly equate the body and the image, rather than oppose these as the thing in itself is opposed to its representation. Both evacuate the image, or the body, of all its usual accretions: depth, interiority, significance, symbolic resonance. Both abjure theatrical conventions of verisimilitude in presentation and expressiveness in acting, in order instead to affirm the absolute coincidence of being and appearance, and to show the construction of subjectivity through a purely reactive "movement from the exterior to the interior" (Bresson 1986, 4). And most important, Warhol and Bresson alike reject all that is commonly thought of as emotion, in favor of a rigorous, yet oddly seductive, neutrality and indifference. But in so doing, they display and explore the hitherto neglected realm of asubjective affect: the passions and affections, the stresses and transformations of the body. Warhol's films oscillate between a disquieting stillness—positive inscription of coldness, intensity of the flesh even at degree zero—and the frenetic orgies of an unrestrained exhibitionism. Bresson's films, quite differently, articulate an exaltation and pain rooted in the sufferings, the endurance, and the ascetic metamorphoses of the subjugated and humiliated body. But both directors exhibit a strange, impersonal kind of affect, one that is irreducible to psychological sentiment, that in fact can be liberated only through the rupturing of personal identity and the fragmentation of homogeneous space and time.

Bresson thus emerges, paradoxically perhaps, as a powerfully materialist filmmaker. The reticence, austerity, and minimalism of his films are not the result of any supposed holding back of emotion, but in their own right constitute a new, positive and affirmative, form of expression. The body is central to the work of this director, even though he is generally celebrated for his rejection of the concerns of pleasure, politics, and the flesh. Far from clearing a space for disembodied spiritual reflection, Bresson's films work to produce and intensify affect, to render experience fully incarnate. His cinematography exalts whatever it encounters, raising everything to its utmost level of carnal intensity, its highest possible degree of embodiment. These films refuse psychological involvement and identification, the better to concentrate upon the body, and the body alone. They reveal and communicate the secret life of the flesh, a life so compressed and so extreme that it is nearly impossible to bear. The spiritual is itself finally a quality, an affection, of the body: it is what can also be called—with equal inadequacy—the intolerable. Bresson grasps the flesh with such directness and such intensity that he necessarily presents a vision in which grace is indistinguishable from suffering and abjection.

viii

Conclusions

The Cinematic Body

CINEMA'S GREATEST power may be its ability to evacuate meanings and identities, to proliferate resemblances without sense or origin. When I watch a film I suffer from a sort of "similarity disorder." I have great difficulty associating faces and names, remembering which actor or character is which. Thus, I am unable to "identify" properly. Instead, I am affected by continuities and cuts, movements and stillnesses, gradations of color or of brightness. This does not mean that my experience of film is nonmimetic or abstract: these variations have to do with the actions and events being enacted, and not just with the plastic or formal qualities of the image. I laugh and cry, I shudder and scream, I get tense or pissed off or bored, I restlessly glance at my watch and at the person next to me, or I sink into a state of near-catatonic absorption. But in any case, I do not actively interpret or seek to control; I just sit back and blissfully consume. I passively enjoy or endure certain rhythms of duration: the passage of time, with its play of retention and anticipation, and with its relentless accumulation, transformation, and destruction of sounds and images. There is no structuring lack, no primordial division, but a continuity between the physiological and affective responses of my own body and the appearances and disappearances, the mutations and perdurances, of the bodies and images on screen. The important distinction is not the hierarchical, binary one between bodies and images, or between the real and its representations. It is rather a question of discerning multiple and continually varying interactions among what can be defined indifferently as bodies and as images: degrees of stillness and motion, of action and passion, of clutter and emptiness, of light and dark.

Throughout this book, I have therefore tried to inflect the current critical debates surrounding the issues of simulation and cinematic representation by foregrounding the presence of the body in the circuits of postmodern power and of mechanical and electronic reproduction. The flesh is intrinsic to the cinematic apparatus, at once its subject, its substance, and its limit. All the films I have been discussing display a mute insistence of the body, beyond or beneath the limits of linguistic articulation and (social and cinematic) representation. Bigelow, Romero, Lewis, Cronenberg, Fassbinder, Warhol, and Bresson all show in various ways that the body is not volatilized in cinematic and electronic reproduction; it is never merely the lost object of a (supposedly disembodied) gaze. The image cannot be opposed to the body, as representation is opposed to its unattainable referent. For a fugitive, supplemental materiality haunts the (allegedly) idealizing processes of mechanical reproduction. If the filmed body seems distant and untouchable, this is because it withdraws into its likeness, its literal appearance, that hyperbolic resemblance to itself that Blanchot (1981) explicitly compares to the perturbing presence of an unburied cadaver, "the insupportable image and the figure of the unique becoming anything at all" (p. 82).

This "body wholly body" exhibits an inertia, a torpid persistence and resistance, a dull opacity that refuses transcendence or illumination. Featureless, anonymous, and forever inauthentic, this body lacks self-identity, but it thereby *also* manifests an alarming capacity for metamorphosis, which is only the other side of its inertia. The cinematic apparatus is a new mode of embodiment; it is a technology for containing and controlling bodies, but also for affirming, perpetuating, and multiplying them, by grasping them in the terrible, uncanny immediacy of their images. The cinematic body is then neither phenomenologically given nor fantasmatically constructed. It stands at the limits of both of these categories, and it undoes them. This body is a necessary condition and support of the cinematic process: it makes that process possible, but also continually interrupts it, unlacing its sutures and swallowing up its meanings. Film theory should be less a theory of fantasy (psychoanalytic or otherwise) than a theory of the affects and transformations of bodies.

Thinking the Body

But what can be said or shown of the body, independent of its meanings and representations? In Western thought, the body has generally been regarded as an affront to the intelligence, an obstacle to both thought and action. The body is passive matter waiting to be shaped by the logos's articulating form. Or it is something that needs to be regulated and contained—this is why it is subjected to the canons of representation. Metaphysics tends to set up dualisms of body and mind, nature and culture, presence and signification. Sartre's "practico-inert" and the Lacanian themes of "lack," of the passage through the defile of the patriarchal signifier, and of the radical difference between the penis and the phallus, are recent avatars of this tradition. But Gilles Deleuze traces a countertradition, a "philosophical reversal" found in the writings of Spinoza and Nietzsche (among others). This countertradition does not oppose body and thought, but instead posits a parallelism between them: it affirms the powers of the body, and it sees the very opacity and insubordination of the flesh as a stimulus to thought and as its necessary condition. Spinoza foregrounds the affects and passions of the body, as he argues *that the body surpasses the knowledge that we have of it,* and that thought likewise surpasses the consciousness that we have of it.... *The model of the body, according to Spinoza, does not imply any devaluation of thought in relation to extension, but, much more important, a devaluation of consciousness in relation to thought: a discovery of the unconscious, of an* unconscious of thought *just as profound as the* unknown of the body. *(Deleuze 1988b, 18–19)*

Deleuze (1989) suggests that a similar reversal takes place in cinema, when the camera explores the minutiae of bodily postures and behaviors, investing, investigating, and embracing the flesh; then,

the body is no longer the obstacle that separates thought from itself, that which it has to overcome to reach thinking. It is on the contrary that which it plunges into or must plunge into, in order to reach the unthought, that is life. Not that the body thinks, but, obstinate and stubborn, it forces us to think, and forces us to think what is concealed from thought, life. (p. 189)

This life of the body cannot be grasped or defined; it remains unconscious, untheorized, and unrepresented. But we "perceive" this unreachable excess; we are affected by it in a new way. As Walter Benjamin (1969) puts it, film brings about a "deepening of apperception" of "entirely new structural formations" of the physical world: "The camera introduces us to unconscious optics as does psychoanalysis to unconscious impulses" (pp. 235–37). The very proximity of the body, conducted and hyperbolically magnified by the cinematic apparatus, provokes and compels us, forcing us to move beyond a certain limit. Cinema is a kind of nonrepresentational contact, dangerously mimetic and corrosive, thrusting us into the mysterious life of the body.

This contact implies a radical immanence, an anti-Cartesian inherence of thought to the body, of epistemology to physiology, of the self to the world. The cinematic unconscious may be in a certain sense a Freudian one, but it is surely not the Lacanian one of radical separation, in which "the symbol manifests itself first of all as the murder of the thing, and this death constitutes in the subject the eternalization of its desire" (Lacan 1977, 104). I have been arguing throughout this book that the cinematic apparatus perpetuates the object rather than absents us from it; or, to put it differently, cinematic fetishism is an affirmative, primary process rather than a secondary and defensive one. The fetish is not fascinating and disturbing because it substitutes for, and frantically denies, a more primordial absence, a foreclosure of the real (Silverman 1988, 1–41); we must invert this formulation and say instead that the fetish is compulsively attractive and repulsive precisely because it is perfectly real, and because its material insistence is what prevents there from ever being such a thing as absence or lack. In the tradition of dialectical thought, from Hegel and Marx through Kojève to Sartre and Lacan, negativity is the motor of change: it provides the distance and leverage that permit us to work upon the world, to alter it and to control it. Even though it denies us the prospect of an ultimate dialectical reconciliation, a theory of negation such as Lacan's remains profoundly comforting in the most traditional humanist-idealist way, in that it preserves, through the mediating processes of linguistic alienation and symbolic castration, the possibilities of theoretical comprehension and transformative agency. In Lacanian theory, I am never able to coincide with myself; but such a law of separation also keeps Otherness at a safe distance, replacing its intense, exciting, and intolerable proximity with a more manageable gap.

Film, however, ignores such dialectics: it brings me compulsively, convulsively face to face with an Otherness that I can neither incorporate nor expel. It stimulates and affects my own body, even as it abolishes the distances between my own and other bodies. Boundaries and outlines dissolve; representation gives way to a violently affective, more-than-immediate, and nonconceptualizable contact. Cinema allows me and forces me to see what I cannot assimilate or grasp. It assaults the eye and ear, it touches and it wounds. It foregrounds the body, apart from the comforting representations that I use to keep it at a distance.

       This touch, this contact, is excessive: it threatens my very sense of self. Is my body ever truly "my own"? I *am* my body, and for that very reason it resists my intelligence, I am unable to possess it. Its very immanence is obscene and pornographic. The inertia of the flesh, and its unappeasable demands, are experienced as invasive, frightening, and disgusting. The body is at once captivating and violently repulsive: I come to regard its very presence as an aggression, a rejection, a monstrous Otherness forever out of my control. The body is *abject*, and every abjection is ultimately a posture and reaction of or to the body. As Julia Kristeva (1982) theorizes, the abject is "ejected beyond the scope of the possible, the tolerable, the thinkable. It lies there quite close, but it cannot be assimilated.... [The abject] is radically excluded and draws me toward the place where meaning collapses" (pp. 1–2). (Kristeva seeks to oppose abjection to a normative and regulated, dialectically and psychoanalytically defined, notion of desire; but the power and suggestiveness of her text reside entirely in her evocations of abjection, rather than in her attempts to police it and to reduce it.) The more intensely my body is affected, and the more it is put in contact with appearances, the closer I approach abjection. The flesh becomes ever more alien and unassimilable, inspiring vertigo and nausea. There is no longer any clear distinction between inside and outside. I am disgusted, terrified. But I need, I *want*, this closeness and this vertigo. Every abjection is also an exaltation: there is a deep, unresolvable ambivalence in the contact of the flesh, a continual affective oscillation. This indeterminacy is not empty, but overly, insufferably full: a hypertrophic surplus of irreconcilable sensations and passions, the bodily contours of my desire.

Two Films

Nagisa Oshima's *In the Realm of the Senses*, in jubilantly affirming a sexual passion culminating in strangulation and castration, only pushes to an ecstatic extreme the logic of desire and sexuality that is always implicit in cinema. Peter Lehman (1987) rightly notes that Oshima "overthrows the usual phallic representation of the male in order to present a literal body, mercifully free from its usual symbolic function"; but he disappointingly vitiates his own insight when he goes on to claim that Oshima's consequent "extraordinary overemphasis of the penis ... places the film paradoxically back in a phallocentric order" (p. 22). The penis, in this film, is emphatically not the phallus; there is no phallic function beyond the immediately physiological one. The literal—graphic and immediate—presentation of the lovers' genitals and bodies, together with the obsessive insistence upon Kichi's penis as a detachable, physically operative organ of pleasure (for Sada more than for himself), effectively prevents there from being any phallic "surplus value," any translation of desire into the abstract and transcendent terms of the Symbolic order.

With hard-core explicitness, Oshima presents desire affectively and materially, as a matter of bodily pleasures and intensities, of the multiplication of affects and sensations. The film overwhelms us with its repetitive insistence upon the act of fucking, with its determination to make every aspect of the conjunction of these bodies visible. Sexual desire must be located in concrete acts and practices, in the surfaces and depths of the body, in the incision and penetration of the flesh, rather than in the mythology of infinite substitution and of the quest for the unattainable object. The castration that ends the film—presented in excruciating close-up—is a literal and not a symbolic one: the ultimate extension and embodiment of Kichi and Sada's orgasmic games. The male organ, isolated and fetishized, is at once the concrete token of passion-as-possession (Sada's insistence that Kichi's penis be always available to service her, and only her) and the physical remnant and evidence of passion-exceeding-possession (Kichi's inability to remain forever hard, and more generally the ecstatic stresses of lovemaking that exhaust and tear apart the body).

Sada and Kichi's violently intense erotic play is rooted in materiality, not in fantasy. It does not negate the real, but embodies and intensifies it. This is why Katurah Hutcheson (1986) rightly criticizes conventional interpretations of the film, which tend to see Kichi and Sada's *folie à deux* as a radical, utopian rejection of the militaristic Japanese society of the 1930s. She argues that patriarchal power relations and tensions are in fact reproduced and regenerated in the small world of the brothel. If Sada and Kichi's private space has any subversive privilege at all, it is that of being a zone in which power is intensified, hyperbolized, and "demystified" by being made flesh. We must say that it is *because* the film is so excessively penis centered that it is *not* "phallocentric."

In the Realm of the Senses literally displays the male organ as the "substance" to which structures of domination (war, virility, masculine privilege) are secondarily "attributed"; it is this physical display of the workings of power that reveals the phallic or Symbolic order outside the brothel to be an imposture. Sada and Kichi do not in any sense escape relations of power; they precisely bring the forces of the Outside, the powers and pleasures that traverse the social order, to a point of maximal corporeal saturation. It is thus that they experience, and forcibly incorporate, movements and relations that their flesh cannot contain or sustain, affects that exceed the capacity of their bodies to respond. Physical castration then expresses the primordially ambivalent intrication of power and resistance as it plays over the body, together with the inherence of destabilizing pain in erotic pleasure. Castration is a hyperbolic manifestation of the excess of Kichi and Sada's desire, of its immanence in the real, rather than a sign of deprivation and lack. For

Oshima as for Bataille, sexuality is "impossible," tied to limits and to death, only because it involves and expresses so great a multiplication and intensification of bodily pleasures, and because it implicates us in transpersonal relations of power. The life of the body is disorienting and destabilizing, impelling us beyond ourselves in spite of ourselves, forcing the discharge of an irrecuperable expenditure.

A very different example of the problematic intrication of pleasure, desire, and power, their mutual intensification at the very point where social relations are embodied literally rather than just being articulated symbolically, is provided by Katt Shea's *Poison Ivy*. The film concerns a friendship between two lonely and alienated teenage girls: Ivy (Drew Barrymore) is a "bad girl" from a broken home, while Cooper (Sara Gilbert) is a sensitive only child trapped in an affluent, but loveless and dysfunctional, suburban family. The girls are drawn together by a common experience of loneliness, neglect, and alienation. But the girls' friendship is doomed from the beginning, because it is grounded only in their illusions about one another. Ivy envies the closeness and love that she imagines Cooper to possess; she wants so intensely to belong to a "real" family that she is unable to perceive the actual emotional emptiness of the Cooper household. Cooper, for her part, envies the freedom and assurance signified for her by Ivy's bad-girl clothes and mannerisms. In the course of the film, Ivy takes over and destroys Cooper's family: she kills the invalid and terminally depressed mother (Cheryl Ladd), and then assumes the roles of both mother and daughter by seducing the emotionally stunted and confused father (Tom Skerrit). But Ivy never becomes simply an "evil" character; throughout the film, it remains clear that her manipulativeness is a consequence of her prior victimization. She is merely trying to compel or to fabricate—to extort—the love and sympathy that she has always been taught that she has a right to expect.

As *Poison Ivy* escalates from a seriocomic depiction of teenage depression to a shocker involving murder and metaphorical incest, it also moves from fantasy to embodiment, playing out to exhaustion the basic American myth of the nuclear family. Ivy's crime is finally just that she overinvests in the glamorous images of familial togetherness, paternal authority, and suburban affluence that have proliferated so abundantly and so sickeningly in post-Reagan America. She simply takes these media images "at their word," enacting them in her own flesh, on the level of lived reality. *Poison Ivy* as a whole plays with and questions social power relations in the same way that it plays with and perverts the constraints and genre conventions of low-budget filmmaking: not by distancing us from these manifestations of power, but precisely by actualizing them in the most extreme way possible. Social forces are grasped at the point of their material emergence, which is also that of their most violent compression and ambivalence. The bourgeois patriarchal order implodes under the weight of its own literal embodiment.

Postmodernism and Film Theory

In this book, I have been exploring the relations between the cinematic apparatus and the life of the body. I have tried to suggest that these two realms are not alien or extrinsic to one another: their more-than-marriage, their symbiotic and parasitic interpenetration, is an inescapable feature of postmodern culture, which is to say of late capitalist social and technological relations. Our bodies have been decisively altered by the mass media of mechanical reproduction; we perceive our bodies in new ways, and our bodies are agitated and affected in new ways. At the same time, the mechanism of cinema itself—by which I mean its social and economic organization, its modes of production and distribution, as well as its technology—works only in relation to, and is thinkable only on the basis of, a certain dynamics of the body. We film viewers are "chimeras, theorized and fabricated hybrids of machine and organism," *cyborgs* in the multiple senses brilliantly defined by Donna Haraway (1991) in her "Cyborg Manifesto" (pp. 150, 149–81).

Given this mutual dependency of body and apparatus—or, better, their inextricable impropriety—the theory of film needs radical rethinking. In particular, the themes of specular representation, of identification and suture, of idealization and fantasy, of lack and disavowal, and of the supremacy of the signifier, must be abandoned. That old phallogocentric metaphysics is a poor instrument for coming to grips with the specificities of cinematic experience, let alone with the dizzying complexities of politics on a larger scale in the postmodern world. We are at the point of a momentous paradigm shift. We need a new politics and aesthetics of culture, a new kinetics and economics of power and resistance, of pleasure and pain, one oriented toward the multiple perceptions, affects, and subjectivity effects intrinsic to cyborgs and simulacra, to our deorganicized, hypersexualized, technologized bodies.

Of course, when one is at the cusp of a paradigm shift it is impossible to say what the new paradigm will look like. Still less is it possible to foresee the ways in which that new paradigm will in its own turn need eventually to be contested and shattered. But being on a cusp also has its distinct advantages. Deleuze and Guattari (1987) advise us to insinuate ourselves in the middle of things, "to move between things, establish a logic of the AND, overthrow ontology, do away with foundations, nullify endings and beginnings" (p. 25). The point is never to make definitive, totalizing claims.

Throughout this book, I have tried to trace some of the vectors of postmodern cinematic practice, to search out various points of intersection between the concerns of film theory and film study, of an aesthetics and metaphysics of the body, and of the micropolitics of contemporary culture. I have tried to "read" various films and oeuvres in ways that are as textually specific as possible, and yet that continue to resonate with larger theoretical concerns. I do not claim that my choice of works and directors is typical and representative of cinematic process in general, or of postmodern culture as a whole. I attempt rather to be postmodern enough so as to reject the very notion of typicality. I have deliberately sought to make my choices as heterogeneous, as singular and idiosyncratic, as possible. I have been guided in this both by the aberrancies of my individual taste and by broader strategic considerations, for I believe that such eclecticism is the best way for postmodern theory to avoid the old philosophical traps of universal legislation and of dialectical subsumption and totalization. Relativism and contextualism must reign. But the common practices of culture studies and of left academic criticism, much as I've learned from them, are to my mind not nearly relativistic and contextualist enough. Delimiting and situating particular practices, locating them in their specific circumstances and contexts, is often just a way for the critic to maintain a position of superior comprehension and mastery, since he or she is then able to present the Big Picture of which various cultural phenomena are just so many little pieces. And so, rather than move hierarchically from the specific to the general, from epiphenomena to underlying structures, from individual symptoms to the social totality, I have pursued the *paralogical* strategy recommended by Jean-François Lyotard (1984) and already practiced implicitly by the Wittgenstein of *Philosophical Investigations* (1968). I have endeavored to jump directly, and discontinuously, between the singular and the paradigmatic. I have shunned generality, and have instead "universalized" exceptions, counterexamples, and extreme cases. Writing theory thus becomes a monstrous hybrid of empirical description and simulacral fabulation. Theory as 'pataphysics, rather than as dialectics or as metaphysics.

These pages, then, record and perform an obsession. They are the written traces of a tactile and voyeuristic fascination. I have moved among a range of styles: from the still camera and unedited long takes of Warhol's early films to the fragmented, hyperkinetic action editing of Bigelow's genre revisions, and from Warhol's and Fassbinder's fixations upon the surfaces of bodies to Romero's and Cronenberg's attempts to penetrate those bodies' depths, to pull out the viscera, and to render visible the mysteries of interiority. But through all these variations and transformations, I have returned over and over again to the notion of cinema as a technology for oxymoronically intensifying corporeal sensation, for affecting and transforming the body, for at once destabilizing and multiplying the effects of subjectivity. I have insisted upon a primordial passivity and ambiguity, an unsurpassable, promiscuously undecidable intermingling of body and image, of reality and artifice, of passion and subjection, of pleasure and pain. And I have tried to argue that such ambivalence does not disable politics: it should be seen, rather, as a necessary, enabling condition of any political intervention or evaluation. The ambivalent cinematic body is not an object of representation, but a zone of affective intensity, an anchoring point for the articulation of passions and desires, a site of continual political struggle. I have consequently articulated an aesthetic of bodily intensity, of masochism and abjection, presenting it both as a symptomatic effect of postmodern power and as a possible form of resistance to that power. This book seeks to mobilize, within its own discourse, the disconcerting combination of pleasure and anxiety that characterizes the experience of cinematic fascination. It rejects the academic tendency to separate meaning from pleasure and pain, to foreground signification at the expense of affect. I've attempted to write a pornographic and participatory criticism, rather than a detached, judgmental one, for the voyeuristic drive, the passion of film viewing, that inspires and fuels this book is an affair, not of mastery, but of affirmation and abjection.

References

Altman, Rick. *The American Film Musical*. Bloomington: Indiana University Press, 1 9 8 7.

Andrew, Dudley. *The Major Film Theories: An Introduction*. New York: Oxford University Press, 1 9 7 6.

Andrew, Dudley. "The Neglected Tradition of Phenomenology in Film Theory," in *Movies and Methods*, Vol. 2, ed. Bill Nichols, 625–32. Berkeley: University of California Press, 1 9 8 5.

Aranda, Francisco. *Luis Bunuel: A Critical Biography*, trans. and ed. David Robinson. New York: Da Capo, 1 9 7 6.

Arthur, Paul. "Flesh of Absence: Resighting the Warhol Catechism," in *Andy Warhol: Film Factory*, ed. Michael O'Pray. London: British Film Institute, 1 9 8 9.

Bataille, Georges. *Visions of Excess: Selected Writings, 1927–1939*, trans. and ed. Allan Stoekl. Minneapolis: University of Minnesota Press, 1 9 8 5.

Bataille, Georges. *Erotism: Death and Sensuality*, trans. Mary Dalwood. San Francisco: City Lights, 1 9 8 6.

Baudrillard, Jean. *Simulations*, trans. Paul Foss, Paul Patton, and Philip Beitchman. New York: Semiotext(e), 1 9 8 3.

Baudrillard, Jean. *The Ecstasy of Communication*, trans. Bernard Schutze and Caroline Schutze. New York: Semiotext(e), 1 9 8 8.

Baudry, Jean-Louis. "The Apparatus: Metapsychological Approaches to the Impression of Reality in the Cinema," trans. Jean Andrews and Bertrand Augst, in *Narrative, Apparatus, Ideology: A Film Theory Reader*, ed. Philip Rosen, 299–318. New York: Columbia University Press, 1 9 8 6a.

Baudry, Jean-Louis. "Ideological Effects of the Basic Cinematographic Apparatus," trans. Alan Williams, in *Narrative, Apparatus, Ideology: A Film Theory Reader*, ed. Philip Rosen, 286–98. New York: Columbia University Press, 1 9 8 6b.

Bazin, Andre. *What Is Cinema?* Vols. 1–2, trans. Hugh Gray. Berkeley: University of California Press, 1 9 6 7.

Benjamin, Walter. *Illuminations*, ed. Hannah Arendt, trans. Harry Zohn. New York: Schocken, 1 9 6 9.

Benjamin, Walter. *One Way Street and Other Writings*, trans. Edmund Jephcott and Kingsley Shorter. London: Verso, 1 9 8 5a.

Benjamin, Walter. *The Origin of German Tragic Drama*, trans. John Osborne. London: Verso, 1 9 8 5b.

Berg, Gretchen. "Nothing to Lose: An Interview with Andy Warhol," in *Andy Warhol: Film Factory*, ed. Michael O'Pray. London: British Film Institute, 1 9 8 9.

Bergstrom, Janet, and Mary Anne Doane, eds., The Spectatrix (special issue). *Camera Obscura* 20–21 (May–September 1 9 8 9).

Bersani, Leo. *The Freudian Body: Psychoanalysis and Art.* New York: Columbia University Press, 1 9 8 6.

Bersani, Leo. "Is the Rectum a Grave?" *October* 43 (Winter 1 9 8 7): 197–222.

Blanchot, Maurice. *The Gaze of Orpheus*, ed. P. Adams Sitney, trans. Lydia Davis. Barrytown, N.Y.: Station Hill, 1 9 8 1.

Blanchot, Maurice. *When the Time Comes*, trans. Lydia Davis. Barrytown, N.Y.: Station Hill, 1 9 8 5.

Bresson, Robert. *Notes on the Cinematographer*, trans. Jonathan Griffin. London: Quartet, 1 9 8 6.

Brodsky, Michael. *Detour*. Rhinebeck, N.Y.: Guignol, 1 9 8 5.

Buci-Glucksmann, Christine. *La folie du voir: De l'esthétique baroque*. Paris: Galilée, 1 9 8 6.

Bukatman, Scott. "Paralysis in Motion: Jerry Lewis's Life as a Man." *Camera Obscura* 17 (May 1 9 8 8): 195–205.

Carroll, Noel. *Mystifying Movies: Fads and Fallacies in Contemporary Film Theory*. New York: Columbia University Press, 1 9 8 8.

Carroll, Noel. *The Philosophy of Horror, or Paradoxes of the Heart*. New York: Routledge, 1 9 9 0.

Clover, Carol J. *Men, Women, and Chainsaws: Gender in the Modern Horror Film*. Princeton, N.J.: Princeton University Press, 1 9 9 2.

Coursodon, Jean-Pierre. "Jerry Lewis," in *American Directors*, Vol. 2, ed. Jean-Pierre Coursodon, with Pierre Savage, 189–200. New York: McGraw-Hill, 1 9 8 3.

Crary, Jonathan. "Modernizing Vision," in *Vision and Visuality*, ed. Hal Foster, 29–49. Seattle: Bay, 1 9 8 8a.

Crary, Jonathan. "Techniques of the Observer." *October* 45 (Summer 1 9 8 8b): 3–35.

Crary, Jonathan. *Techniques of the Observer: On Vision and Modernity in the Nineteenth Century*. Cambridge: MIT Press, 1 9 9 0.

Deleuze, Gilles. *Masochism: An Interpretation of Coldness and Cruelty*, trans. Jean McNeil. New York: George Braziller, 1 9 7 1.

Deleuze, Gilles. *Proust and Signs*, trans. Richard Howard. New York: George Braziller, 1 9 7 2.

Deleuze, Gilles. *Nietzsche and Philosophy*, trans. Hugh Tomlinson. New York: Columbia University Press, 1 9 8 3.

Deleuze, Gilles. *Kant's Critical Philosophy*, trans. Hugh Tomlinson and Barbara Habberjam. Minneapolis: University of Minnesota Press, 1 9 8 4.

Deleuze, Gilles. *Cinema 1: The Movement-Image*, trans. Hugh Tomlinson and Barbara Habberjam. Minneapolis: University of Minnesota Press, 1 9 8 6.

Deleuze, Gilles. *Foucault*, trans. Sean Hand. Minneapolis: University of Minnesota Press, 1 9 8 8a.

Deleuze, Gilles. *Spinoza: Practical Philosophy*, trans. Robert Hurley. San Francisco: City Lights, 1 9 8 8b.

Deleuze, Gilles. *Cinema 2: The Time-Image*, trans. Hugh Tomlinson and Robert Galeta. Minneapolis: University of Minnesota Press, 1 9 8 9.

Deleuze, Gilles. *The Logic of Sense*, trans. Mark Lester. New York: Columbia University Press, 1 9 9 0.

Deleuze, Gilles, and Félix Guattari. *Anti-Oedipus: Capitalism and Schizophrenia*, trans. Robert Hurley, Mark Seem, and Helen R. Lane. Minneapolis: University of Minnesota Press, 1 9 8 3.

Deleuze, Gilles, and Félix Guattari. *A Thousand Plateaus: Capitalism and Schizophrenia*, trans. Brian Massumi. Minneapolis: University of Minnesota Press, 1 9 8 7.

Doane, Mary Anne. *The Desire to Desire: The Woman's Film of the 1940's*. Bloomington: Indiana University Press, 1 9 8 7.

Dyer, Richard. *Now You See It: Studies on Lesbian and Gay Film*. New York: Routledge, 1 9 9 0.

Elsaesser, Thomas. "Primary Identification and the Historical Subject: Fassbinder in Germany," in *Narrative, Apparatus, Ideology: A Film Theory Reader*, ed. Philip Rosen, 535–49. New York: Columbia University Press, 1 9 8 6.

Fassbinder, R. W. *Querelle: The Film Book*, trans. Arthur S. Wensinger and Richard H. Wood. New York: Schirmer, 1 9 8 3.

Feuer, Jane. *The Hollywood Musical*. Bloomington: Indiana University Press, 1 9 8 2.

Flesch, William. " 'New Bright Destruction': 'The Triumph of Life' and Some Versions of the Sublime." Unpublished manuscript, 1 9 8 4.

Flesch, William. "Proximity and Power: Shakespearean and Cinematic Space." *Theatre Journal* (October 1 9 8 7): 277–93.

Foucault, Michel. *Langauge, Counter-Memory, Practice: Selected Essays and Interviews*, ed. Donald Bouchard, trans. Donald Bouchard and Sherry Simon. Ithaca, N.Y.: Cornell University Press, 1 9 7 7.

Foucault, Michel. *Discipline and Punish: The Birth of the Prison*, trans. Alan Sheridan. New York: Vintage, 1 9 7 9.

Foucault, Michel. *The History of Sexuality*. Vol. 1. *An Introduction*, trans. Robert Hurley. New York: Vintage, 1 9 8 0.

Foucault, Michel. "The Discourse on Language," trans. Rupert Sawyer, in *The Archaeology of Knowledge*, 215–37. New York: Pantheon, 1 9 8 2.

Foucault, Michel. "The Subject and Power," in *Michel Foucault: Beyond Structuralism and Hermeneutics*, 2nd ed., ed. Hubert Dreyfus and Paul Rabinow, 208–26. Chicago: University of Chicago Press, 1 9 8 3a.

Foucault, Michel. *This Is Not a Pipe*, trans. James Harkness. Berkeley: University of California Press, 1 9 8 3b.

Genet, Jean. *Querelle*, trans. Anselm Hollo. New York: Grove Press, 1 9 7 4.

Grisham, Therese. "Linguistics as an Indiscipline: Deleuze and Guattari's Pragmatics." *Sub Stance* 20, No. 3 (1 9 9 1): 36–54.

Hammett, Jennifer. "Essentializing Movies: Perceiving Cognitive Film Theory." *Wide Angle* 14 (January 1 9 9 2): 86–94.

Hanlon, Lindley. *Fragments: Bresson's Film Style*. Rutherford, N.J.: Fairleigh Dickinson University Press, 1 9 8 6.

Haraway, Donna J. *Simians, Cyborgs, and Women: The Reinvention of Nature*. New York: Routledge, 1 9 9 1.

Hayman, Ronald. *Fassbinder: Film Maker*. New York: Simon & Schuster, 1 9 8 4.

Haynes, Todd. "Homoaesthetics and *Querelle*." *Subjects/Objects* 3 (1 9 8 5): 71–99.

Hutcheson, Katurah. "The Story of a Man Who Left His Will on Film." Unpublished seminar paper, University of Arizona, 1 9 8 6.

James, David. "The Producer as Author," in *Andy Warhol: Film Factory*, ed. Michael O'Pray. London: British Film Institute, 1 9 8 9.

Koch, Stephen. *Stargazer: Andy Warhol's World and His Films*. New York: Praeger, 1 9 7 3.

Krauss, Rosalind. "Antivision." *October* 36 (Spring 1 9 8 6): 147–54.

Kristeva, Julia. *Powers of Horror: An Essay on Abjection*, trans. Leon S. Roudiez. New York: Columbia University Press, 1 9 8 2.

Lacan, Jacques. *Ecrits: A Selection*, trans. Alan Sheridan. New York: Norton, 1 9 7 7.

Lacan, Jacques, et al. *Feminine Sexuality*, trans. Jacqueline Rose, ed. Juliet Mitchell and Jacqueline Rose. New York: Norton, 1 9 8 3.

Lehman, Peter. "Oshima: The Avant-Garde Artist without an Avant-Garde Style." *Wide Angle* 9, No. 2 (1 9 8 7): 18–31.

Lyotard, Jean-François. *The Postmodern Condition: A Report on Knowledge*, trans. Geoff Bennington and Brian Massumi. Minneapolis: University of Minnesota Press, 1 9 8 4.

MacBean, James Roy. "Between Kitsch and Fascism: Notes on Fassbinder, Pasolini, (Homo)sexual Politics, the Exotic, the Erotic and Other Consuming Passions." *Cineaste* 13, No. 4 (1 9 8 4): 12–19.

Massumi, Brian. "Realer Than Real: The Simulacrum According to Deleuze and Guattari." *Copyright* 1 (1 9 8 7): 90–97.

Massumi, Brian. *A User's Guide to Capitalism and Schizophrenia: Deviations from Deleuze and Guattari*. Cambridge: MIT Press, 1 9 9 2.

McNeese, Casy. "The Devil Is a Double." Unpublished seminar paper, University of Washington, 1 9 8 9.

Metz, Christian. *The Imaginary Signifier: Psychoanalysis and the Cinema*, trans. Celia Britton, Annwyl Williams, Ben Brewster, and Alfred Guzzetti. Bloomington: Indiana University Press, 1 9 8 2.

Michaelson, Annette. " 'Where Is Your Rupture?': Mass Culture and the Gesamtkunstwerk." *October* 56 (Spring 1 9 9 1): 43–63.

Modleski, Tania. *The Women Who Knew Too Much: Hitchcock and Feminist Theory*. New York: Methuen, 1 9 8 8.

Mulvey, Laura. "Visual Pleasure and Narrative Cinema," in *Feminism and Film Theory*, ed. Constance Penley, 57–68. New York: Routledge, 1 9 8 8.

Newman, Kim. *Nightmare Movies: A Critical Guide to Contemporary Horror Films*. New York: Harmony, 1 9 8 8.

Nietzsche, Friedrich. *Twilight of the Idols and The Anti-Christ*, trans. R. J. Hollingdale. New York: Penguin, 1 9 6 8.

Olalquiaga, Celeste. *Megalopolis: Contemporary Cultural Sensibilities*. Minneapolis: University of Minnesota Press, 1 9 9 2.

O'Pray, Michael, ed. *Andy Warhol: Film Factory*. London: British Film Institute, 1 9 8 9.

Owens, Craig. "The Allegorical Impulse: Toward a Theory of Postmodernism," in *Art after Modernism: Rethinking Representation*, ed. Brian Wallis. New York: New Museum of Contemporary Art, in association with David R. Godine, 1 9 8 4.

Penley, Constance. *The Future of an Illusion: Film, Feminism, and Psychoanalysis*. Minneapolis: University of Minnesota Press, 1 9 8 9.

Ratcliff, Carter. *Andy Warhol*. New York: Abbeville, 1 9 8 3.

Rees, A. L. "Warhol Waves: The Influences of Andy Warhol on the British Avant-garde Film," in *Andy Warhol: Film Factory*, ed. Michael O'Pray. London: British Film Institute, 1 9 8 9.

Rodley, Chris, ed. *Cronenberg on Cronenberg*. London: Faber & Faber, 1 9 9 2.

Rodowick, D. N. *The Difficulty of Difference: Psychoanalysis, Sexual Difference, and Film Theory*. New York: Routledge, 1 9 9 1.

Sarduy, Severo. *Written on a Body*, trans. Carol Meier. New York: Lumen, 1 9 8 9.

Schrader, Paul. *Transcendental Style in Film: Ozu, Bresson, Dreyer*. New York: Da Capo, 1 9 8 8.

Sharrett, Christopher. "The Last Stranger: *Querelle* and Cultural Simulation." *Canadian Journal of Political and Social Theory* 13, Nos. 1–2 (1 9 8 9): 115–28.

Silverman, Kaja. *The Acoustic Mirror: The Female Voice in Psychoanalysis and Cinema*. Bloomington: Indiana University Press, 1 9 8 8.

Silverman, Kaja. *Male Subjectivity at the Margins*. New York: Routledge, 1 9 9 2.

Smith, Patrick S. *Andy Warhol's Art and Films*. Ann Arbor: UMI Research Press, 1 9 8 6.

Sontag, Susan. *A Susan Sontag Reader*. New York: Vintage, 1 9 8 3.

Steinberg, Leo. *Other Criteria: Confrontations with Twentieth-Century Art*. New York: Oxford University Press, 1 9 7 2.

Studlar, Gaylyn. "Masochism and the Perverse Pleasures of the Cinema," in *Movies and Methods*, Vol. 2, ed. Bill Nichols, 602–21. Berkeley: University of California Press, 1 9 8 5.

Studlar, Gaylyn. *In the Realm of Pleasure: Von Sternberg, Dietrich, and the Masochistic Aesthetic*. Urbana: University of Illinois Press, 1 9 8 8.

Taussig, Michael. *The Nervous System*. New York: Routledge, 1 9 9 2.

Tavel, Ronald. "The Banana Diary," in *Andy Warhol: Film Factory*, ed. Michael O'Pray. London: British Film Institute, 1 9 8 9.

Vertov, Dziga. *Kino-Eye*, ed. Annette Michelson, trans. Kevin O'Brien. Berkeley: University of California Press, 1 9 8 4.

Warhol, Andy. *The Philosophy of Andy Warhol*. New York: Harvest/HBJ, 1 9 7 5.

Warhol, Andy, and Pat Hackett. *POPism: The Warhol Sixties*. San Diego: Harvest/HBJ, 1 9 9 0.

Watney, Simon. "The Warhol Effect," in *The Work of Andy Warhol* (Dia Art Foundation, Discussions in Contemporary Culture, No. 3), ed. Gary Garrels. Seattle: Bay, 1 9 8 9.

Williams, Linda. "When the Woman Looks," in *Re-Vision: Essays in Feminist Film Criticism*, ed. Mary Ann Doane, Patricia Mellencamp, and Linda Williams, 83–99. Frederick, Md.: University Publications of America, 1 9 8 3.

Williams, Linda. *Hard Core: Power, Pleasure, and the Frenzy of the Visual*. Berkeley: University of California Press, 1 9 8 9.

Wittgenstein, Ludwig. *Philosophical Investigations*, trans. G. E. M. Anscombe. New York: Macmillan, 1 9 6 8.

Wollen, Peter. "Raiding the Icebox," in *Andy Warhol: Film Factory*, ed. Michael O'Pray. London: British Film Institute, 1 9 8 9.

Wood, Robin. "An Introduction to the American Horror Film," in *Movies and Methods*, Vol. 2, ed. Bill Nichols, 195–200. Berkeley: University of California Press, 1 9 8 5.

Wood, Robin. *Hollywood from Vietnam to Reagan*. New York: Columbia University Press, 1 9 8 6.

Index

Steven Shaviro
is associate professor of English
and comparative literature at the University of Washington.
He is the author of
Passion and Excess: Blanchot, Bataille, and Literary Theory (1990)
and of several articles on the politics of difference,
libidinal economy,
and theories of sexuality.